WONDER
WHEEL
Go up it's Great
VISIT
CONEY
LAND
SHINE
10¢

Fulton Street, 1935

BOOTBLACK

Thanks to Yves Schlirf, Valérie Beniest, and the whole Dargaud team.

Thanks also to Jean-Louis Tripp, Tristan Roulot, Francesca Carpentier, and Séverine Dantas.

For my parents, Évelyne and Jean-Claude.

M.

ISBN 978-1-68112-296-0
© 2019, 2020 Dargaud Benelux (Dargaud-Lombard s.a.) - Mikaël
Originally published in French as Bootblack, vols. 1 & 2
Library of Congress Control Number: 2022931289
Book design by Philippe Ghielmetti
Translation by Matt Maden
Lettering by Cromatik Ltd.
Printed in Malaysia

This graphic novel is also available as an e-book, ISBN 978-1-68112-297-7

MIKAËL

BOOTBLACK

nbm GRAPHIC NOVELS

Nantier · Beall · Minoustchine
NEW YORK

CHAPTER 1

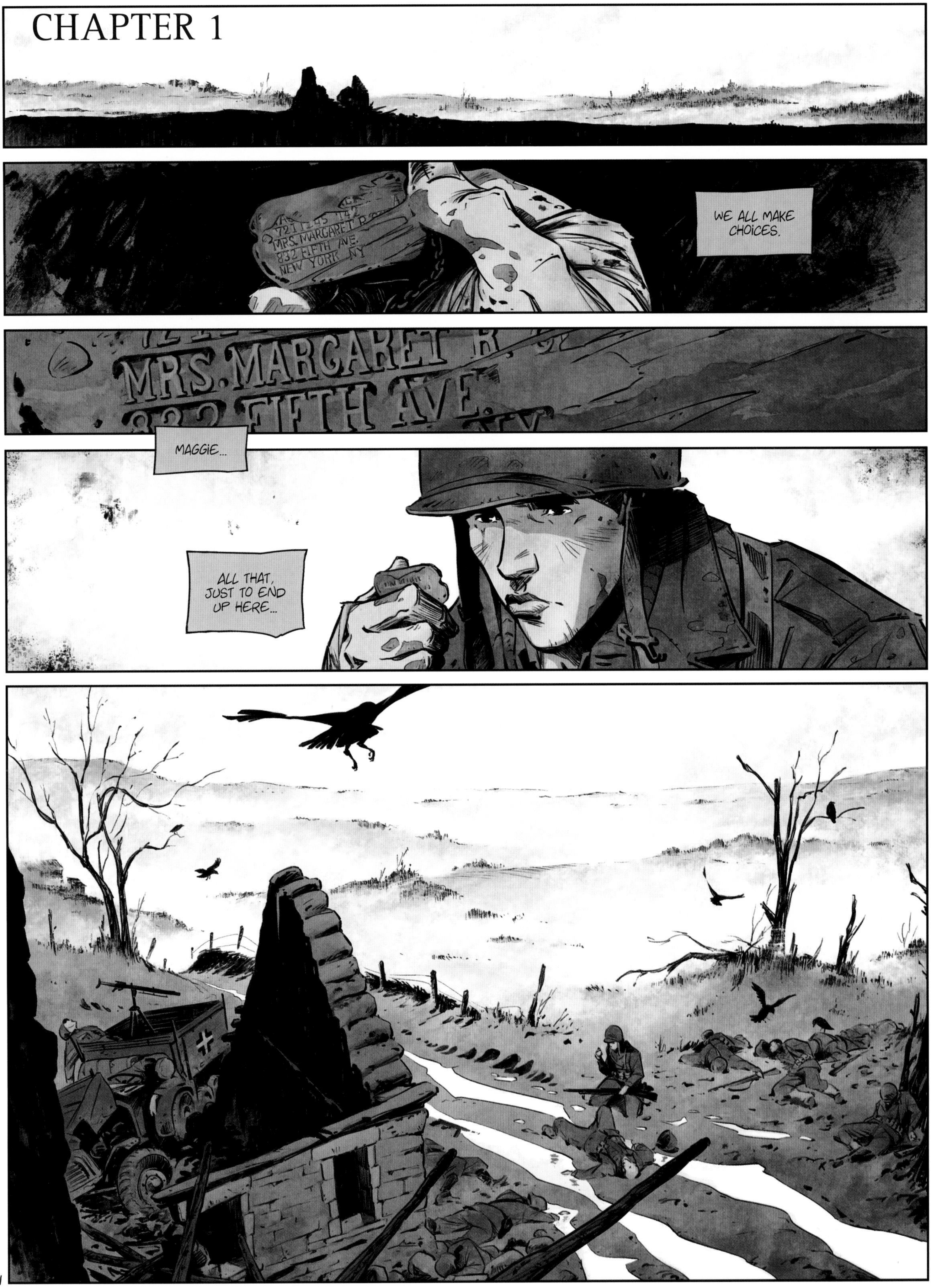
WE ALL MAKE CHOICES.
MAGGIE...
ALL THAT, JUST TO END UP HERE...

...WHAT A MESS.

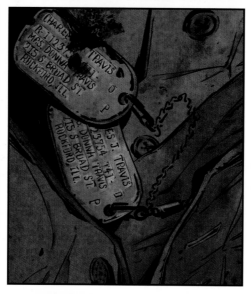

AND WHAT'S MY ROLE IN THIS MESS?

...WHO AM I?

WHO AM I, REALLY?

ALTENBERG!

2

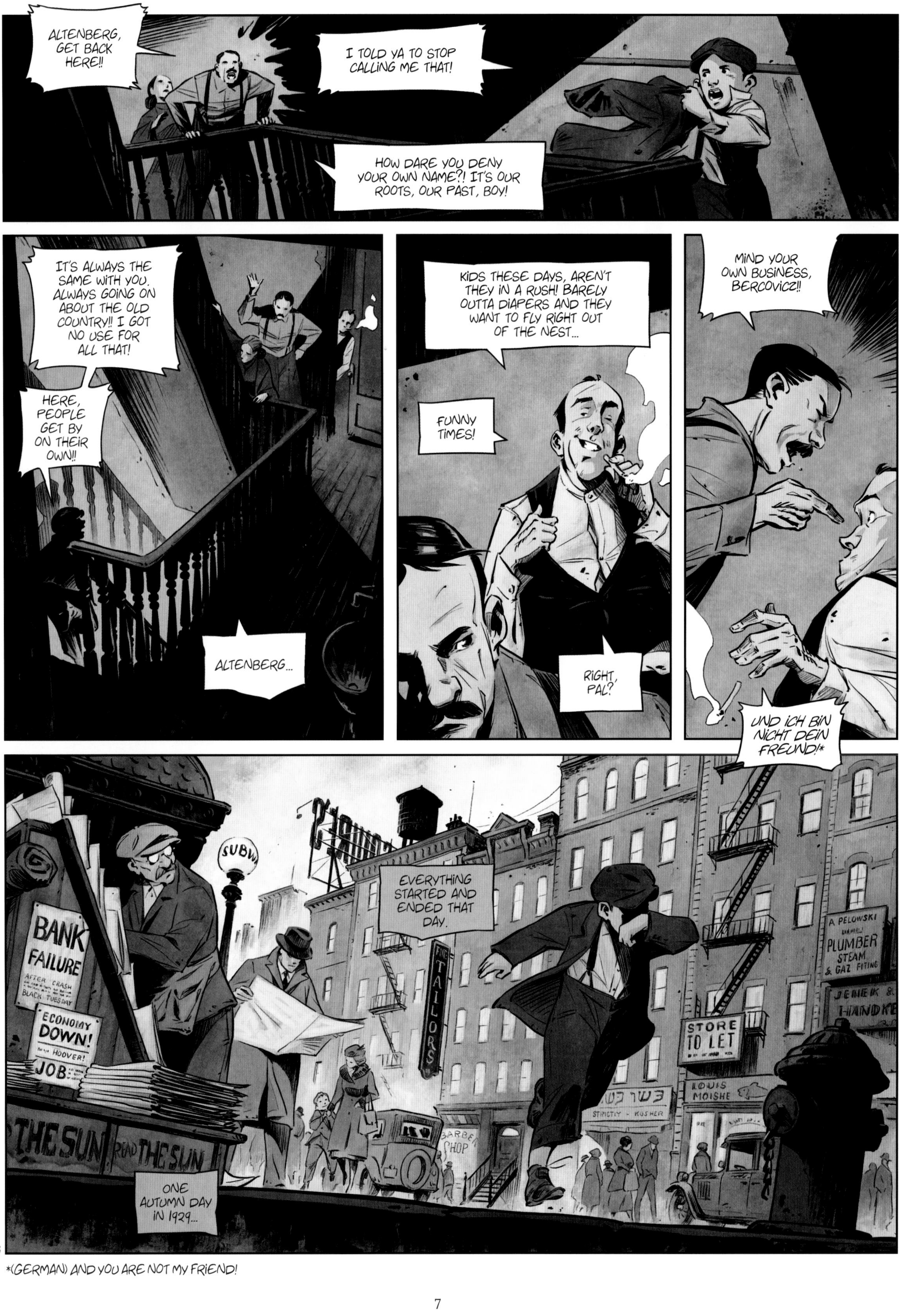

ALTENBERG, GET BACK HERE!!
I TOLD YA TO STOP CALLING ME THAT!
HOW DARE YOU DENY YOUR OWN NAME?! IT'S OUR ROOTS, OUR PAST, BOY!
IT'S ALWAYS THE SAME WITH YOU. ALWAYS GOING ON ABOUT THE OLD COUNTRY!! I GOT NO USE FOR ALL THAT!
HERE, PEOPLE GET BY ON THEIR OWN!!
ALTENBERG...
KIDS THESE DAYS, AREN'T THEY IN A RUSH! BARELY OUTTA DIAPERS AND THEY WANT TO FLY RIGHT OUT OF THE NEST...
FUNNY TIMES!
RIGHT, PAL?
MIND YOUR OWN BUSINESS, BERCOVICZ!!
UND ICH BIN NICHT DEIN FREUND!*
EVERYTHING STARTED AND ENDED THAT DAY.
SUBW
BANK FAILURE
ECONOMY DOWN!
HOOVER
JOB
THE SUN
READ THE SUN
TAILORS
A PELOWSKI
PLUMBER STEAM & GAZ FITING
STORE TO LET
LOUIS MOISHE
STRICTLY KOSHER
BARBER SHOP
ONE AUTUMN DAY IN 1929...

*(GERMAN) AND YOU ARE NOT MY FRIEND!

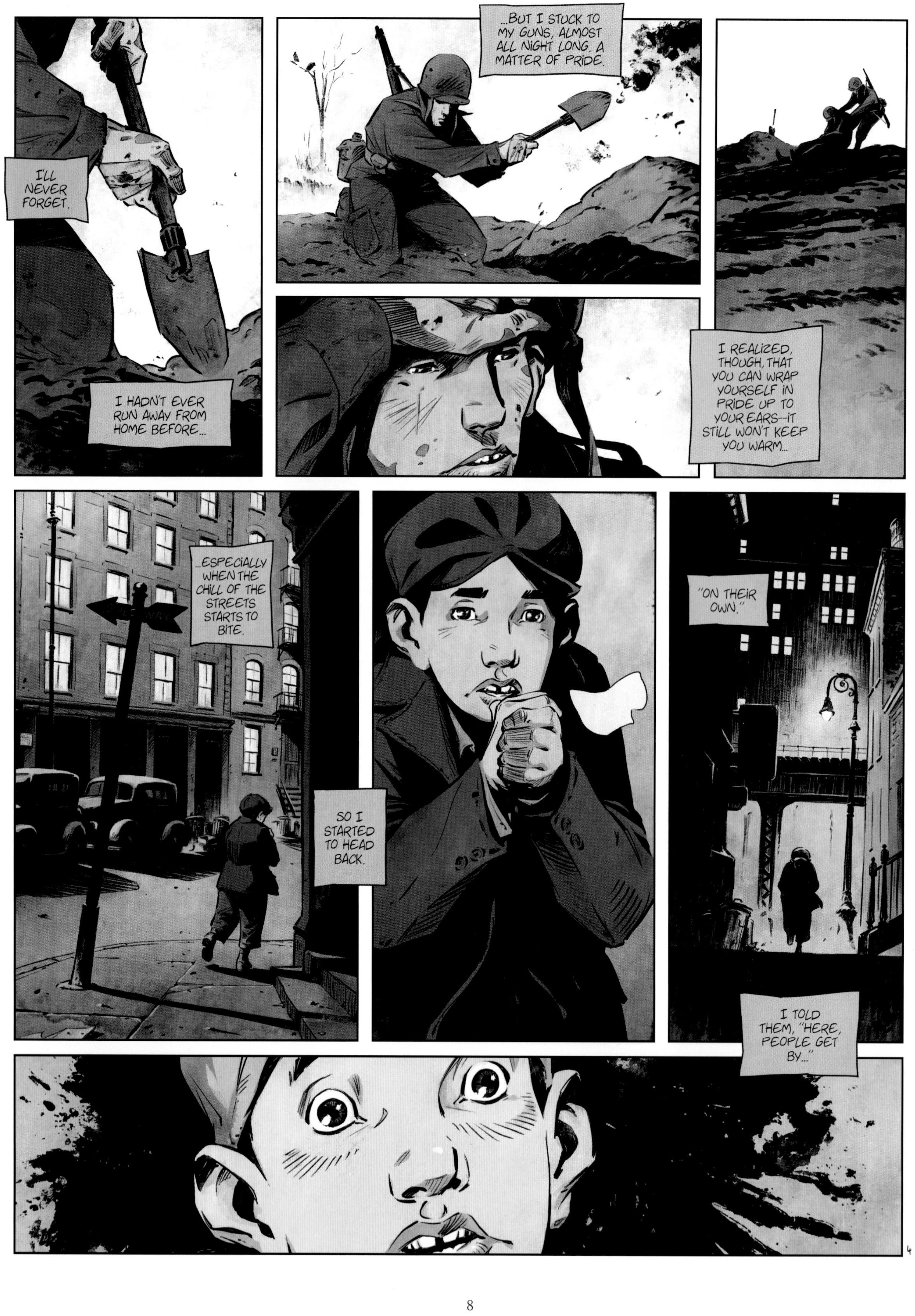

I'LL NEVER FORGET.
I HADN'T EVER RUN AWAY FROM HOME BEFORE...
...BUT I STUCK TO MY GUNS, ALMOST ALL NIGHT LONG. A MATTER OF PRIDE.
I REALIZED, THOUGH, THAT YOU CAN WRAP YOURSELF IN PRIDE UP TO YOUR EARS--IT STILL WON'T KEEP YOU WARM...
...ESPECIALLY WHEN THE CHILL OF THE STREETS STARTS TO BITE.
SO I STARTED TO HEAD BACK.
"ON THEIR OWN."
I TOLD THEM, "HERE, PEOPLE GET BY..."

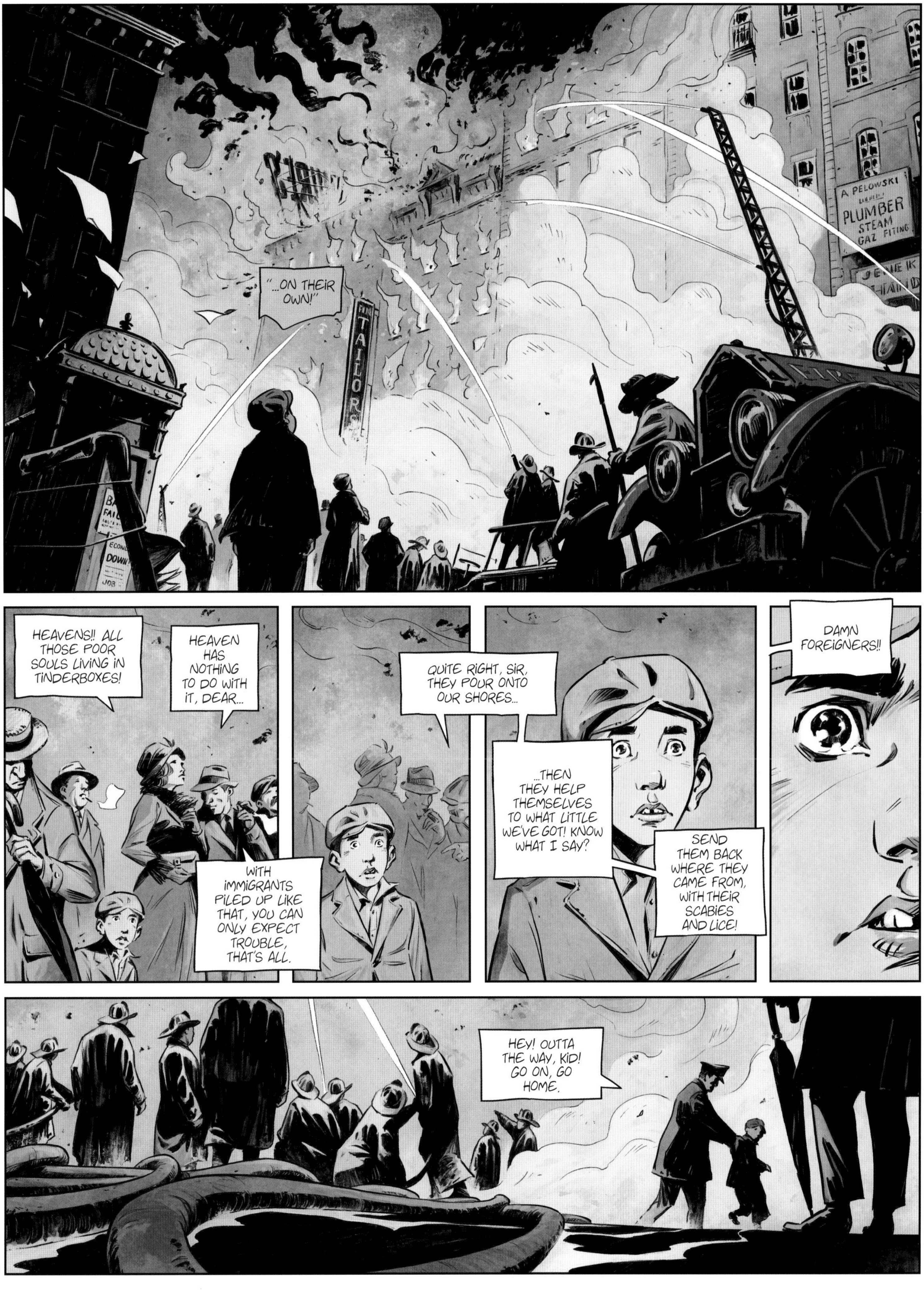
"...ON THEIR OWN!"
TAILORS
A PELOWSKI
PLUMBER
STEAM
GAZ FITING
HEAVENS!! ALL THOSE POOR SOULS LIVING IN TINDERBOXES!
HEAVEN HAS NOTHING TO DO WITH IT, DEAR...
WITH IMMIGRANTS PILED UP LIKE THAT, YOU CAN ONLY EXPECT TROUBLE, THAT'S ALL.
QUITE RIGHT, SIR, THEY POUR ONTO OUR SHORES...
...THEN THEY HELP THEMSELVES TO WHAT LITTLE WE'VE GOT! KNOW WHAT I SAY?
SEND THEM BACK WHERE THEY CAME FROM, WITH THEIR SCABIES AND LICE!
DAMN FOREIGNERS!!
HEY! OUTTA THE WAY, KID! GO ON, GO HOME.

5

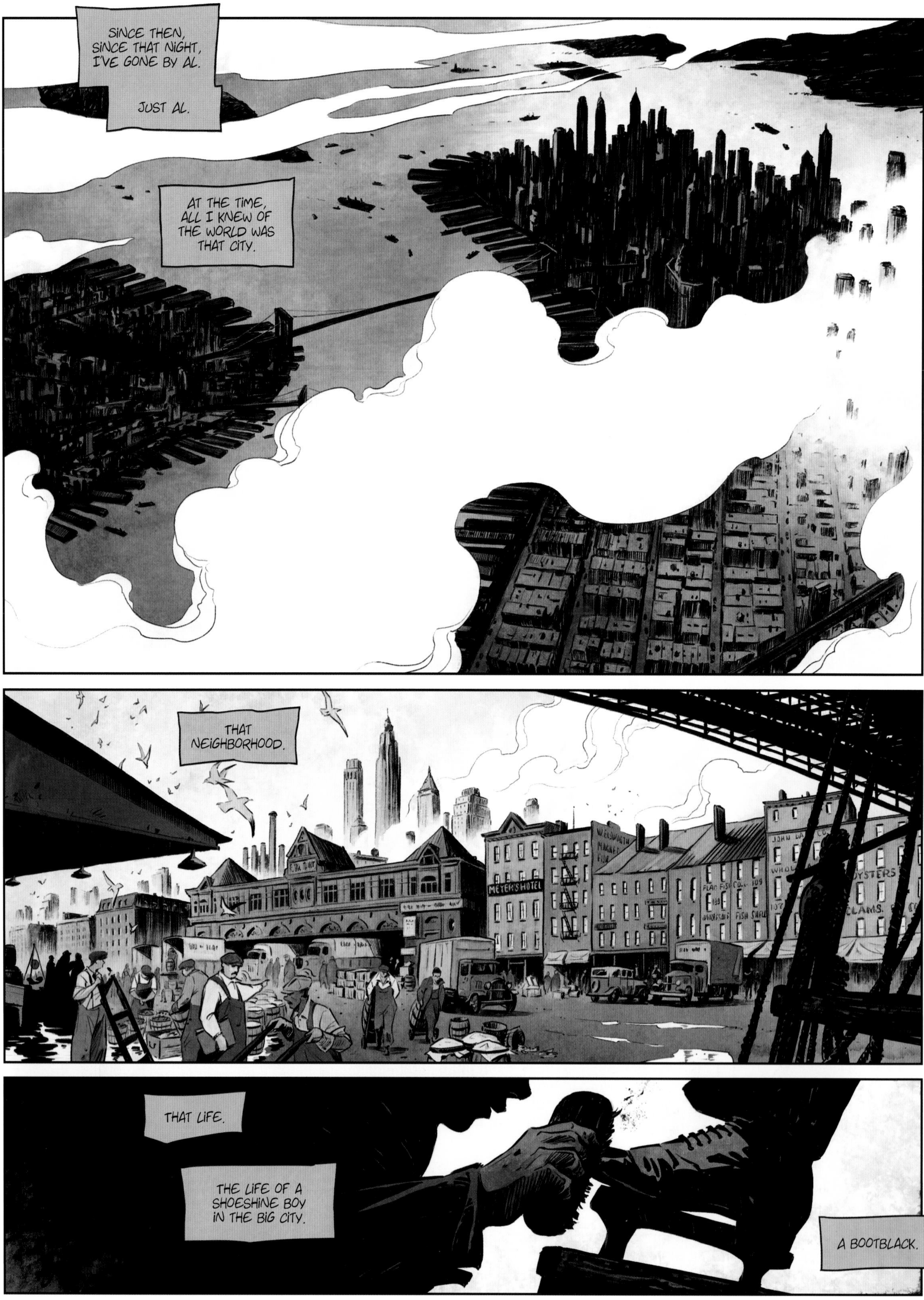
SINCE THEN, SINCE THAT NIGHT, I'VE GONE BY AL.
JUST AL.
AT THE TIME, ALL I KNEW OF THE WORLD WAS THAT CITY.
THAT NEIGHBORHOOD.
OYSTERS
CLAMS.
THAT LIFE.
THE LIFE OF A SHOESHINE BOY IN THE BIG CITY.
A BOOTBLACK.

6

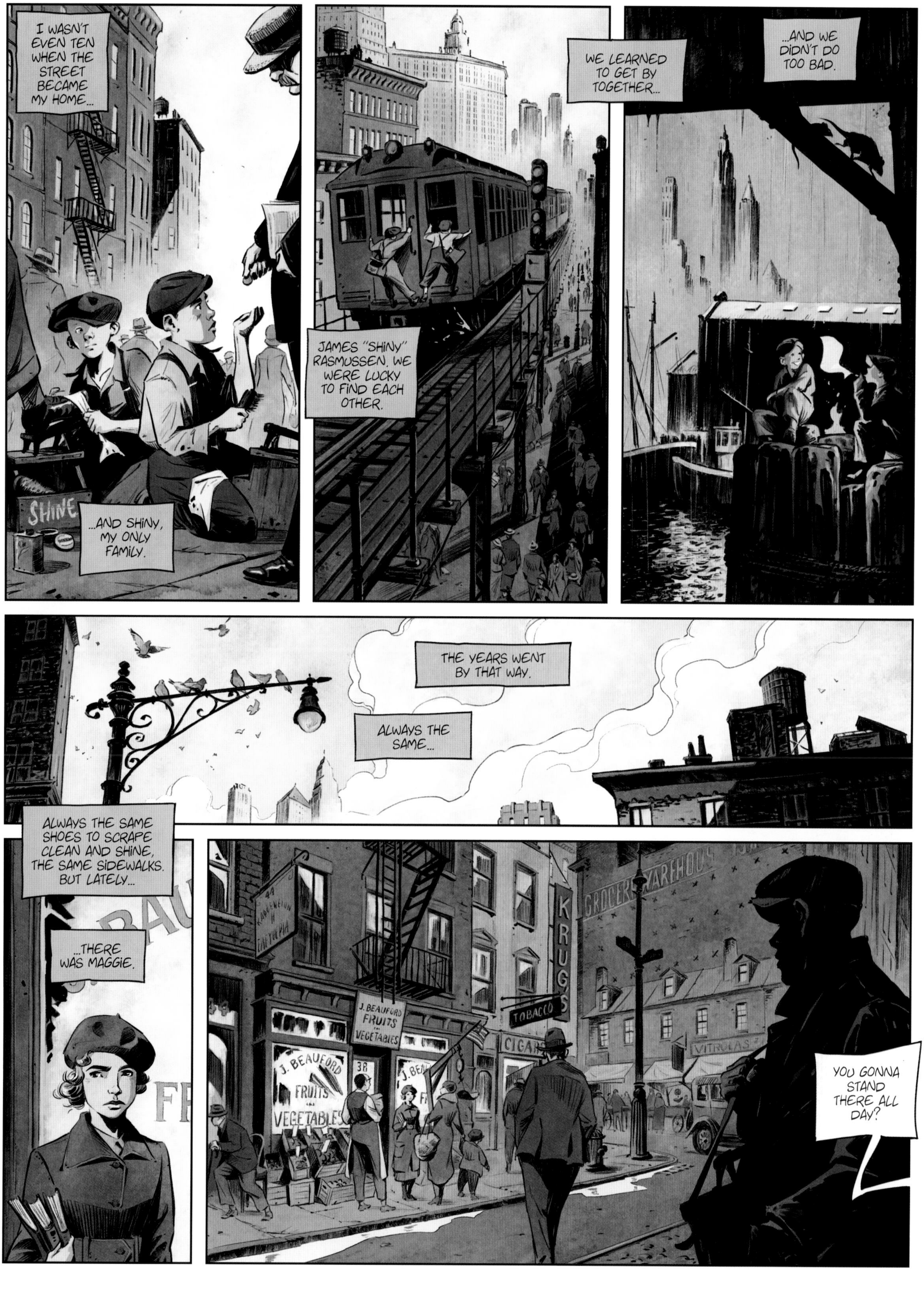
I WASN'T EVEN TEN WHEN THE STREET BECAME MY HOME...
SHINE
...AND SHINY, MY ONLY FAMILY.
WE LEARNED TO GET BY TOGETHER...
JAMES "SHINY" RASMUSSEN. WE WERE LUCKY TO FIND EACH OTHER.
...AND WE DIDN'T DO TOO BAD.
THE YEARS WENT BY THAT WAY.
ALWAYS THE SAME...
ALWAYS THE SAME SHOES TO SCRAPE CLEAN AND SHINE, THE SAME SIDEWALKS. BUT LATELY...
...THERE WAS MAGGIE.
J. BEAUFORD FRUITS VEGETABLES
KRUGS
TOBACCO
CIGARS
VITROLAS
YOU GONNA STAND THERE ALL DAY?

7

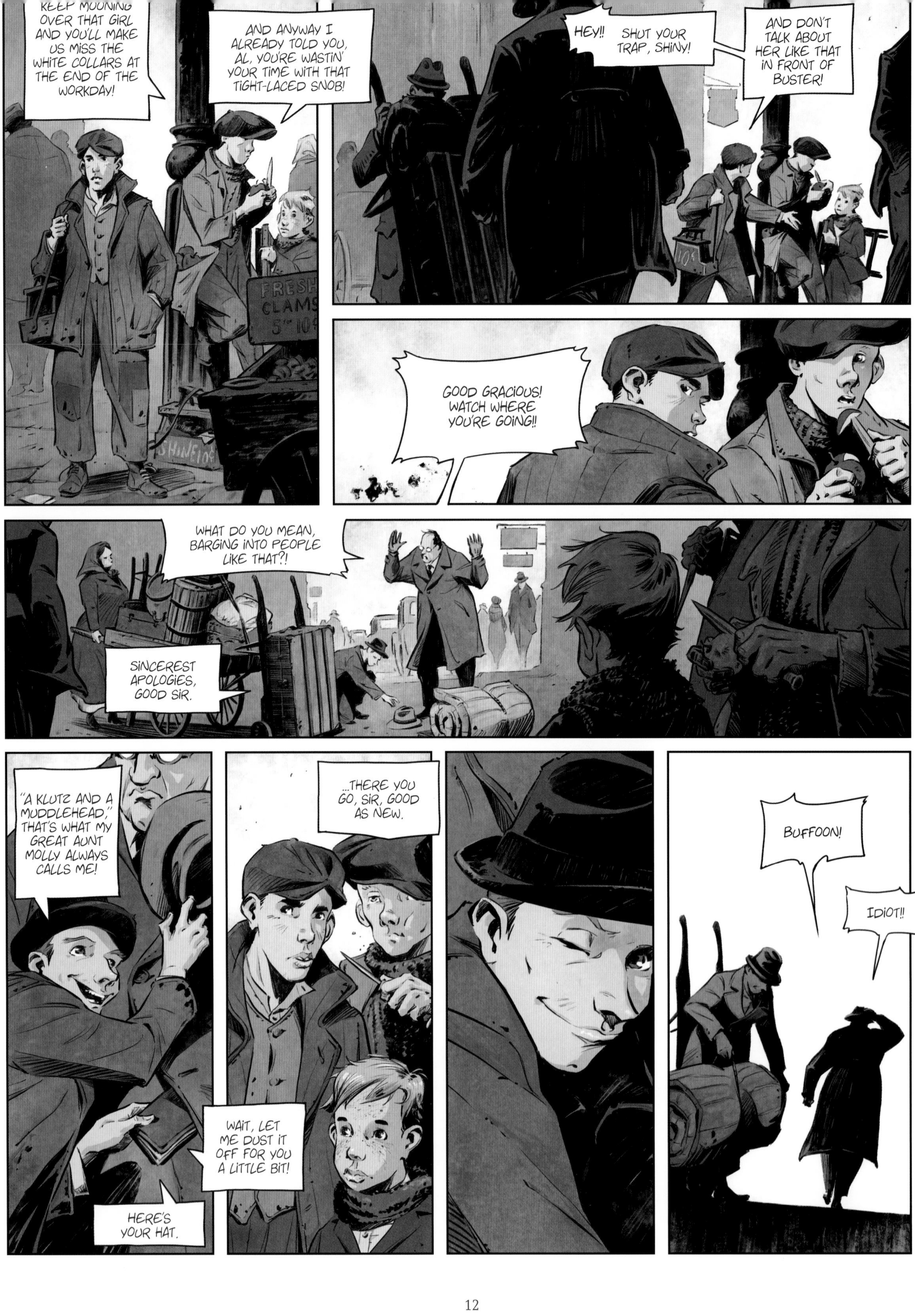
KEEP MOONING OVER THAT GIRL AND YOU'LL MAKE US MISS THE WHITE COLLARS AT THE END OF THE WORKDAY!
AND ANYWAY I ALREADY TOLD YOU, AL, YOU'RE WASTIN' YOUR TIME WITH THAT TIGHT-LACED SNOB!
FRESH CLAMS
HEY!!
SHUT YOUR TRAP, SHINY!
AND DON'T TALK ABOUT HER LIKE THAT IN FRONT OF BUSTER!
GOOD GRACIOUS! WATCH WHERE YOU'RE GOING!!
WHAT DO YOU MEAN, BARGING INTO PEOPLE LIKE THAT?!
SINCEREST APOLOGIES, GOOD SIR.
"A KLUTZ AND A MUDDLEHEAD," THAT'S WHAT MY GREAT AUNT MOLLY ALWAYS CALLS ME!
HERE'S YOUR HAT.
WAIT, LET ME DUST IT OFF FOR YOU A LITTLE BIT!
...THERE YOU GO, SIR, GOOD AS NEW.
BUFFOON!
IDIOT!!
8

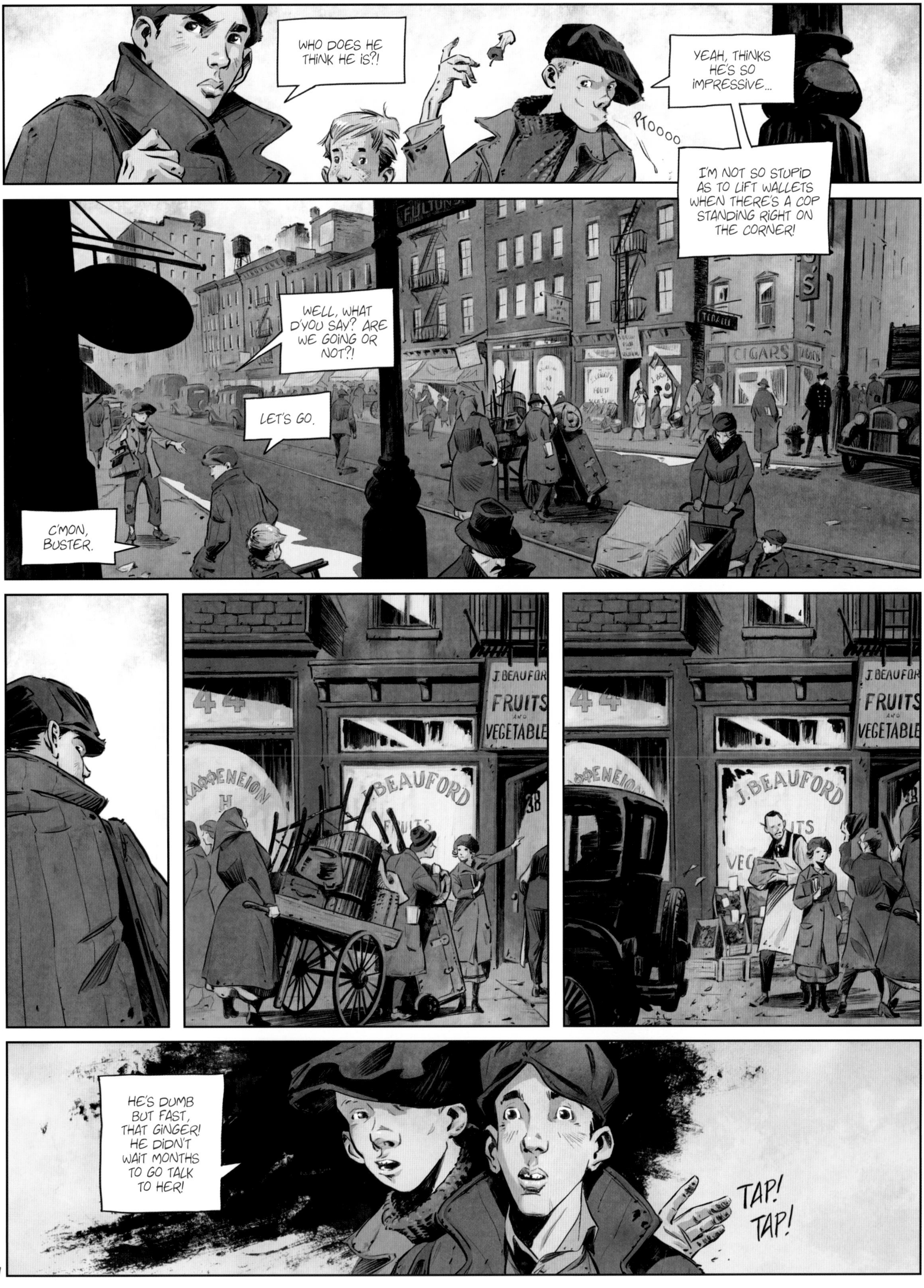

WHO DOES HE THINK HE IS?!
YEAH, THINKS HE'S SO IMPRESSIVE...
PTOOOO
I'M NOT SO STUPID AS TO LIFT WALLETS WHEN THERE'S A COP STANDING RIGHT ON THE CORNER!
FULTON ST
WELL, WHAT D'YOU SAY? ARE WE GOING OR NOT?!
LET'S GO.
CIGARS
C'MON, BUSTER.
44
J. BEAUFORD
FRUITS AND VEGETABLES
J. BEAUFORD
ΚΑΦΦΕΝΕΙΟΝ
HE'S DUMB BUT FAST, THAT GINGER! HE DIDN'T WAIT MONTHS TO GO TALK TO HER!
TAP! TAP!

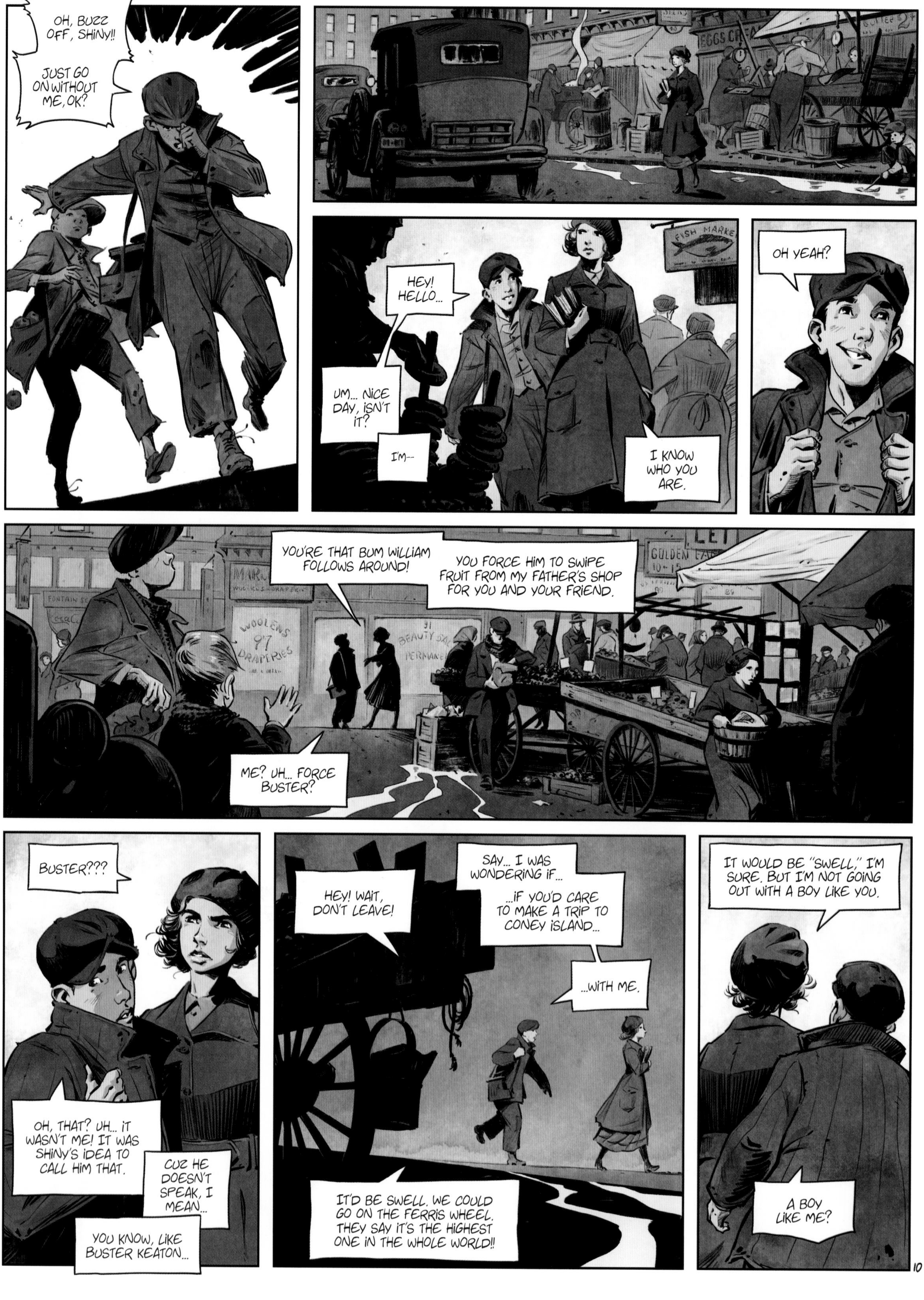
OH, BUZZ OFF, SHINY!!
JUST GO ON WITHOUT ME, OK?
HEY! HELLO...
UM... NICE DAY, ISN'T IT?
I'M--
I KNOW WHO YOU ARE.
OH YEAH?
YOU'RE THAT BUM WILLIAM FOLLOWS AROUND!
YOU FORCE HIM TO SWIPE FRUIT FROM MY FATHER'S SHOP FOR YOU AND YOUR FRIEND.
ME? UH... FORCE BUSTER?
BUSTER???
OH, THAT? UH... IT WASN'T ME! IT WAS SHINY'S IDEA TO CALL HIM THAT.
CUZ HE DOESN'T SPEAK, I MEAN...
YOU KNOW, LIKE BUSTER KEATON...
HEY! WAIT, DON'T LEAVE!
SAY... I WAS WONDERING IF...
...IF YOU'D CARE TO MAKE A TRIP TO CONEY ISLAND...
...WITH ME.
IT'D BE SWELL. WE COULD GO ON THE FERRIS WHEEL. THEY SAY IT'S THE HIGHEST ONE IN THE WHOLE WORLD!!
IT WOULD BE "SWELL," I'M SURE. BUT I'M NOT GOING OUT WITH A BOY LIKE YOU.
A BOY LIKE ME?

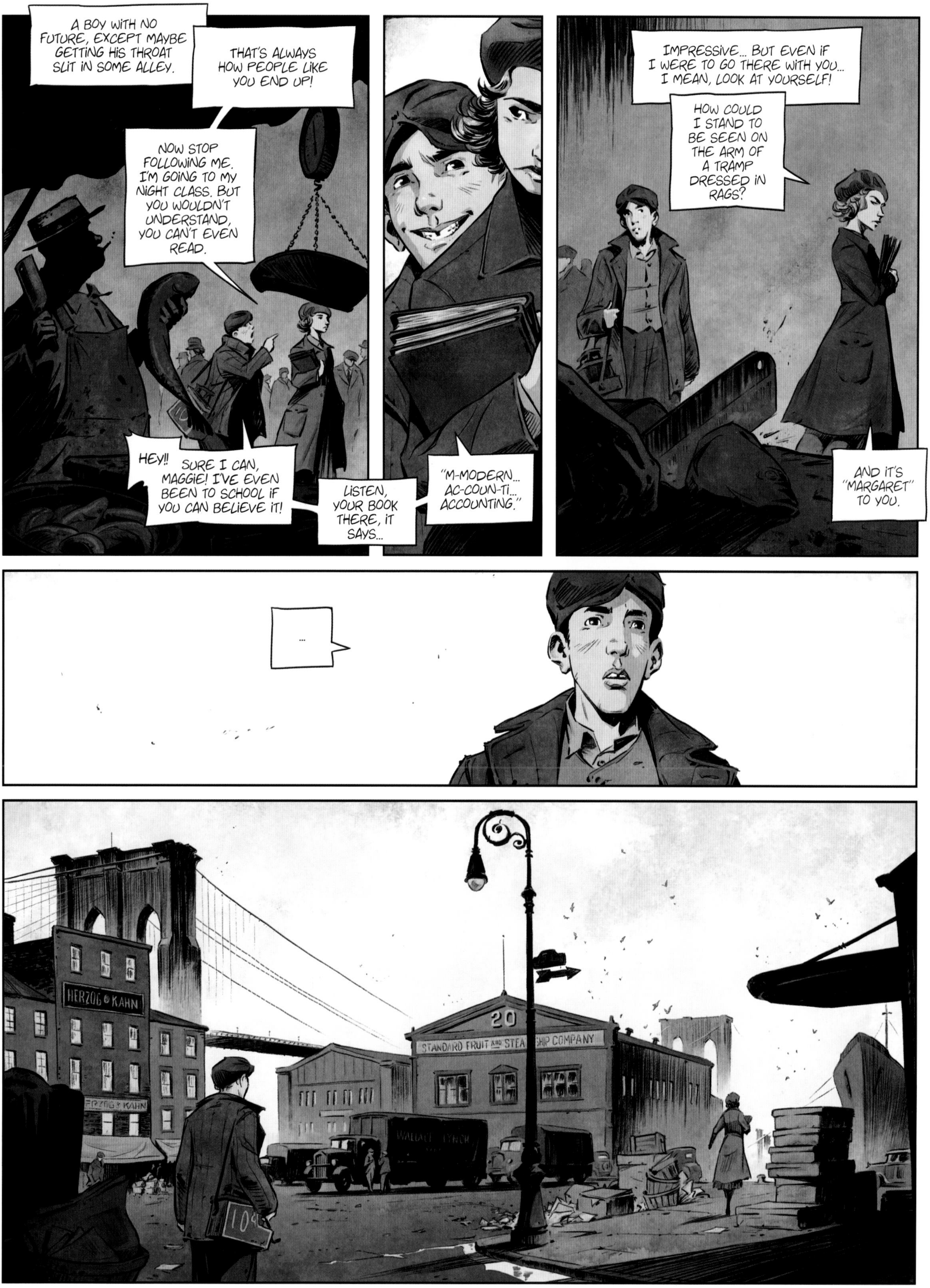
A BOY WITH NO FUTURE, EXCEPT MAYBE GETTING HIS THROAT SLIT IN SOME ALLEY.
THAT'S ALWAYS HOW PEOPLE LIKE YOU END UP!
NOW STOP FOLLOWING ME. I'M GOING TO MY NIGHT CLASS. BUT YOU WOULDN'T UNDERSTAND, YOU CAN'T EVEN READ.
HEY!! SURE I CAN, MAGGIE! I'VE EVEN BEEN TO SCHOOL IF YOU CAN BELIEVE IT!
LISTEN, YOUR BOOK THERE, IT SAYS...
"M-MODERN... AC-COUN-TI... ACCOUNTING."
IMPRESSIVE... BUT EVEN IF I WERE TO GO THERE WITH YOU... I MEAN, LOOK AT YOURSELF!
HOW COULD I STAND TO BE SEEN ON THE ARM OF A TRAMP DRESSED IN RAGS?
AND IT'S "MARGARET" TO YOU.
...
HERZOG & KAHN
20
STANDARD FRUIT AND STEA SHIP COMPANY

11

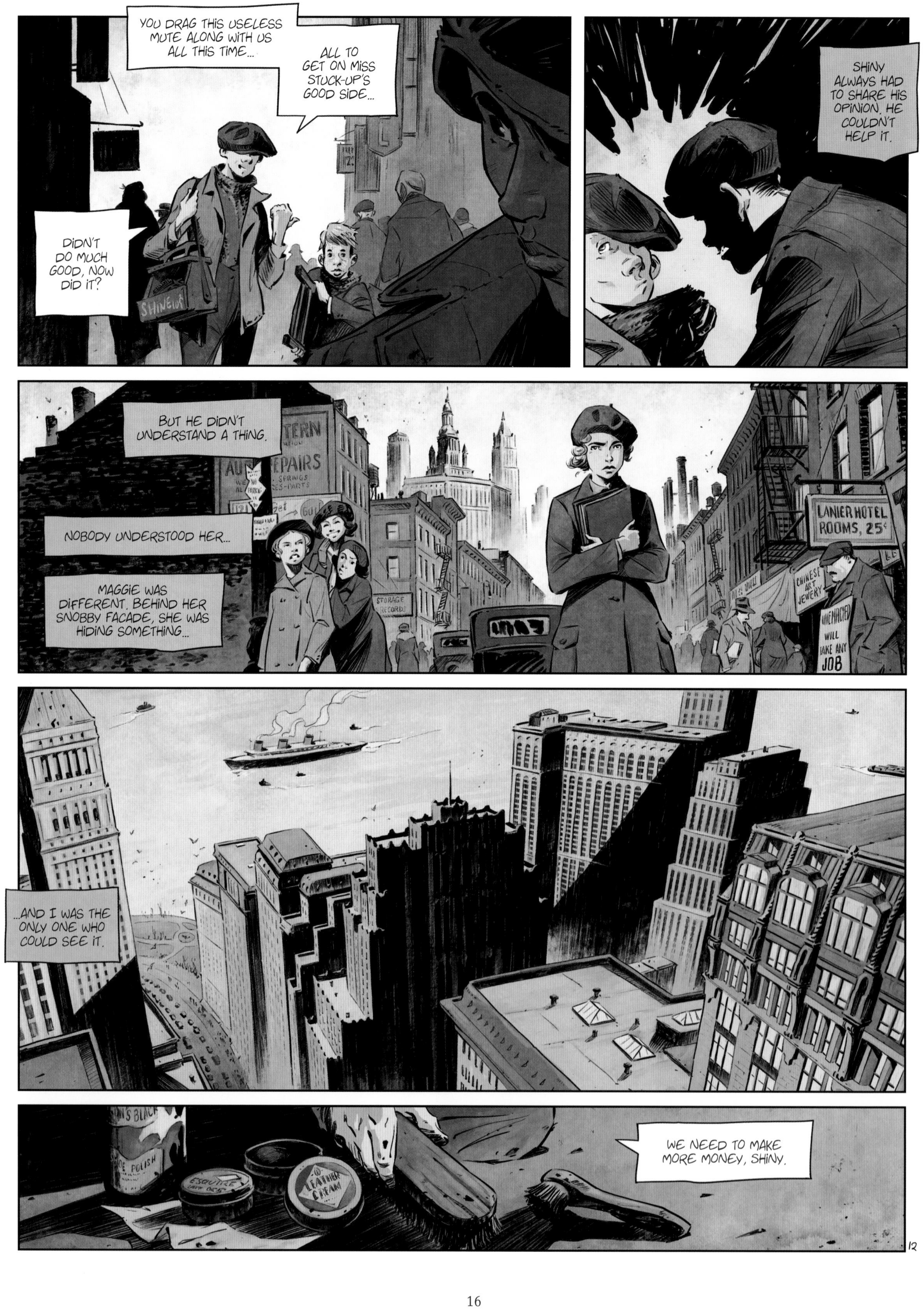

YOU DRAG THIS USELESS MUTE ALONG WITH US ALL THIS TIME...
ALL TO GET ON MISS STUCK-UP'S GOOD SIDE...
DIDN'T DO MUCH GOOD, NOW DID IT?
SHINY ALWAYS HAD TO SHARE HIS OPINION. HE COULDN'T HELP IT.
BUT HE DIDN'T UNDERSTAND A THING.
NOBODY UNDERSTOOD HER...
MAGGIE WAS DIFFERENT. BEHIND HER SNOBBY FACADE, SHE WAS HIDING SOMETHING...
LANIER HOTEL ROOMS, 25¢
CHINESE ART JEWERY
WILL TAKE ANY JOB
STORAGE RECORDS
...AND I WAS THE ONLY ONE WHO COULD SEE IT.
ESQUIRE
LEATHER CREAM
WE NEED TO MAKE MORE MONEY, SHINY.

ALWAYS, AL, ALWAYS!

THE PRICE OF WAX AND SHOE POLISH KEEPS GOIN' UP!

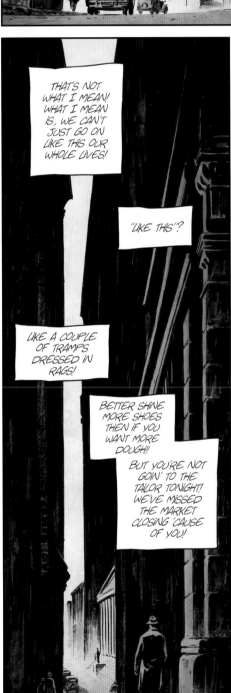

THAT'S NOT WHAT I MEAN! WHAT I MEAN IS, WE CAN'T JUST GO ON LIKE THIS OUR WHOLE LIVES!

"LIKE THIS"?

LIKE A COUPLE OF TRAMPS DRESSED IN RAGS!

BETTER SHINE MORE SHOES THEN IF YOU WANT MORE DOUGH!!

BUT YOU'RE NOT GOIN' TO THE TAILOR TONIGHT! WE'VE MISSED THE MARKET CLOSING 'CAUSE OF YOU!

AND WHAT'S WRONG WITH THESE DUDS, ANYWAY?

PAF!

PAF!

HEY!! YOU TWO!

STOP YAMMERING AND GET TO SHINING!

LOOKS LIKE 1935 WILL BE OL' BABE RUTH'S LAST SEASON...

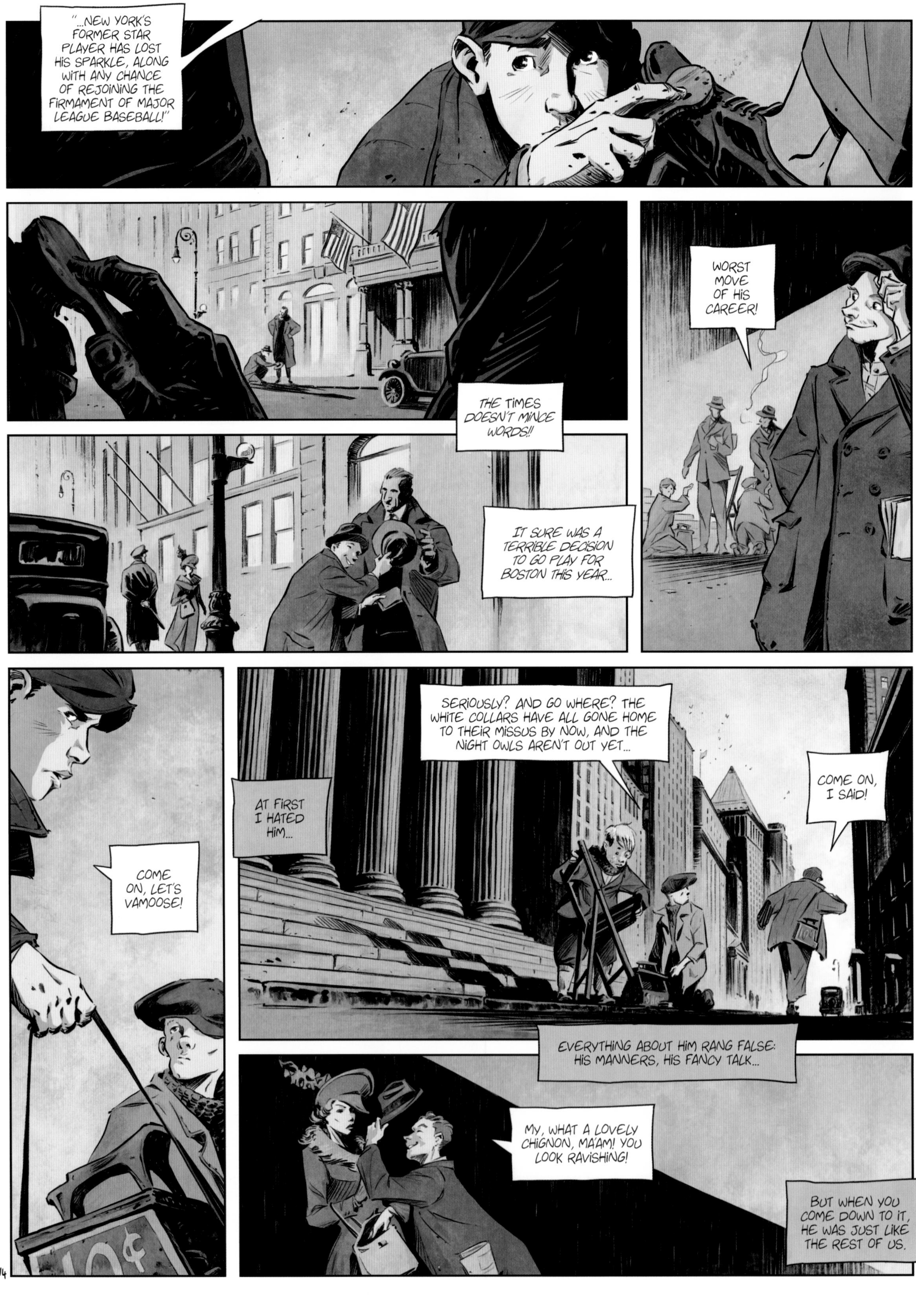
"...NEW YORK'S FORMER STAR PLAYER HAS LOST HIS SPARKLE, ALONG WITH ANY CHANCE OF REJOINING THE FIRMAMENT OF MAJOR LEAGUE BASEBALL!"
THE TIMES DOESN'T MINCE WORDS!!
IT SURE WAS A TERRIBLE DECISION TO GO PLAY FOR BOSTON THIS YEAR...
WORST MOVE OF HIS CAREER!
COME ON, LET'S VAMOOSE!
10¢
AT FIRST I HATED HIM...
SERIOUSLY? AND GO WHERE? THE WHITE COLLARS HAVE ALL GONE HOME TO THEIR MISSUS BY NOW, AND THE NIGHT OWLS AREN'T OUT YET...
COME ON, I SAID!
EVERYTHING ABOUT HIM RANG FALSE: HIS MANNERS, HIS FANCY TALK...
MY, WHAT A LOVELY CHIGNON, MA'AM! YOU LOOK RAVISHING!
BUT WHEN YOU COME DOWN TO IT, HE WAS JUST LIKE THE REST OF US.
14

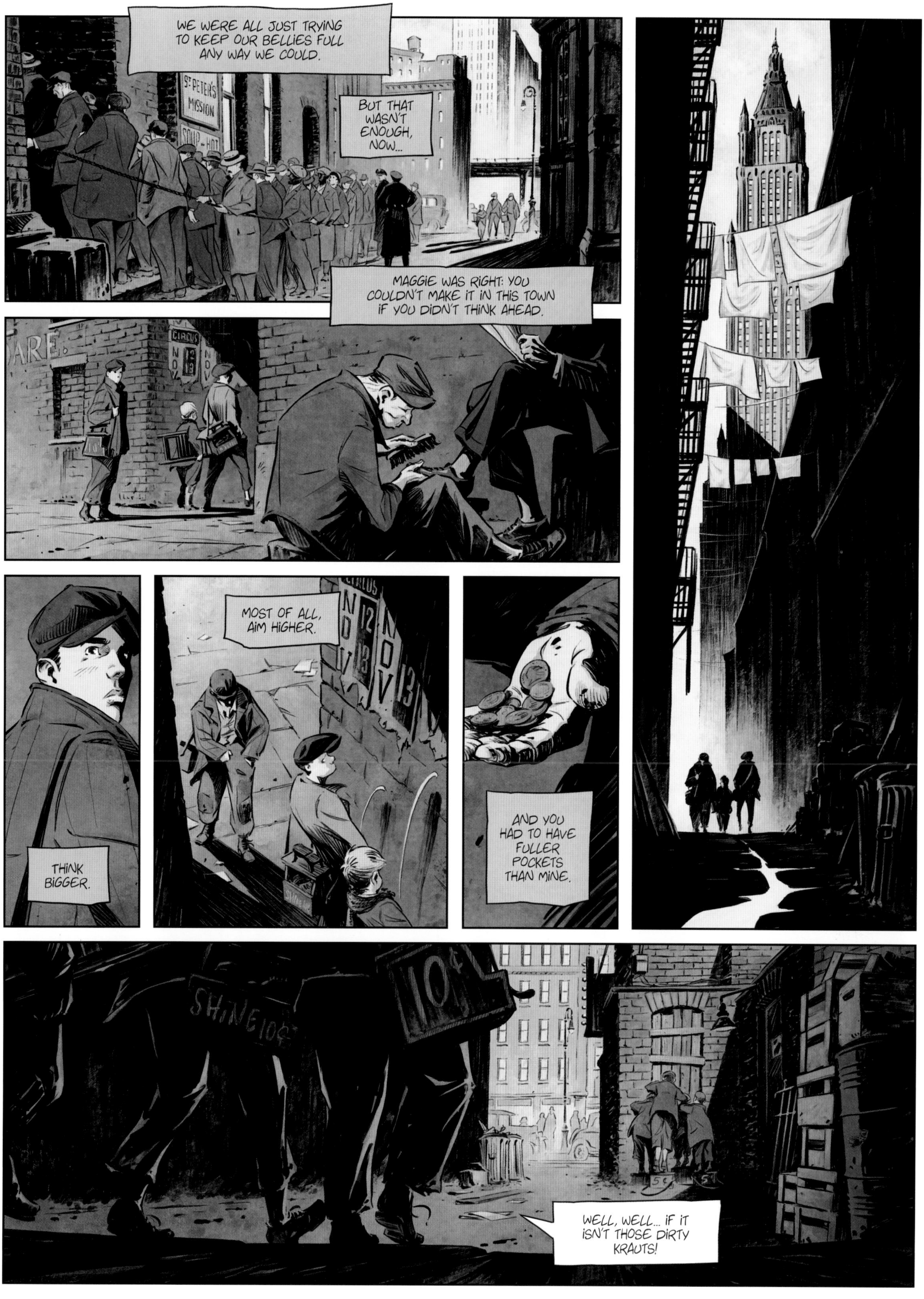
WE WERE ALL JUST TRYING TO KEEP OUR BELLIES FULL ANY WAY WE COULD.
ST. PETER'S MISSION
SOUP - HOT
BUT THAT WASN'T ENOUGH, NOW...
MAGGIE WAS RIGHT: YOU COULDN'T MAKE IT IN THIS TOWN IF YOU DIDN'T THINK AHEAD.
CIRCUS NOV 13 NOV
THINK BIGGER.
MOST OF ALL, AIM HIGHER.
AND YOU HAD TO HAVE FULLER POCKETS THAN MINE.
SHINE 10¢
10¢
WELL, WELL... IF IT ISN'T THOSE DIRTY KRAUTS!
15

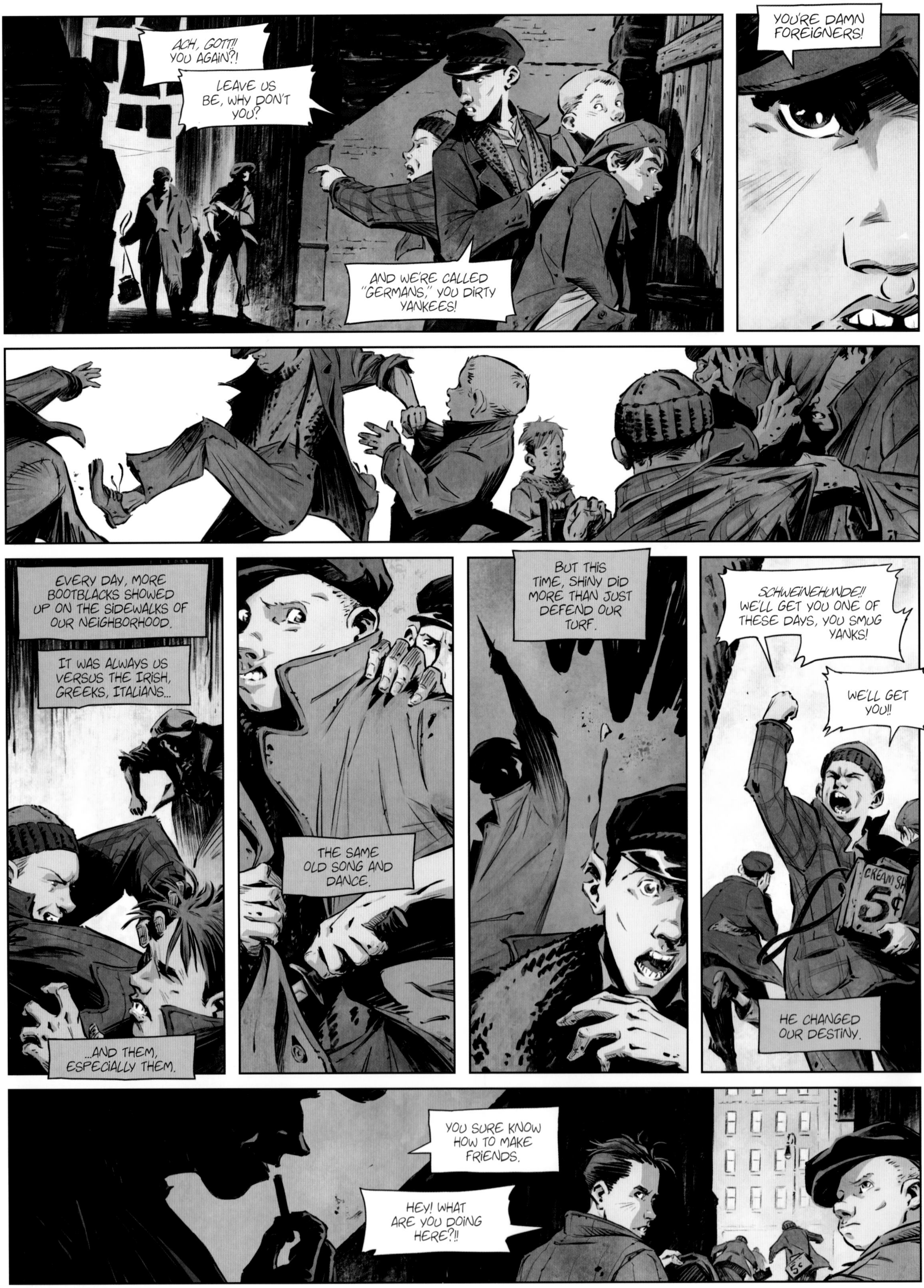
ACH, GOTT!! YOU AGAIN?!
LEAVE US BE, WHY DON'T YOU?
AND WE'RE CALLED "GERMANS," YOU DIRTY YANKEES!
YOU'RE DAMN FOREIGNERS!
EVERY DAY, MORE BOOTBLACKS SHOWED UP ON THE SIDEWALKS OF OUR NEIGHBORHOOD.
IT WAS ALWAYS US VERSUS THE IRISH, GREEKS, ITALIANS...
...AND THEM, ESPECIALLY THEM.
THE SAME OLD SONG AND DANCE.
BUT THIS TIME, SHINY DID MORE THAN JUST DEFEND OUR TURF.
SCHWEINEHUNDE!! WE'LL GET YOU ONE OF THESE DAYS, YOU SMUG YANKS!
WE'LL GET YOU!!
HE CHANGED OUR DESTINY.
YOU SURE KNOW HOW TO MAKE FRIENDS.
HEY! WHAT ARE YOU DOING HERE?!!
16

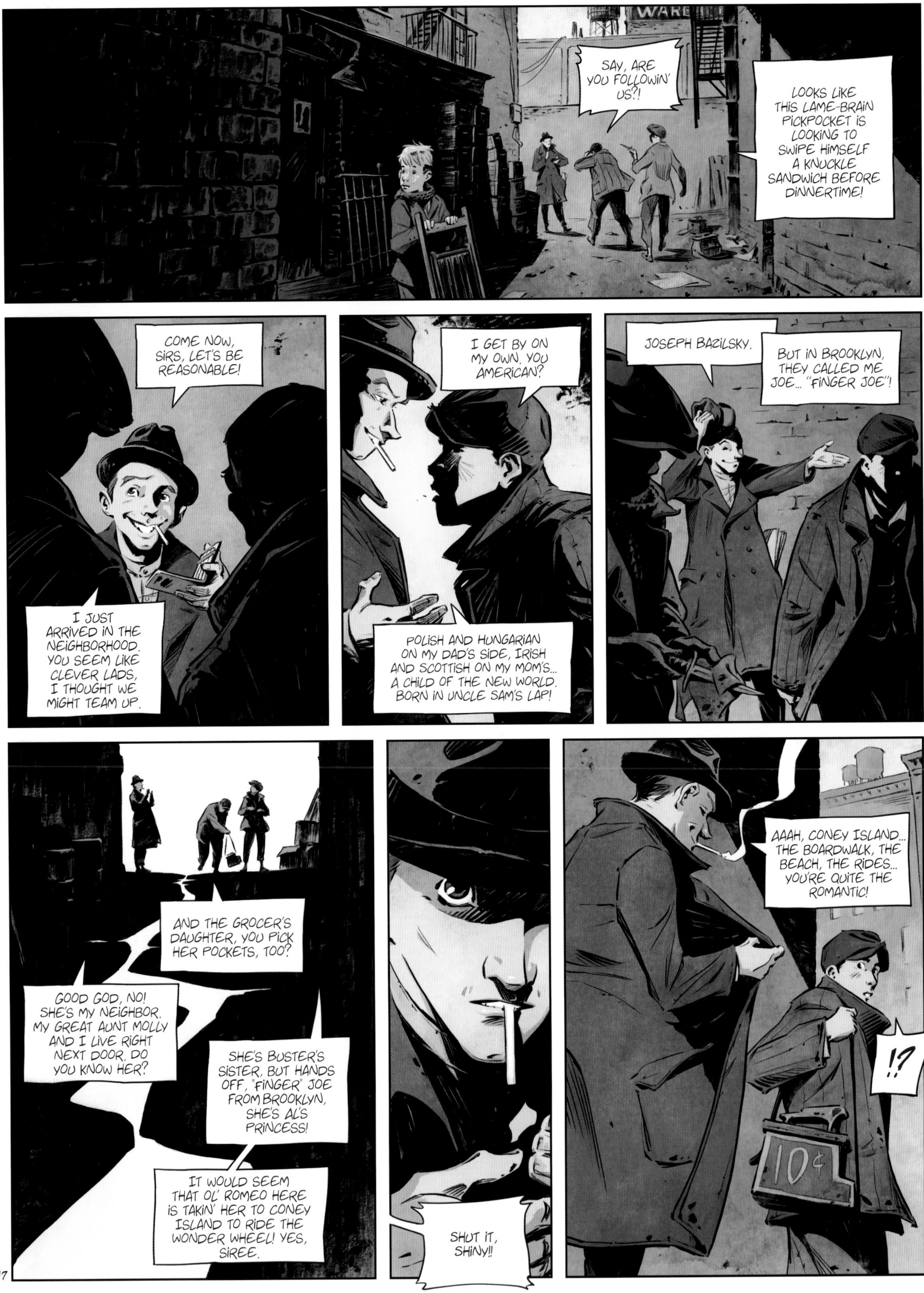

SAY, ARE YOU FOLLOWIN' US?!
LOOKS LIKE THIS LAME-BRAIN PICKPOCKET IS LOOKING TO SWIPE HIMSELF A KNUCKLE SANDWICH BEFORE DINNERTIME!
COME NOW, SIRS, LET'S BE REASONABLE!
I JUST ARRIVED IN THE NEIGHBORHOOD. YOU SEEM LIKE CLEVER LADS, I THOUGHT WE MIGHT TEAM UP.
I GET BY ON MY OWN. YOU AMERICAN?
POLISH AND HUNGARIAN ON MY DAD'S SIDE, IRISH AND SCOTTISH ON MY MOM'S... A CHILD OF THE NEW WORLD. BORN IN UNCLE SAM'S LAP!
JOSEPH BAZILSKY.
BUT IN BROOKLYN, THEY CALLED ME JOE... "FINGER JOE"!
AND THE GROCER'S DAUGHTER, YOU PICK HER POCKETS, TOO?
GOOD GOD, NO! SHE'S MY NEIGHBOR. MY GREAT AUNT MOLLY AND I LIVE RIGHT NEXT DOOR. DO YOU KNOW HER?
SHE'S BUSTER'S SISTER, BUT HANDS OFF, "FINGER" JOE FROM BROOKLYN, SHE'S AL'S PRINCESS!
IT WOULD SEEM THAT OL' ROMEO HERE IS TAKIN' HER TO CONEY ISLAND TO RIDE THE WONDER WHEEL! YES, SIREE.
SHUT IT, SHINY!!
AAAH, CONEY ISLAND... THE BOARDWALK, THE BEACH, THE RIDES... YOU'RE QUITE THE ROMANTIC!
!?
10¢

17

"IF YOU GOT NOTHING, TAKE SOMETHING!" THAT'S MY MOTTO.

THAT SAID, IF YOU'D RATHER GET BY "ON YOUR OWN" AS A TRIO...

PLUS, I'VE GOT CONTACTS IN THE BUSINESS. I CAN GET ANY KIND OF DEAL GOIN'...

YOU TALK BIG, BUT YOU'LL GET CAUGHT SOONER OR LATER! MANHATTAN COPS AIN'T LIKE THE ONES BACK IN BROOKLYN!!

PSSH! THE POLICE ARE THE SAME, NO MATTER WHICH SIDE OF THE BRIDGE YOU'RE ON...

...YOU JUST NEED TO KNOW HOW TO HANDLE THEM!

French Madame

2:30 P.M. AND 8:30 P.M.

NEW SHOW EVERY FRIDAY MIDNIGHT SHOW SATURDAYS

2½ HOUR SHOW

French Madame BURLESQUE

SNAPPY! SAUCY! SPICY!

LOOK OUT!! A COP!

QUICK, SHINE MY BOOTS!!

NO WAY, WHAT D'YOU--?

DO IT NOW!!

ALL WELL, HERE?

18

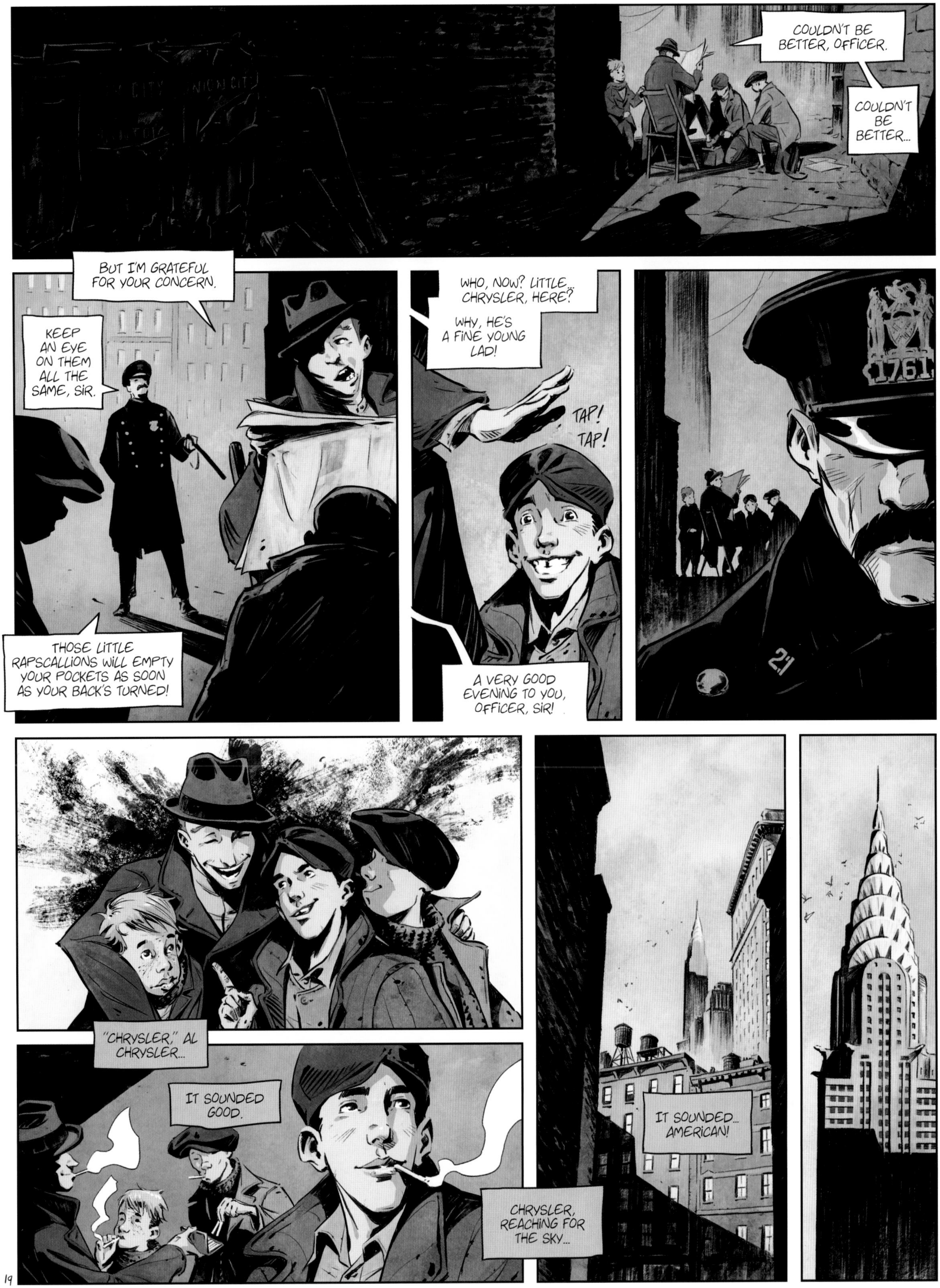
COULDN'T BE BETTER, OFFICER.
COULDN'T BE BETTER...
BUT I'M GRATEFUL FOR YOUR CONCERN.
KEEP AN EYE ON THEM ALL THE SAME, SIR.
THOSE LITTLE RAPSCALLIONS WILL EMPTY YOUR POCKETS AS SOON AS YOUR BACK'S TURNED!
WHO, NOW? LITTLE CHRYSLER, HERE?
WHY, HE'S A FINE YOUNG LAD!
TAP! TAP!
A VERY GOOD EVENING TO YOU, OFFICER, SIR!
1761
21
"CHRYSLER," AL CHRYSLER...
IT SOUNDED GOOD.
IT SOUNDED... AMERICAN!
CHRYSLER, REACHING FOR THE SKY...
19

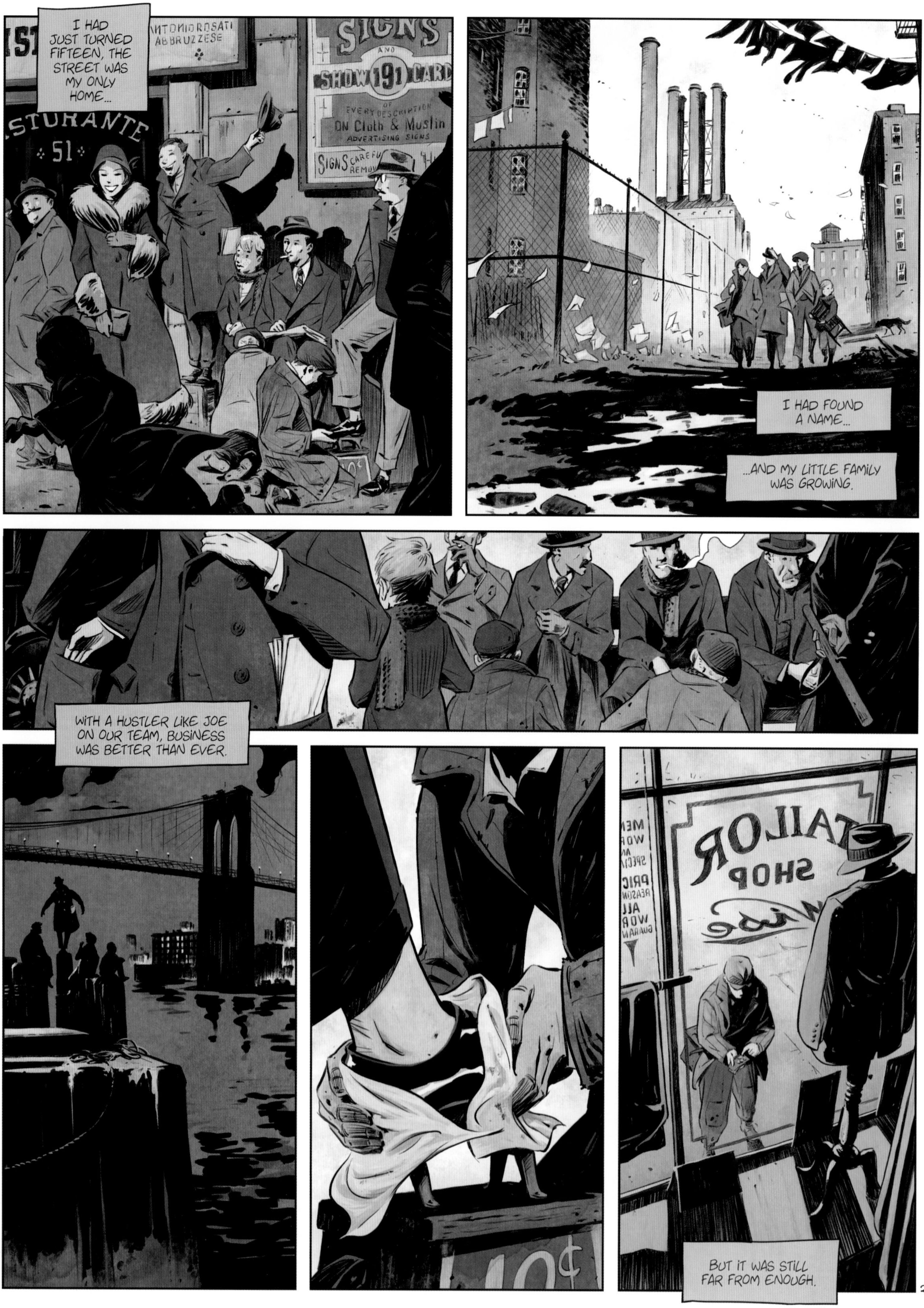
I HAD JUST TURNED FIFTEEN, THE STREET WAS MY ONLY HOME...
ANTONIO ROSATI ABBRUZZESE
SIGNS AND SHOW 191 CARDS OF EVERY DESCRIPTION ON Cloth & Muslin ADVERTISING SIGNS
I HAD FOUND A NAME...
...AND MY LITTLE FAMILY WAS GROWING.
WITH A HUSTLER LIKE JOE ON OUR TEAM, BUSINESS WAS BETTER THAN EVER.
BUT IT WAS STILL FAR FROM ENOUGH.
20

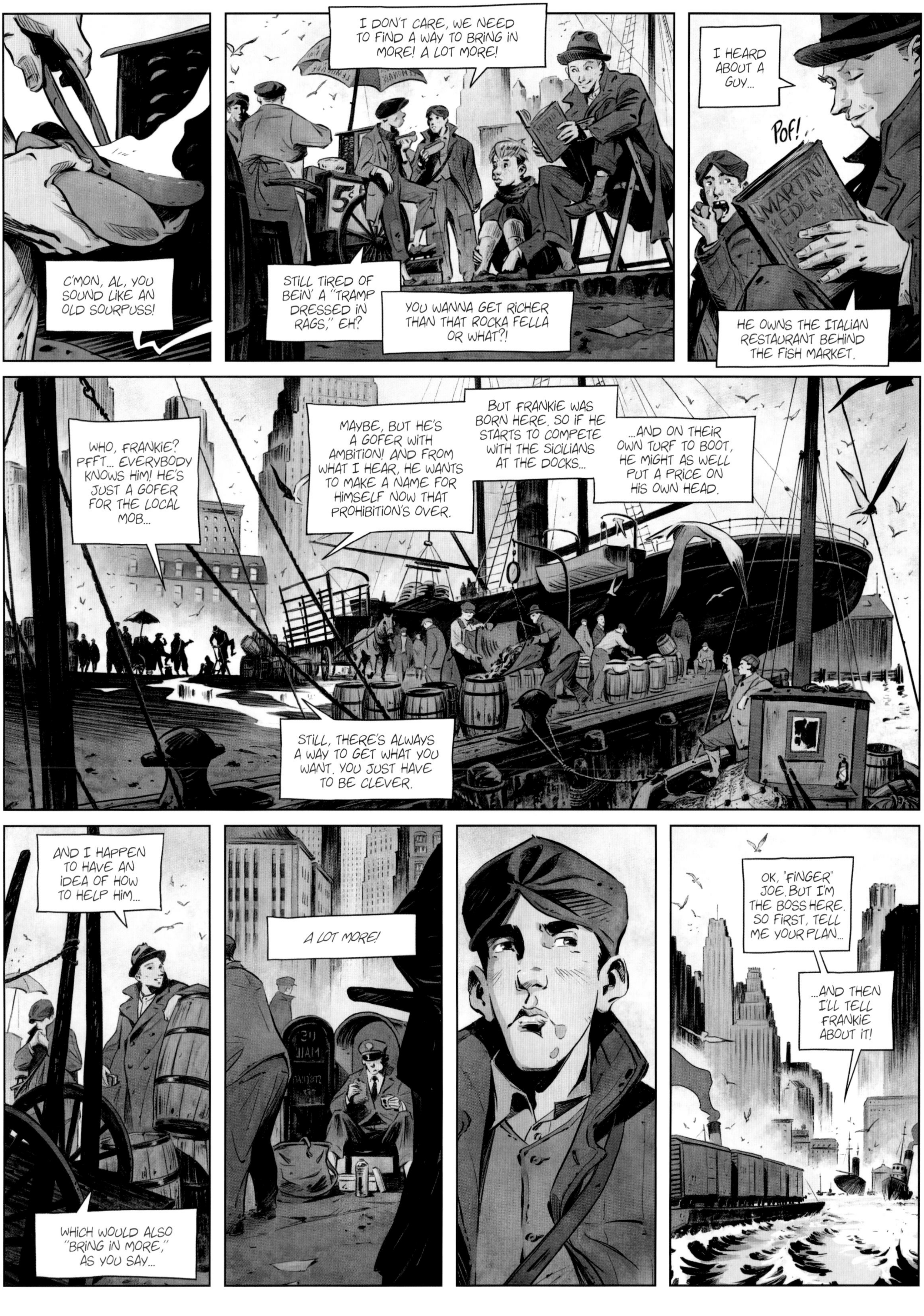
C'MON, AL, YOU SOUND LIKE AN OLD SOURPUSS!
I DON'T CARE, WE NEED TO FIND A WAY TO BRING IN MORE! A LOT MORE!
STILL TIRED OF BEIN' A "TRAMP DRESSED IN RAGS," EH?
YOU WANNA GET RICHER THAN THAT ROCKA FELLA OR WHAT?!
I HEARD ABOUT A GUY...
POF!
HE OWNS THE ITALIAN RESTAURANT BEHIND THE FISH MARKET.
WHO, FRANKIE? PFFT... EVERYBODY KNOWS HIM! HE'S JUST A GOFER FOR THE LOCAL MOB...
MAYBE, BUT HE'S A GOFER WITH AMBITION! AND FROM WHAT I HEAR, HE WANTS TO MAKE A NAME FOR HIMSELF NOW THAT PROHIBITION'S OVER.
BUT FRANKIE WAS BORN HERE. SO IF HE STARTS TO COMPETE WITH THE SICILIANS AT THE DOCKS...
...AND ON THEIR OWN TURF TO BOOT, HE MIGHT AS WELL PUT A PRICE ON HIS OWN HEAD.
STILL, THERE'S ALWAYS A WAY TO GET WHAT YOU WANT. YOU JUST HAVE TO BE CLEVER.
AND I HAPPEN TO HAVE AN IDEA OF HOW TO HELP HIM...
WHICH WOULD ALSO "BRING IN MORE," AS YOU SAY...
A LOT MORE!
OK, "FINGER" JOE. BUT I'M THE BOSS HERE. SO FIRST, TELL ME YOUR PLAN...
...AND THEN I'LL TELL FRANKIE ABOUT IT!

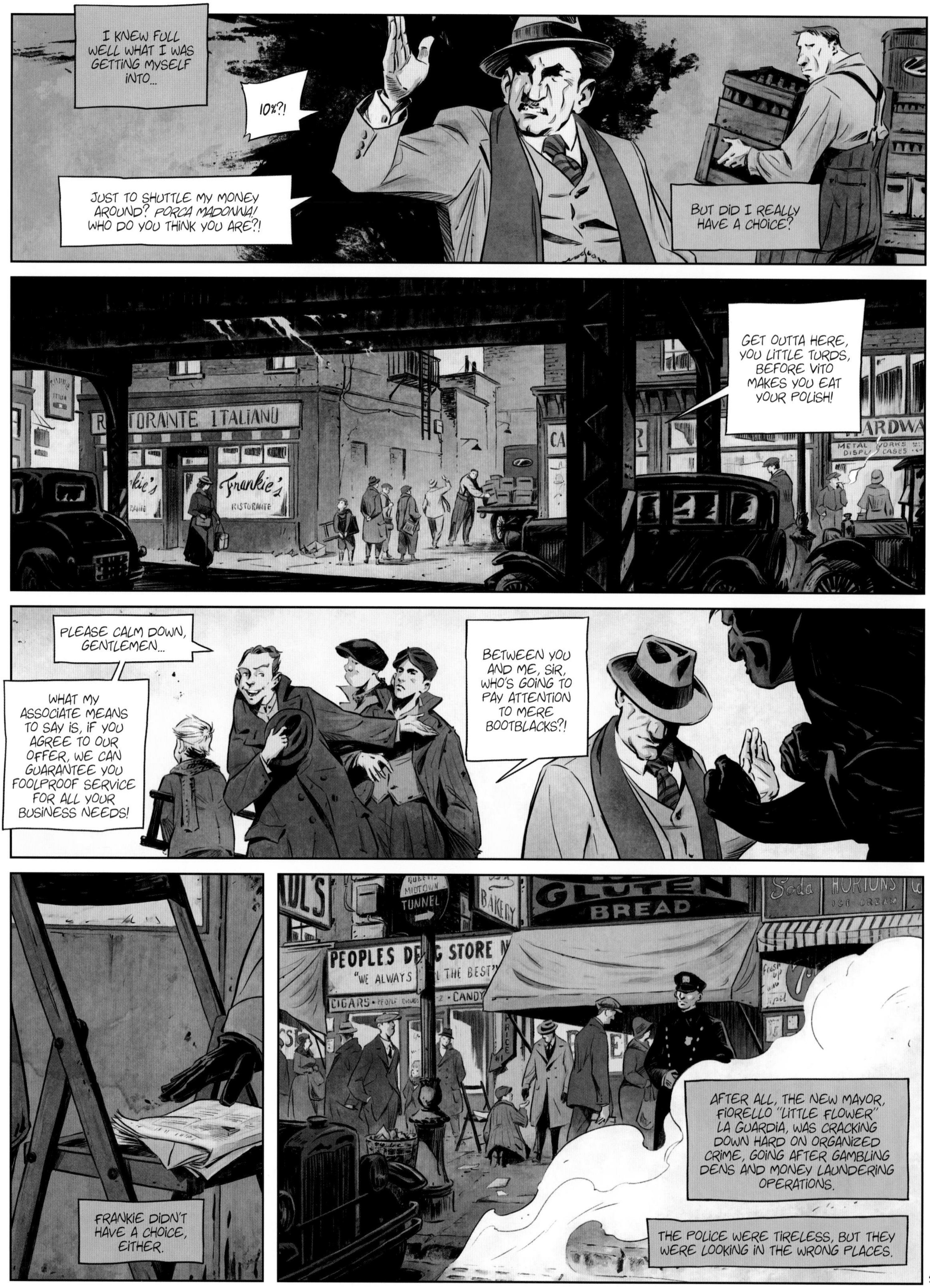

I KNEW FULL WELL WHAT I WAS GETTING MYSELF INTO...
10%?!
JUST TO SHUTTLE MY MONEY AROUND? *PORCA MADONNA!* WHO DO YOU THINK YOU ARE?!
BUT DID I REALLY HAVE A CHOICE?
GET OUTTA HERE, YOU LITTLE TURDS, BEFORE VITO MAKES YOU EAT YOUR POLISH!
Frankie's
RISTORANTE
PLEASE CALM DOWN, GENTLEMEN...
WHAT MY ASSOCIATE MEANS TO SAY IS, IF YOU AGREE TO OUR OFFER, WE CAN GUARANTEE YOU FOOLPROOF SERVICE FOR ALL YOUR BUSINESS NEEDS!
BETWEEN YOU AND ME, SIR, WHO'S GOING TO PAY ATTENTION TO MERE BOOTBLACKS?!
FRANKIE DIDN'T HAVE A CHOICE, EITHER.
TUNNEL
BAKERY
GLUTEN
BREAD
CIGARS
CANDY
AFTER ALL, THE NEW MAYOR, FIORELLO "LITTLE FLOWER" LA GUARDIA, WAS CRACKING DOWN HARD ON ORGANIZED CRIME, GOING AFTER GAMBLING DENS AND MONEY LAUNDERING OPERATIONS.
THE POLICE WERE TIRELESS, BUT THEY WERE LOOKING IN THE WRONG PLACES.

22

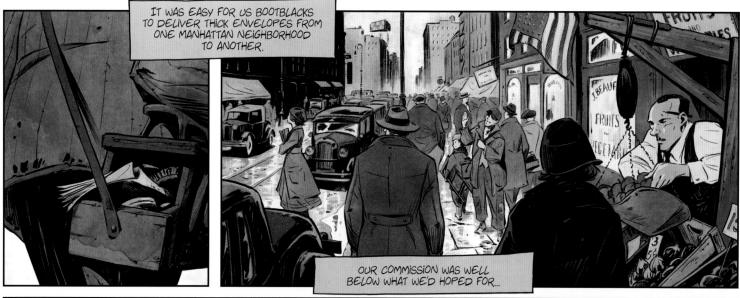

IT WAS EASY FOR US BOOTBLACKS TO DELIVER THICK ENVELOPES FROM ONE MANHATTAN NEIGHBORHOOD TO ANOTHER.
FRUITS
OUR COMMISSION WAS WELL BELOW WHAT WE'D HOPED FOR...
THURS. FEB. 15
JORDAN
PRIMO
CARNERA
ADMISSION $2.30
ROOSEVELT
ROT
REELECT
MADISON SQ. GARDEN
15 ROUNDS
JACK "GIANT"
...BUT IT WAS A LOT MORE THAN WHAT WE'D EARNED WEARING OUT OUR KNEES EVERY DAY ON THE CITY'S COLD SIDEWALKS.
AND SO FRANKIE'S MONEY PASSED FROM HAND TO HAND WITHOUT RAISING THE SLIGHTEST SUSPICION.
25¢
Snappy

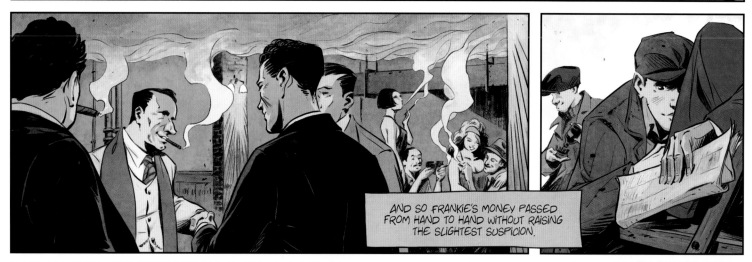

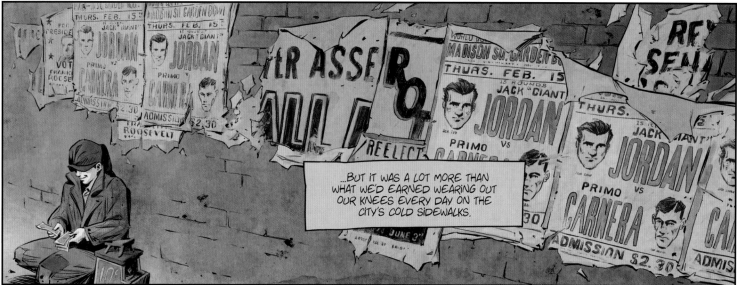

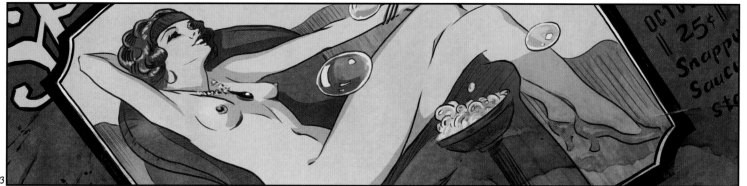

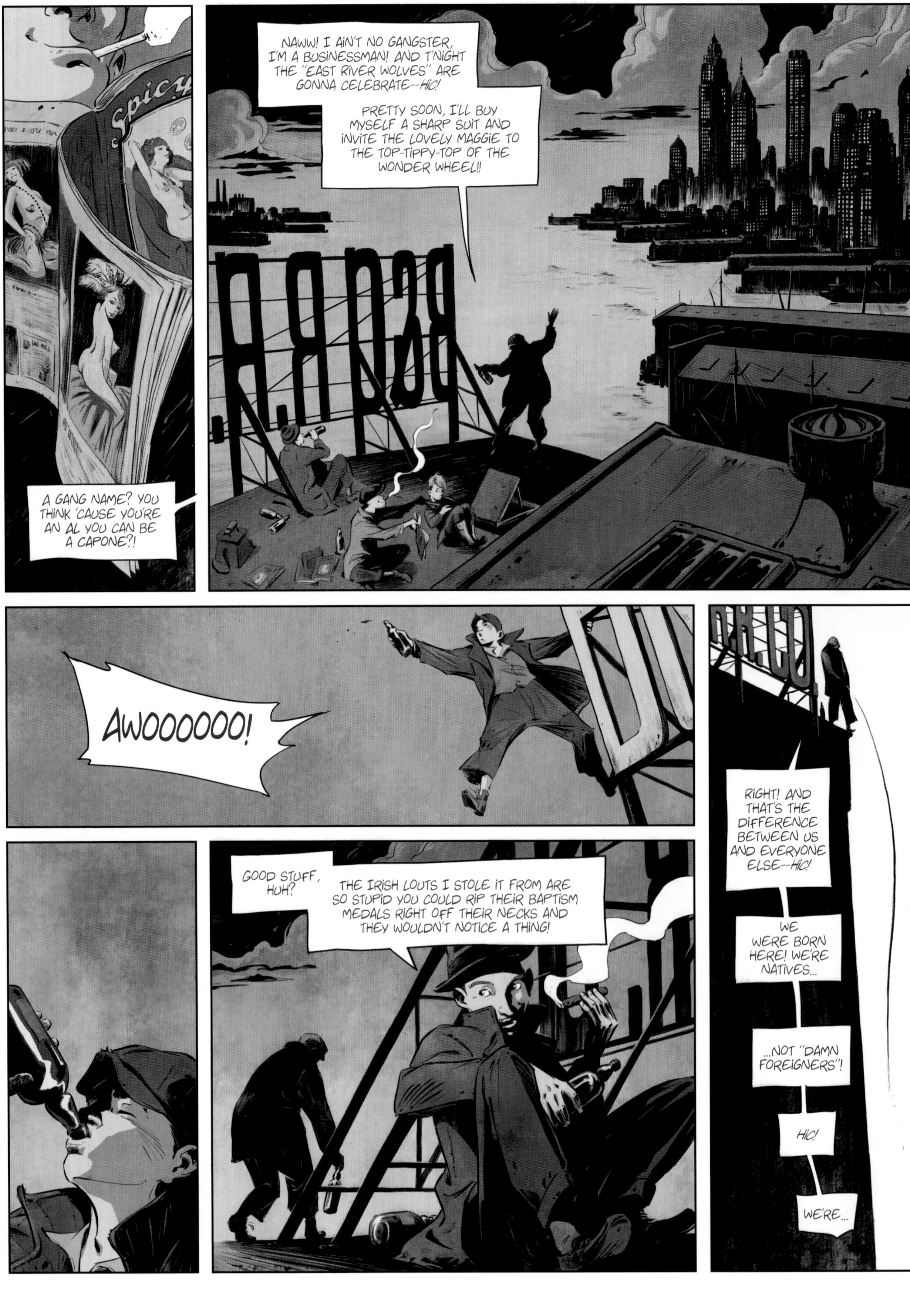
A GANG NAME? YOU THINK 'CAUSE YOU'RE AN AL YOU CAN BE A CAPONE?!
NAWW! I AIN'T NO GANGSTER, I'M A BUSINESSMAN! AND T'NIGHT THE "EAST RIVER WOLVES" ARE GONNA CELEBRATE--HIC!
PRETTY SOON, I'LL BUY MYSELF A SHARP SUIT AND INVITE THE LOVELY MAGGIE TO THE TOP-TIPPY-TOP OF THE WONDER WHEEL!!
AWOOOOOO!
GOOD STUFF, HUH?
THE IRISH LOUTS I STOLE IT FROM ARE SO STUPID YOU COULD RIP THEIR BAPTISM MEDALS RIGHT OFF THEIR NECKS AND THEY WOULDN'T NOTICE A THING!
RIGHT! AND THAT'S THE DIFFERENCE BETWEEN US AND EVERYONE ELSE--HIC!
WE WERE BORN HERE! WE'RE NATIVES...
...NOT "DAMN FOREIGNERS"!
HIC!
WE'RE...
24

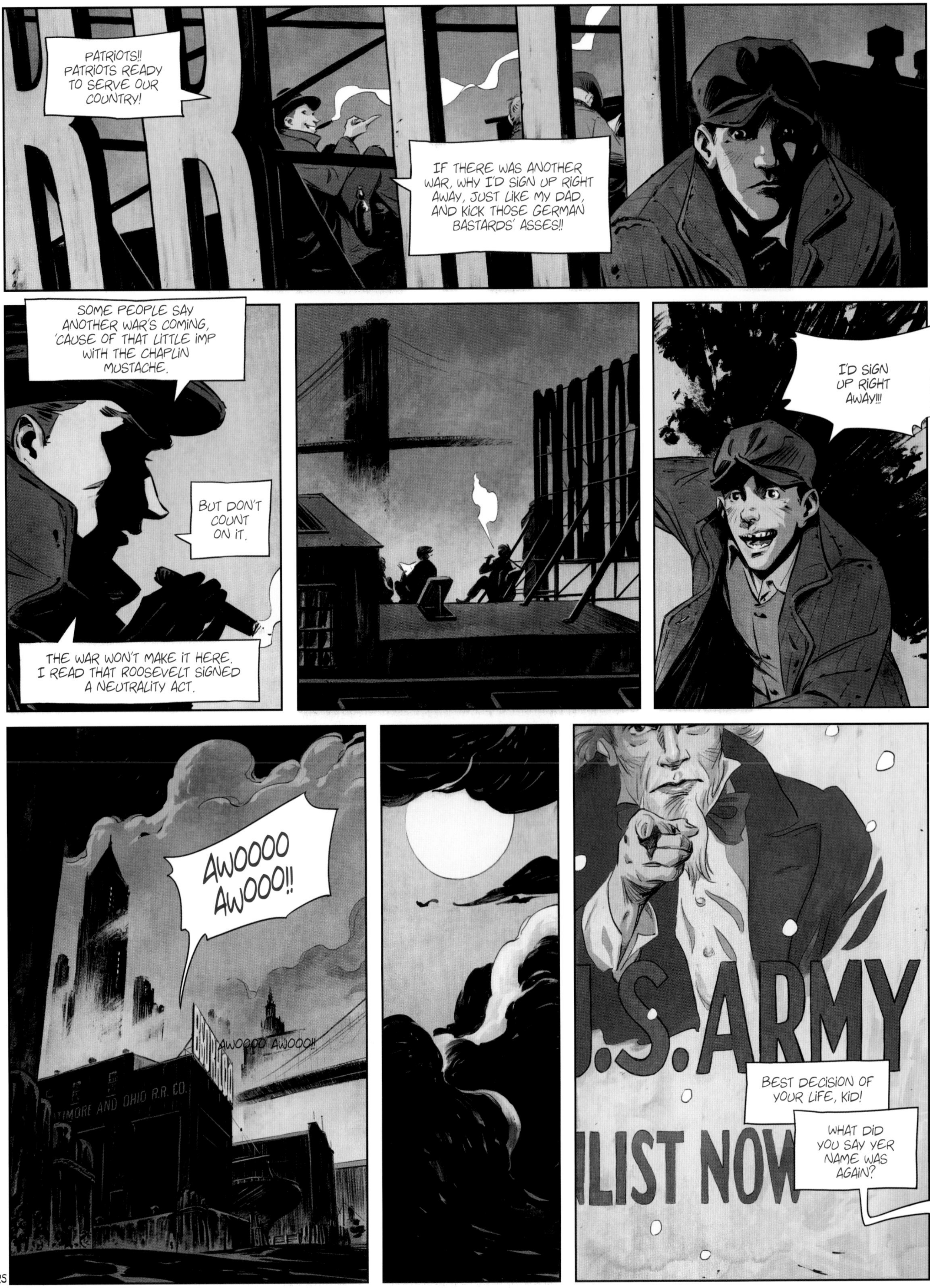

PATRIOTS!! PATRIOTS READY TO SERVE OUR COUNTRY!
IF THERE WAS ANOTHER WAR, WHY I'D SIGN UP RIGHT AWAY, JUST LIKE MY DAD, AND KICK THOSE GERMAN BASTARDS' ASSES!!
SOME PEOPLE SAY ANOTHER WAR'S COMING, 'CAUSE OF THAT LITTLE IMP WITH THE CHAPLIN MUSTACHE.
BUT DON'T COUNT ON IT.
THE WAR WON'T MAKE IT HERE. I READ THAT ROOSEVELT SIGNED A NEUTRALITY ACT.
I'D SIGN UP RIGHT AWAY!!!
AWOOOO AWOOO!!
AWOOOO AWOOO!!
...TIMORE AND OHIO R.R. CO.
U.S. ARMY
...NLIST NOW
BEST DECISION OF YOUR LIFE, KID!
WHAT DID YOU SAY YER NAME WAS AGAIN?

25

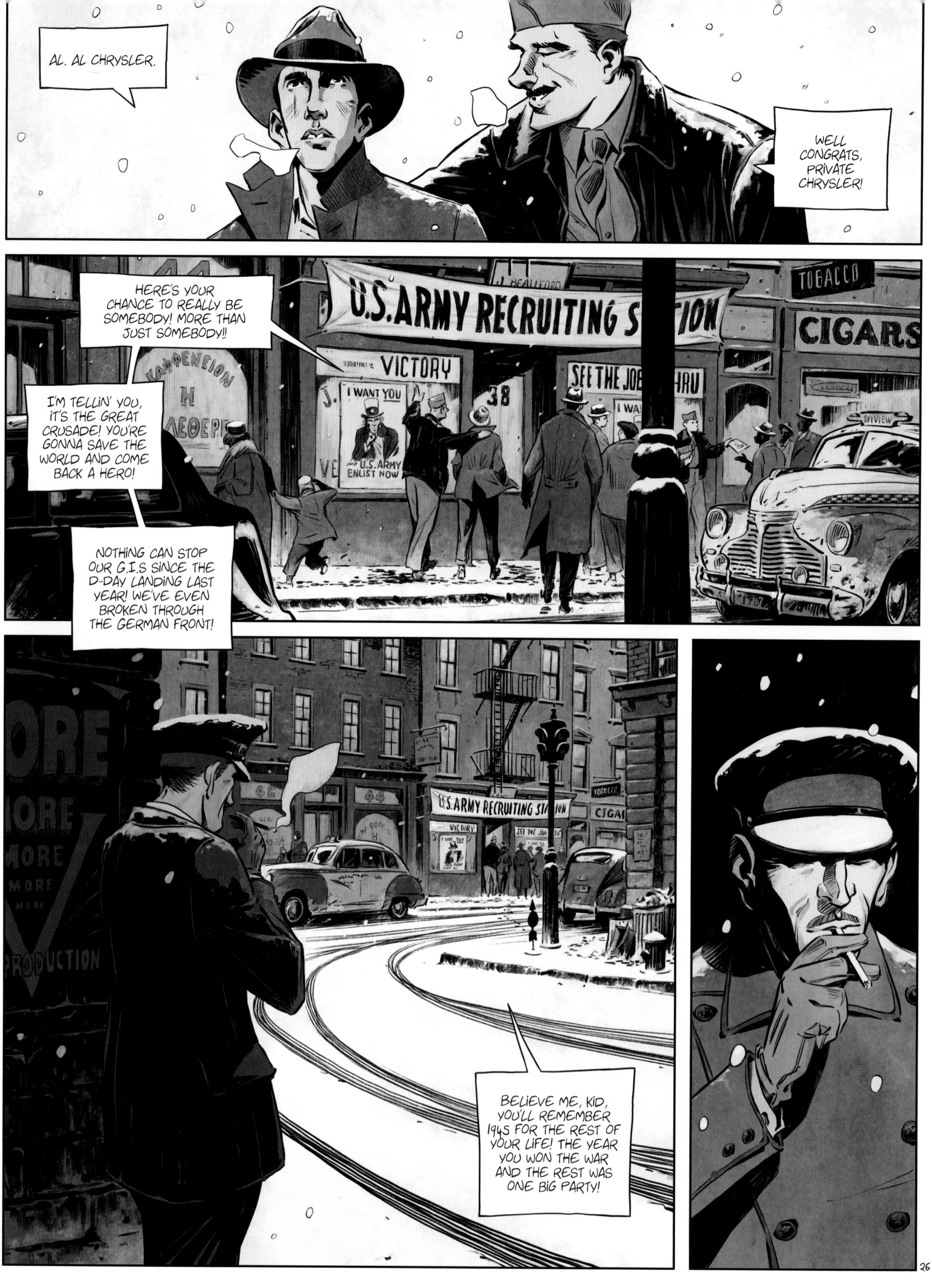
AL. AL CHRYSLER.
WELL CONGRATS, PRIVATE CHRYSLER!
HERE'S YOUR CHANCE TO REALLY BE SOMEBODY! MORE THAN JUST SOMEBODY!!
I'M TELLIN' YOU, IT'S THE GREAT CRUSADE! YOU'RE GONNA SAVE THE WORLD AND COME BACK A HERO!
NOTHING CAN STOP OUR G.I.S SINCE THE D-DAY LANDING LAST YEAR! WE'VE EVEN BROKEN THROUGH THE GERMAN FRONT!
TOBACCO
CIGARS
VICTORY
I WANT YOU
U.S. ARMY
ENLIST NOW
PRODUCTION
BELIEVE ME, KID, YOU'LL REMEMBER 1945 FOR THE REST OF YOUR LIFE! THE YEAR YOU WON THE WAR AND THE REST WAS ONE BIG PARTY!
26

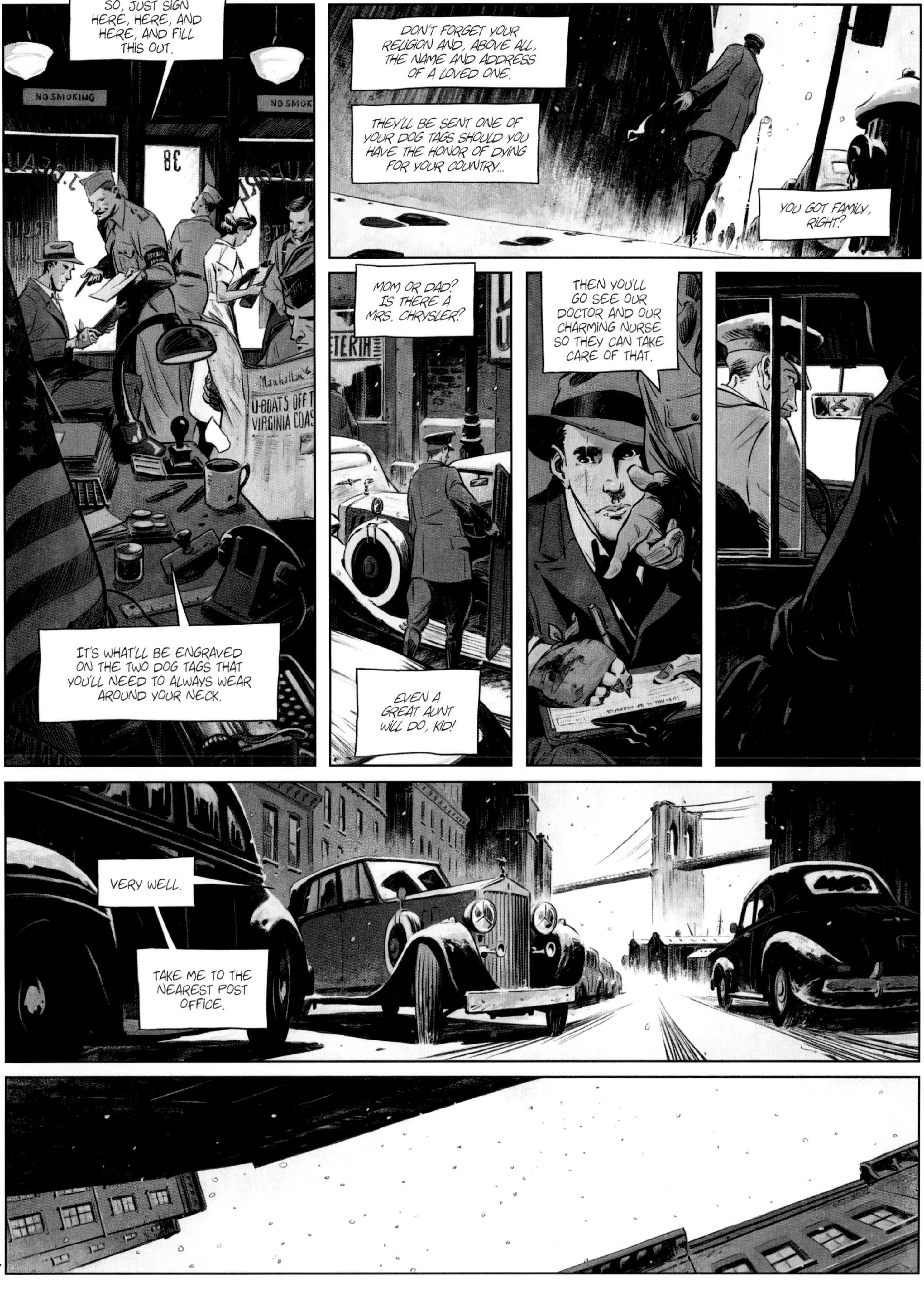

SO, JUST SIGN HERE, HERE, AND HERE, AND FILL THIS OUT.
NO SMOKING
IT'S WHAT'LL BE ENGRAVED ON THE TWO DOG TAGS THAT YOU'LL NEED TO ALWAYS WEAR AROUND YOUR NECK.
DON'T FORGET YOUR RELIGION AND, ABOVE ALL, THE NAME AND ADDRESS OF A LOVED ONE.
THEY'LL BE SENT ONE OF YOUR DOG TAGS SHOULD YOU HAVE THE HONOR OF DYING FOR YOUR COUNTRY...
YOU GOT FAMILY, RIGHT?
MOM OR DAD? IS THERE A MRS. CHRYSLER?
EVEN A GREAT AUNT WILL DO, KID!
THEN YOU'LL GO SEE OUR DOCTOR AND OUR CHARMING NURSE SO THEY CAN TAKE CARE OF THAT.
VERY WELL.
TAKE ME TO THE NEAREST POST OFFICE.

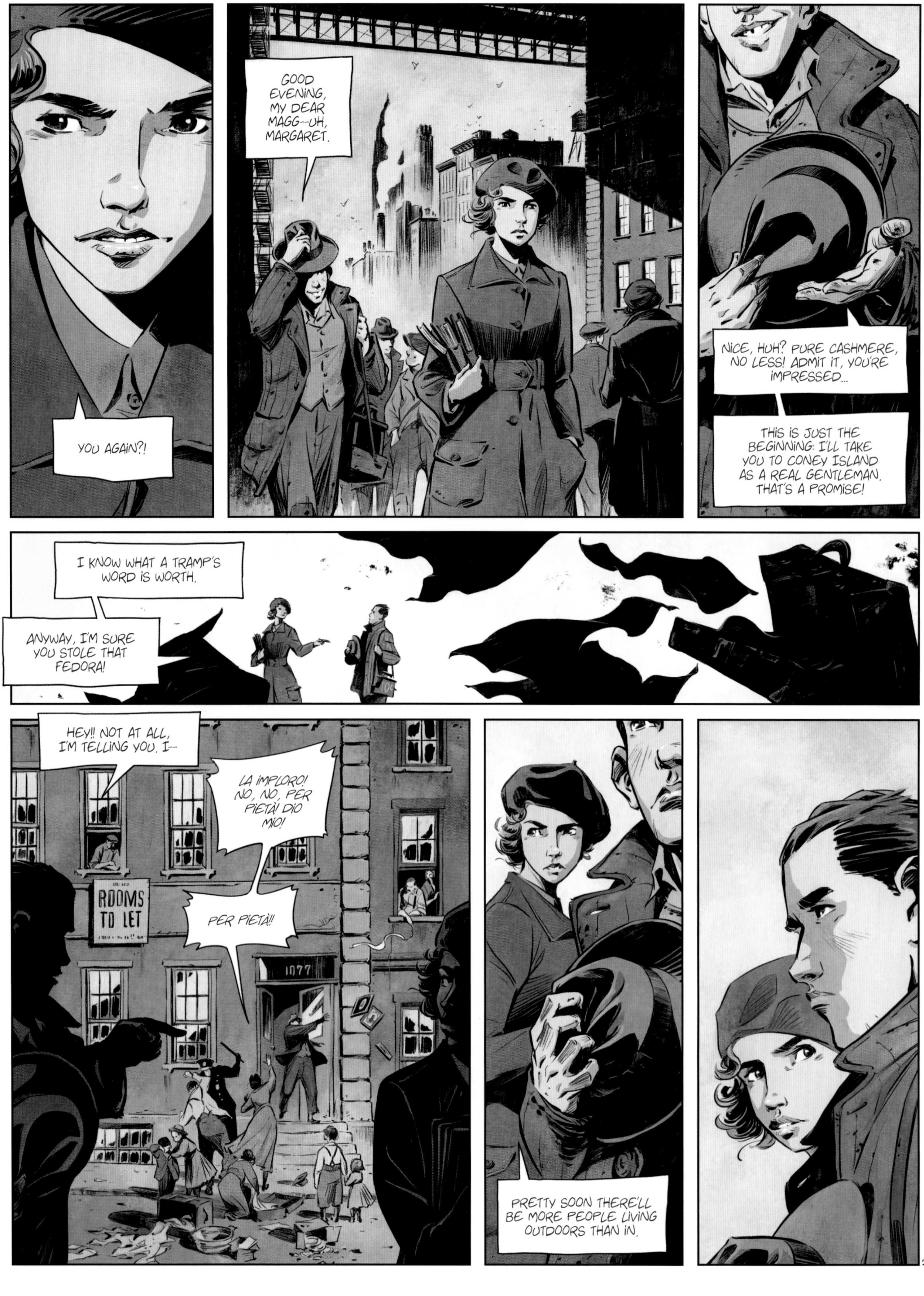
YOU AGAIN?!
GOOD EVENING, MY DEAR MAGG--UH, MARGARET.
NICE, HUH? PURE CASHMERE, NO LESS! ADMIT IT, YOU'RE IMPRESSED...
THIS IS JUST THE BEGINNING: I'LL TAKE YOU TO CONEY ISLAND AS A REAL GENTLEMAN. THAT'S A PROMISE!
I KNOW WHAT A TRAMP'S WORD IS WORTH.
ANYWAY, I'M SURE YOU STOLE THAT FEDORA!
HEY!! NOT AT ALL, I'M TELLING YOU. I--
LA IMPLORO! NO, NO, PER PIETÀ! DIO MIO!
ROOMS TO LET
PER PIETÀ!!
1077
PRETTY SOON THERE'LL BE MORE PEOPLE LIVING OUTDOORS THAN IN.
28

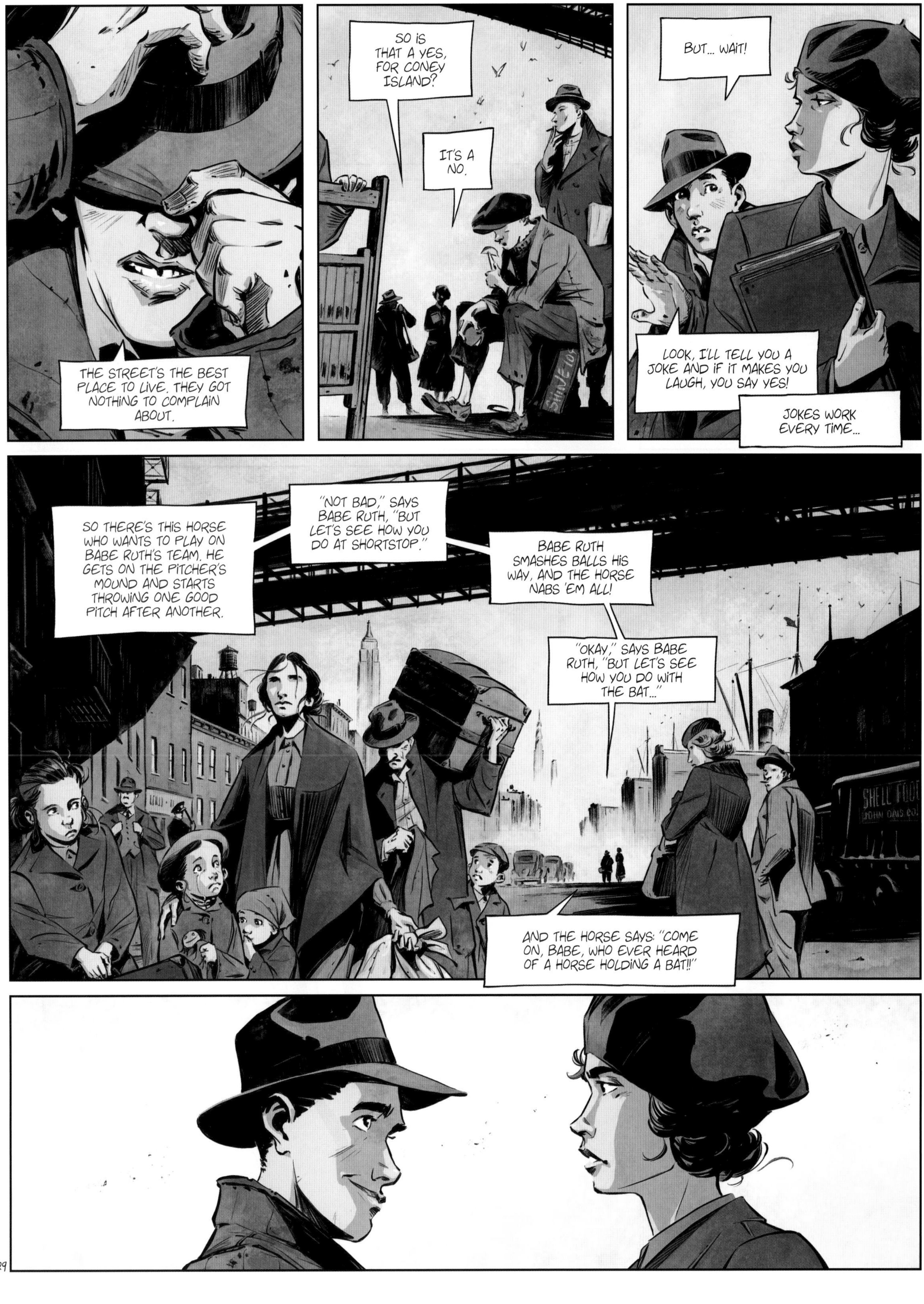
THE STREET'S THE BEST PLACE TO LIVE. THEY GOT NOTHING TO COMPLAIN ABOUT.
SO IS THAT A YES, FOR CONEY ISLAND?
IT'S A NO.
BUT... WAIT!
LOOK, I'LL TELL YOU A JOKE AND IF IT MAKES YOU LAUGH, YOU SAY YES!
JOKES WORK EVERY TIME...
SO THERE'S THIS HORSE WHO WANTS TO PLAY ON BABE RUTH'S TEAM. HE GETS ON THE PITCHER'S MOUND AND STARTS THROWING ONE GOOD PITCH AFTER ANOTHER.
"NOT BAD," SAYS BABE RUTH, "BUT LET'S SEE HOW YOU DO AT SHORTSTOP."
BABE RUTH SMASHES BALLS HIS WAY, AND THE HORSE NABS 'EM ALL!
"OKAY," SAYS BABE RUTH, "BUT LET'S SEE HOW YOU DO WITH THE BAT..."
AND THE HORSE SAYS: "COME ON, BABE, WHO EVER HEARD OF A HORSE HOLDING A BAT!!"

29

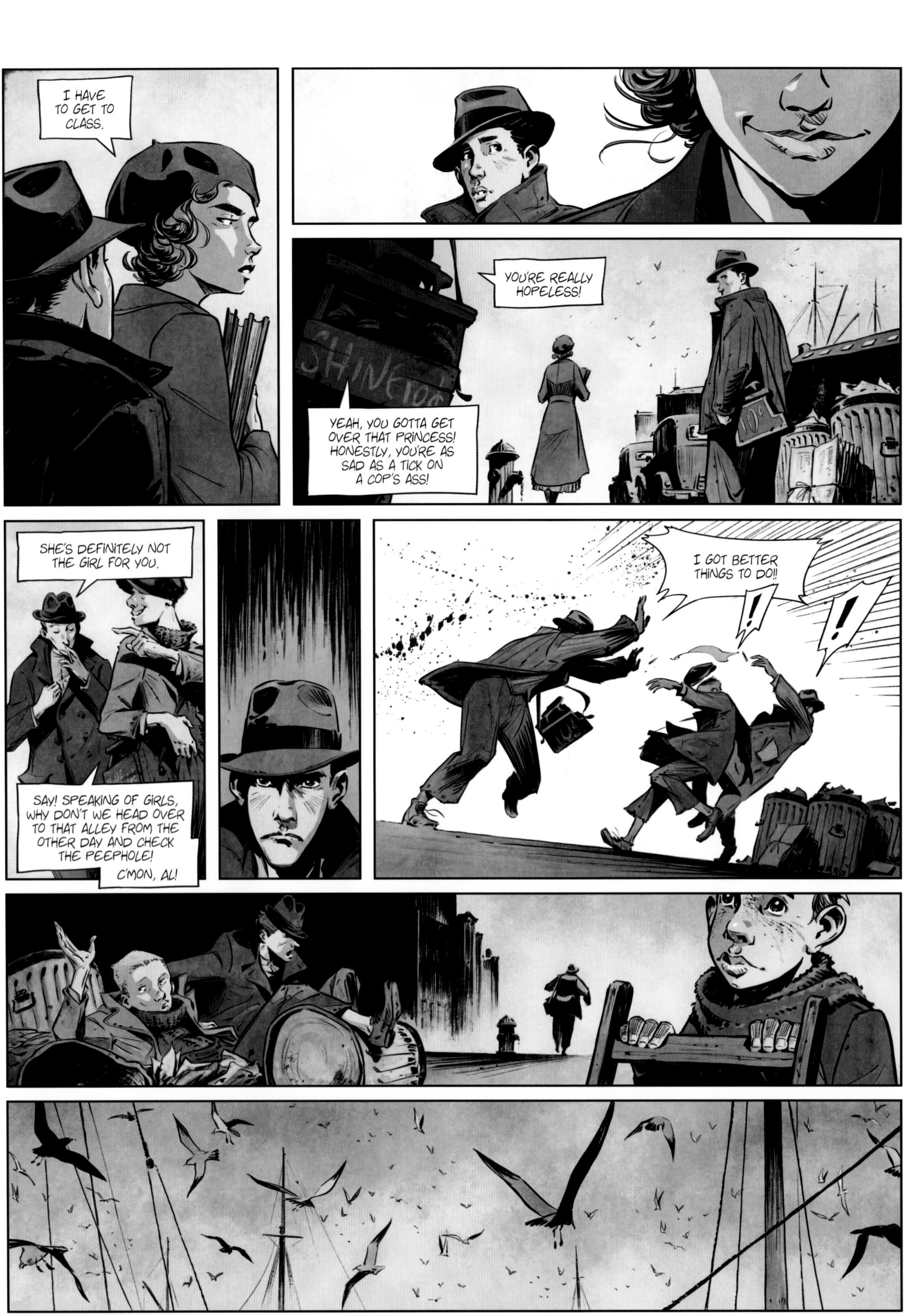
I HAVE TO GET TO CLASS.
YOU'RE REALLY HOPELESS!
YEAH, YOU GOTTA GET OVER THAT PRINCESS! HONESTLY, YOU'RE AS SAD AS A TICK ON A COP'S ASS!
SHE'S DEFINITELY NOT THE GIRL FOR YOU.
SAY! SPEAKING OF GIRLS, WHY DON'T WE HEAD OVER TO THAT ALLEY FROM THE OTHER DAY AND CHECK THE PEEPHOLE!
C'MON, AL!
I GOT BETTER THINGS TO DO!!
!
!
30

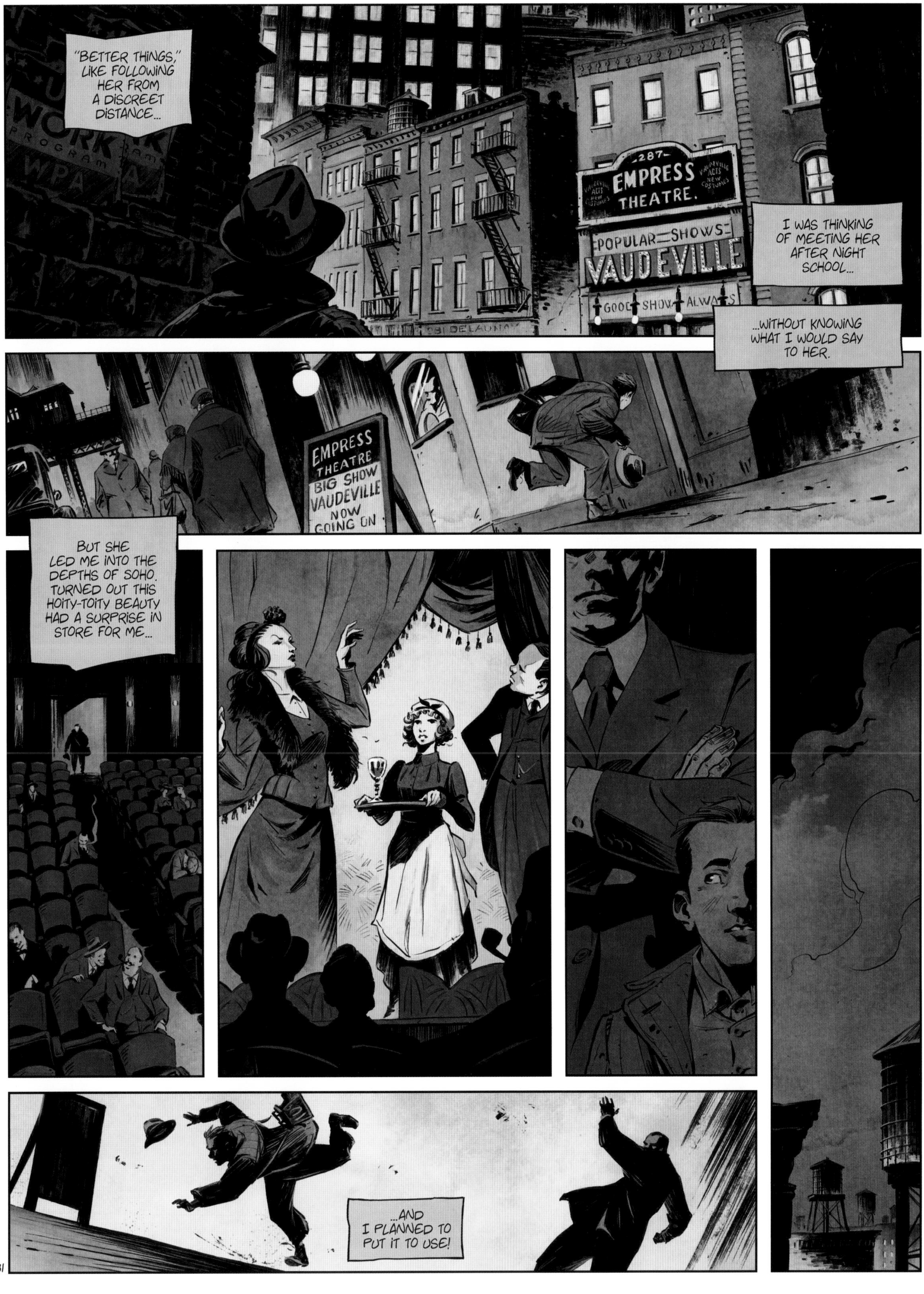
"BETTER THINGS," LIKE FOLLOWING HER FROM A DISCREET DISTANCE...
WORK PROGRAM
WPA
287
EMPRESS THEATRE.
VAUDEVILLE ACTS NEW COSTUMES
POPULAR SHOWS
VAUDEVILLE
GOOD SHOW ALWAYS
I WAS THINKING OF MEETING HER AFTER NIGHT SCHOOL...
...WITHOUT KNOWING WHAT I WOULD SAY TO HER.
EMPRESS THEATRE BIG SHOW VAUDEVILLE NOW GOING ON
BUT SHE LED ME INTO THE DEPTHS OF SOHO. TURNED OUT THIS HOITY-TOITY BEAUTY HAD A SURPRISE IN STORE FOR ME...
...AND I PLANNED TO PUT IT TO USE!
31

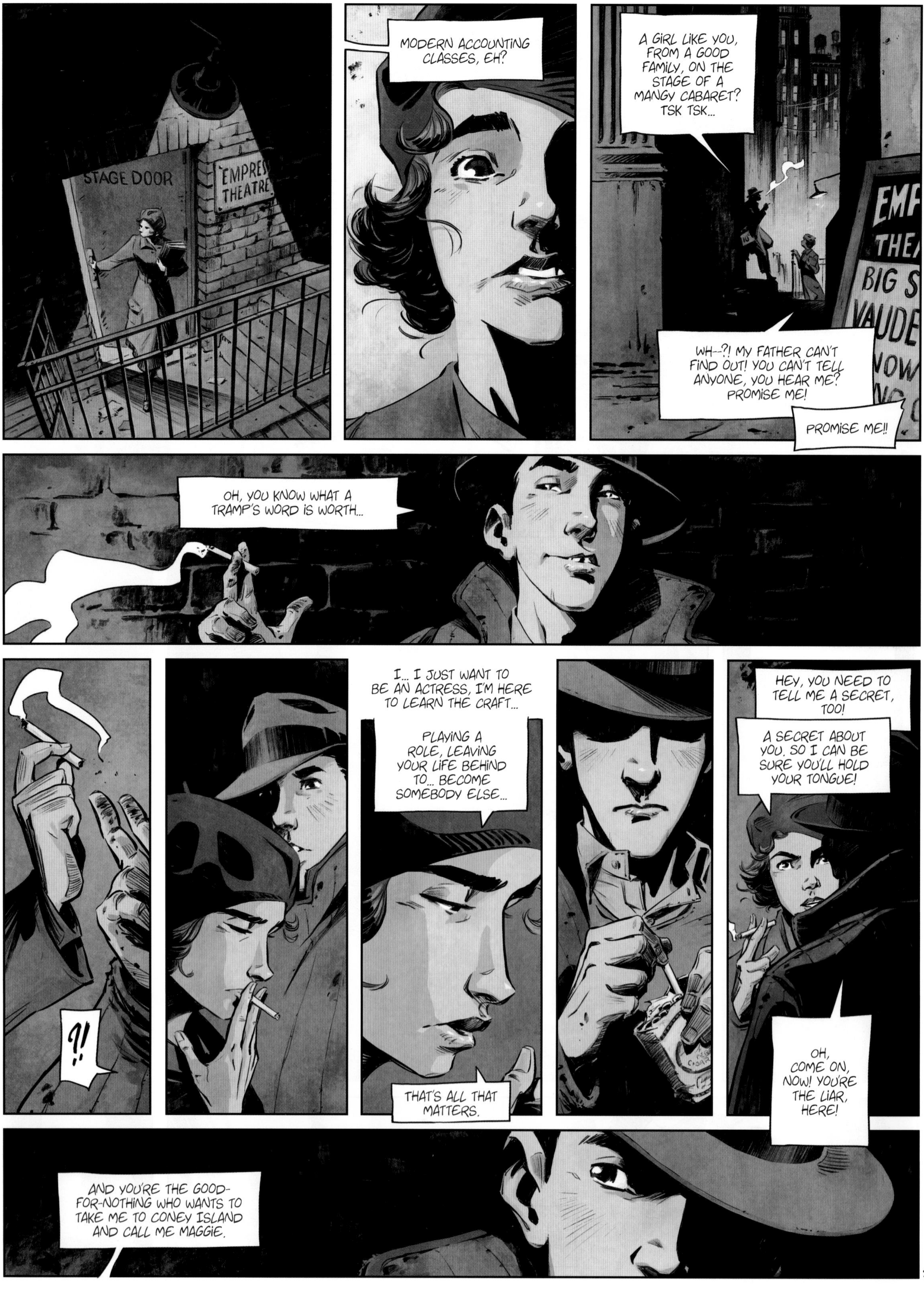
STAGE DOOR
THEATRE
MODERN ACCOUNTING CLASSES, EH?
A GIRL LIKE YOU, FROM A GOOD FAMILY, ON THE STAGE OF A MANGY CABARET? TSK TSK...
WH--?! MY FATHER CAN'T FIND OUT! YOU CAN'T TELL ANYONE, YOU HEAR ME? PROMISE ME!
PROMISE ME!!
OH, YOU KNOW WHAT A TRAMP'S WORD IS WORTH...
?!
I... I JUST WANT TO BE AN ACTRESS, I'M HERE TO LEARN THE CRAFT...
PLAYING A ROLE, LEAVING YOUR LIFE BEHIND TO... BECOME SOMEBODY ELSE...
THAT'S ALL THAT MATTERS.
HEY, YOU NEED TO TELL ME A SECRET, TOO!
A SECRET ABOUT YOU. SO I CAN BE SURE YOU'LL HOLD YOUR TONGUE!
OH, COME ON, NOW! YOU'RE THE LIAR, HERE!
AND YOU'RE THE GOOD-FOR-NOTHING WHO WANTS TO TAKE ME TO CONEY ISLAND AND CALL ME MAGGIE.

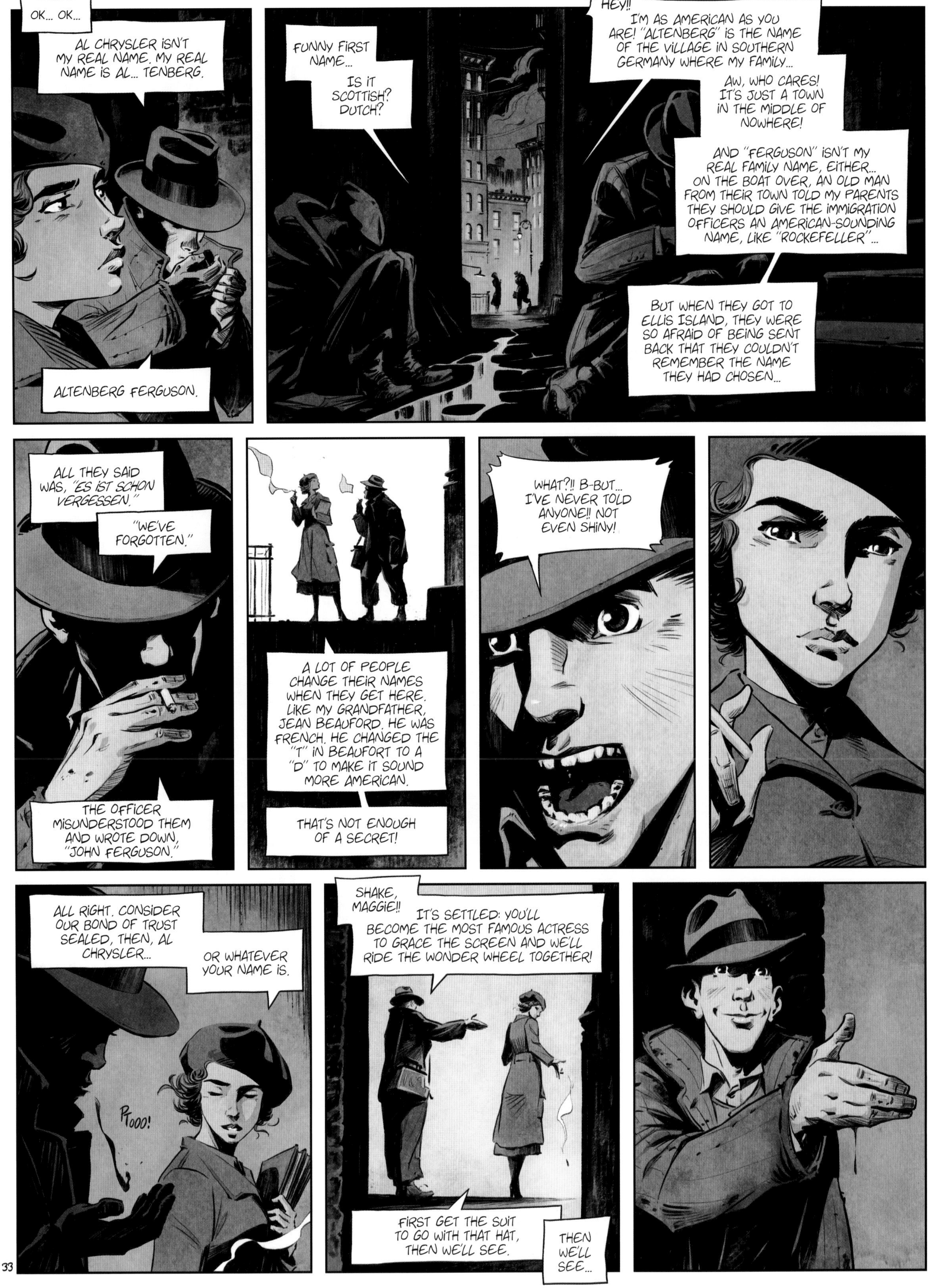
OK... OK...
AL CHRYSLER ISN'T MY REAL NAME. MY REAL NAME IS AL... TENBERG.
ALTENBERG FERGUSON.
FUNNY FIRST NAME...
IS IT SCOTTISH? DUTCH?
HEY!! I'M AS AMERICAN AS YOU ARE! "ALTENBERG" IS THE NAME OF THE VILLAGE IN SOUTHERN GERMANY WHERE MY FAMILY...
AW, WHO CARES! IT'S JUST A TOWN IN THE MIDDLE OF NOWHERE!
AND "FERGUSON" ISN'T MY REAL FAMILY NAME, EITHER... ON THE BOAT OVER, AN OLD MAN FROM THEIR TOWN TOLD MY PARENTS THEY SHOULD GIVE THE IMMIGRATION OFFICERS AN AMERICAN-SOUNDING NAME, LIKE "ROCKEFELLER"...
BUT WHEN THEY GOT TO ELLIS ISLAND, THEY WERE SO AFRAID OF BEING SENT BACK THAT THEY COULDN'T REMEMBER THE NAME THEY HAD CHOSEN...
ALL THEY SAID WAS, "ES IST SCHON VERGESSEN."
"WE'VE FORGOTTEN."
THE OFFICER MISUNDERSTOOD THEM AND WROTE DOWN, "JOHN FERGUSON."
A LOT OF PEOPLE CHANGE THEIR NAMES WHEN THEY GET HERE. LIKE MY GRANDFATHER, JEAN BEAUFORD. HE WAS FRENCH. HE CHANGED THE "T" IN BEAUFORT TO A "D" TO MAKE IT SOUND MORE AMERICAN.
THAT'S NOT ENOUGH OF A SECRET!
WHAT?!! B-BUT... I'VE NEVER TOLD ANYONE!! NOT EVEN SHINY!
ALL RIGHT. CONSIDER OUR BOND OF TRUST SEALED, THEN, AL CHRYSLER...
OR WHATEVER YOUR NAME IS.
PTOOO!
SHAKE, MAGGIE!!
IT'S SETTLED: YOU'LL BECOME THE MOST FAMOUS ACTRESS TO GRACE THE SCREEN AND WE'LL RIDE THE WONDER WHEEL TOGETHER!
FIRST GET THE SUIT TO GO WITH THAT HAT, THEN WE'LL SEE.
THEN WE'LL SEE...
33

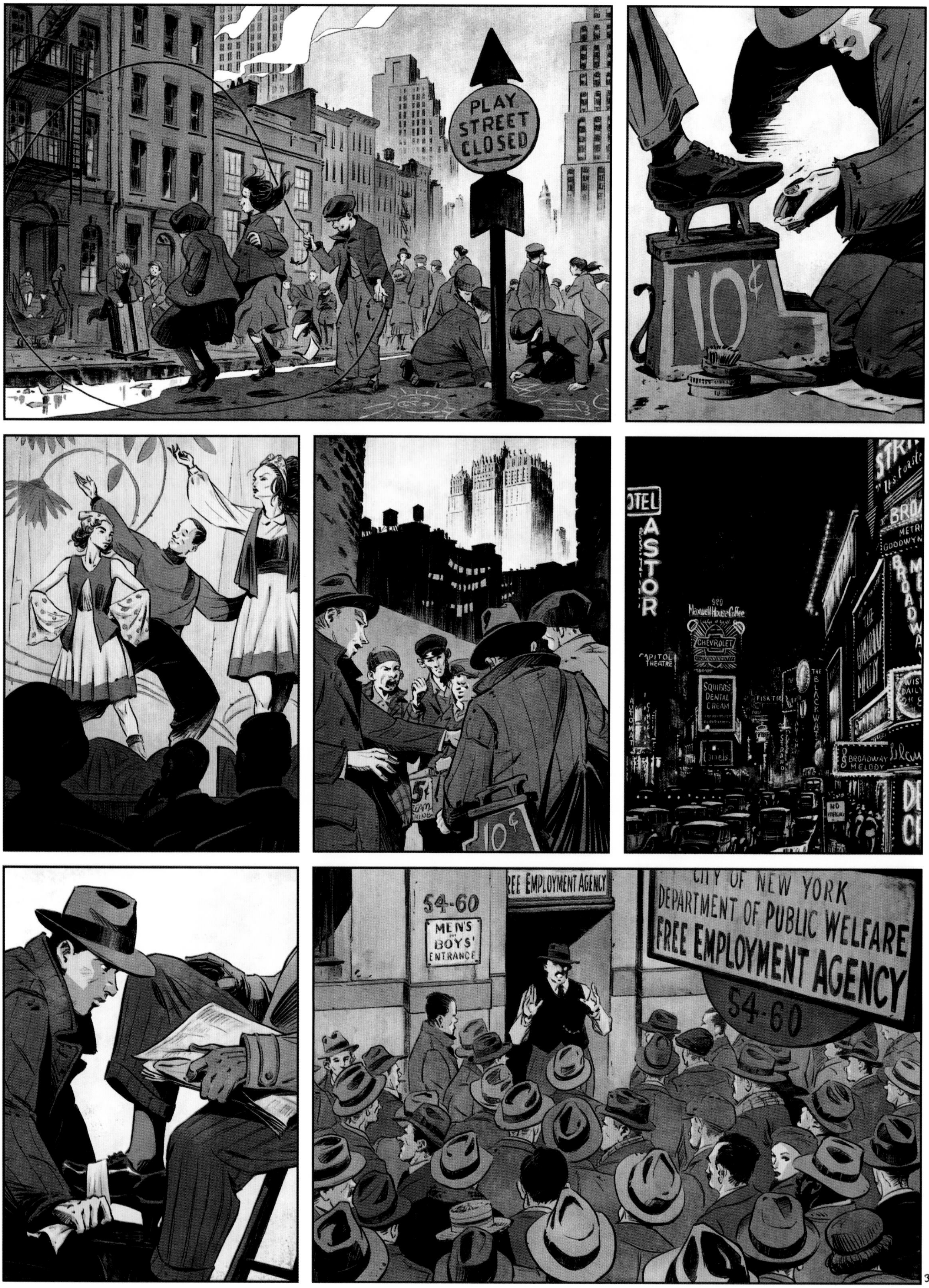
PLAY
STREET
CLOSED
10¢
ASTOR
Maxwell House Coffee
CHEVROLET
CAPITOL THEATRE
SQUIBBS DENTAL CREAM
BROADWAY MELODY
5¢
10¢
54-60
MEN'S BOYS' ENTRANCE
REE EMPLOYMENT AGENCY
CITY OF NEW YORK
DEPARTMENT OF PUBLIC WELFARE
FREE EMPLOYMENT AGENCY
54-60

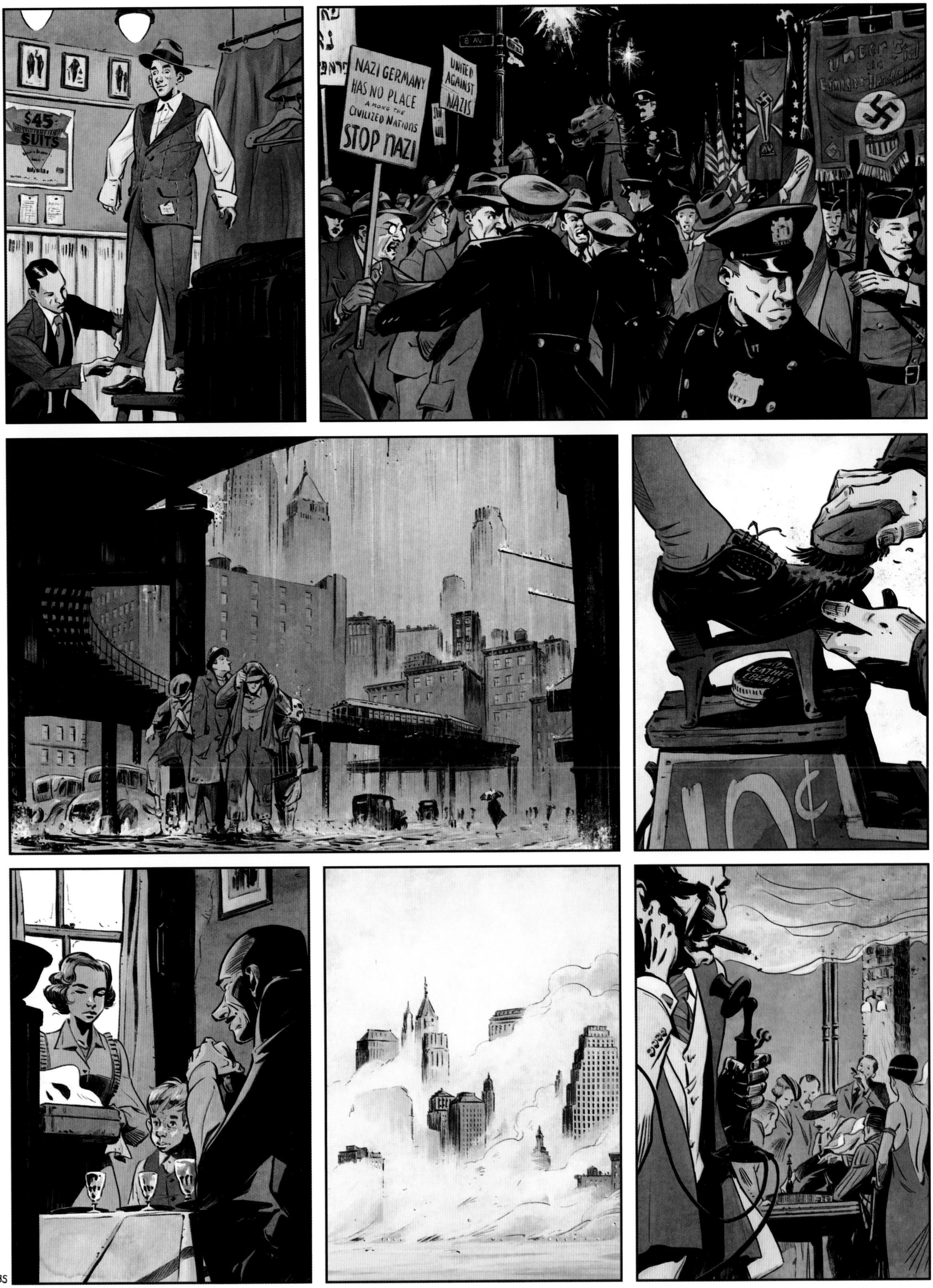
$45
SUITS
8 AV
NAZI GERMANY HAS NO PLACE AMONG THE CIVILIZED NATIONS
STOP NAZI
UNITED AGAINST NAZIS
LEATHER CREAM
10¢

35

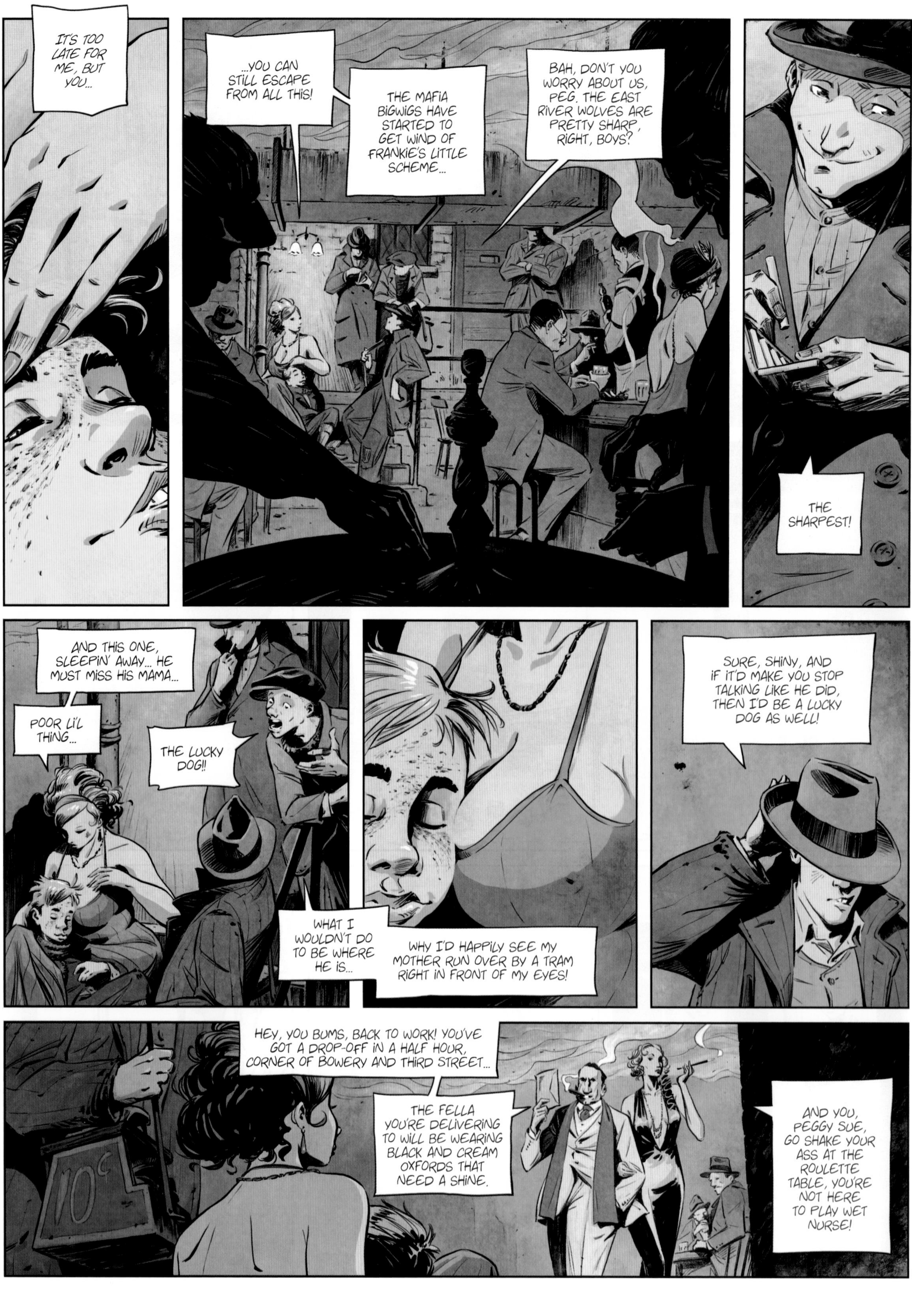

IT'S TOO LATE FOR ME, BUT YOU...
...YOU CAN STILL ESCAPE FROM ALL THIS!
THE MAFIA BIGWIGS HAVE STARTED TO GET WIND OF FRANKIE'S LITTLE SCHEME...
BAH, DON'T YOU WORRY ABOUT US, PEG. THE EAST RIVER WOLVES ARE PRETTY SHARP, RIGHT, BOYS?
THE SHARPEST!
AND THIS ONE, SLEEPIN' AWAY... HE MUST MISS HIS MAMA...
POOR LI'L THING...
THE LUCKY DOG!!
WHAT I WOULDN'T DO TO BE WHERE HE IS...
WHY I'D HAPPILY SEE MY MOTHER RUN OVER BY A TRAM RIGHT IN FRONT OF MY EYES!
SURE, SHINY, AND IF IT'D MAKE YOU STOP TALKING LIKE HE DID, THEN I'D BE A LUCKY DOG AS WELL!
HEY, YOU BUMS, BACK TO WORK! YOU'VE GOT A DROP-OFF IN A HALF HOUR, CORNER OF BOWERY AND THIRD STREET...
THE FELLA YOU'RE DELIVERING TO WILL BE WEARING BLACK AND CREAM OXFORDS THAT NEED A SHINE.
AND YOU, PEGGY SUE, GO SHAKE YOUR ASS AT THE ROULETTE TABLE, YOU'RE NOT HERE TO PLAY WET NURSE!
10¢
36

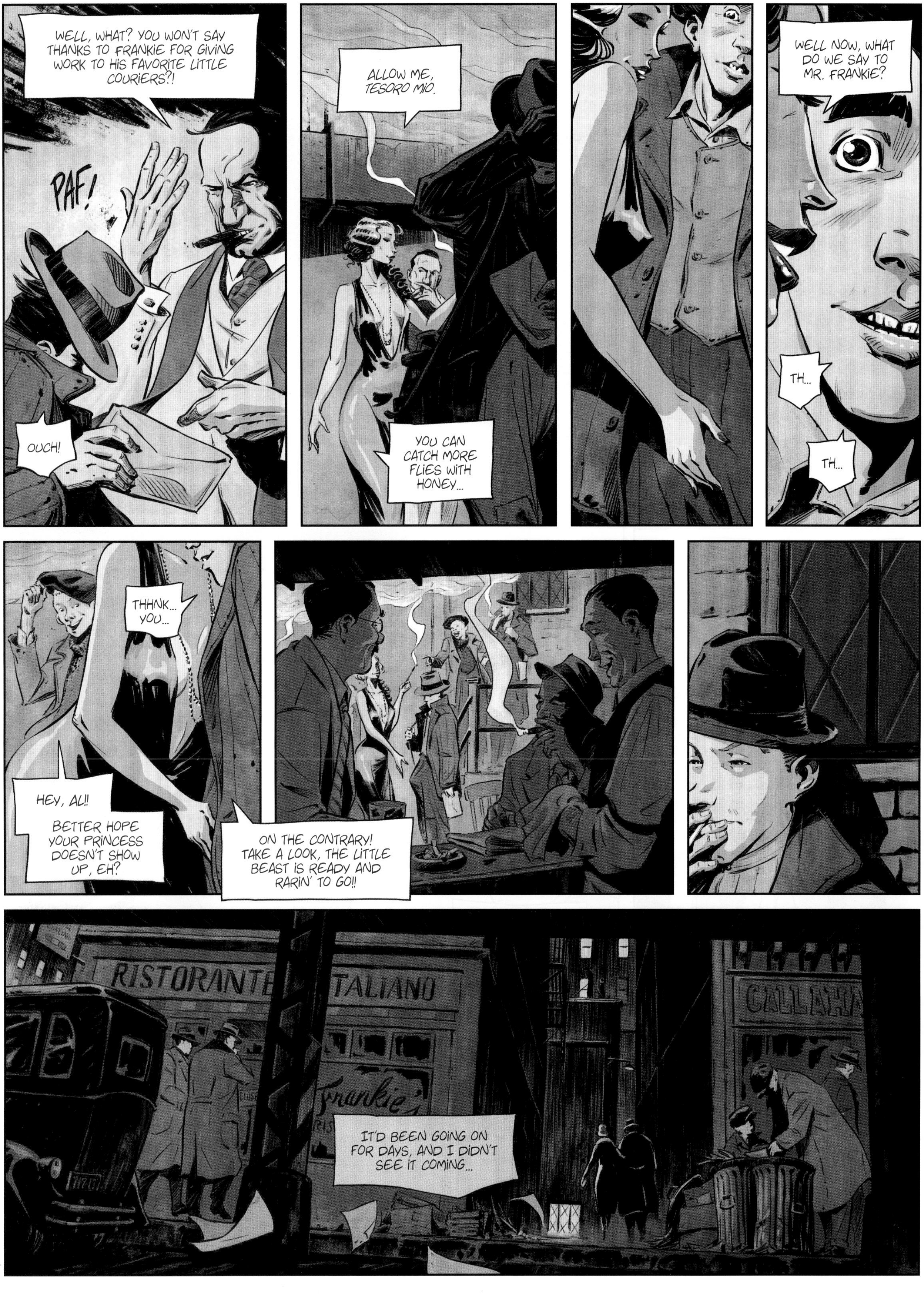
WELL, WHAT? YOU WON'T SAY THANKS TO FRANKIE FOR GIVING WORK TO HIS FAVORITE LITTLE COURIERS?!
PAF!
OUCH!
ALLOW ME, TESORO MIO.
YOU CAN CATCH MORE FLIES WITH HONEY...
WELL NOW, WHAT DO WE SAY TO MR. FRANKIE?
TH...
TH...
THHNK... YOU...
HEY, AL!!
BETTER HOPE YOUR PRINCESS DOESN'T SHOW UP, EH?
ON THE CONTRARY! TAKE A LOOK, THE LITTLE BEAST IS READY AND RARIN' TO GO!!
RISTORANTE ITALIANO
CALLAHA
IT'D BEEN GOING ON FOR DAYS, AND I DIDN'T SEE IT COMING...
37

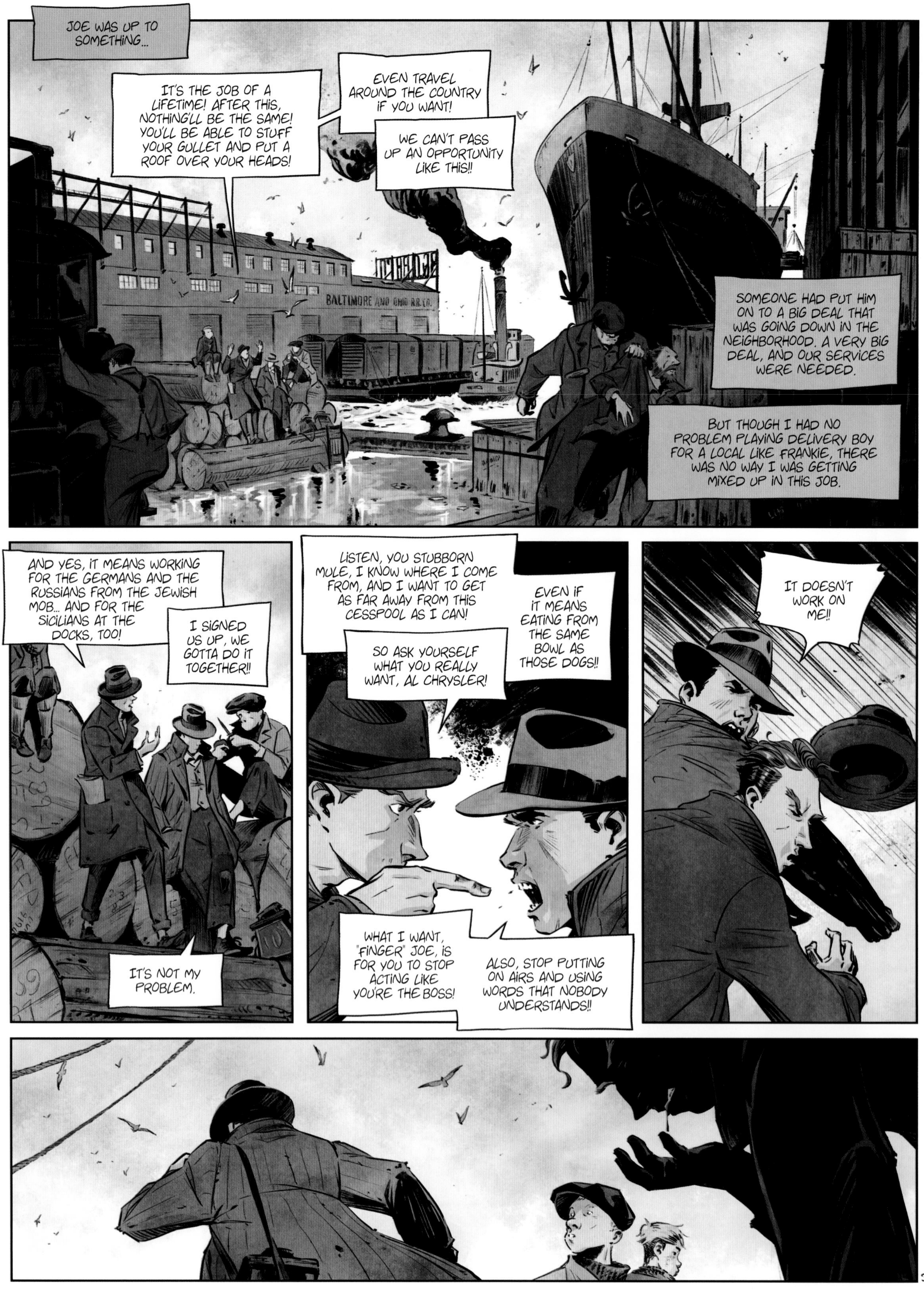
JOE WAS UP TO SOMETHING...
IT'S THE JOB OF A LIFETIME! AFTER THIS, NOTHING'LL BE THE SAME! YOU'LL BE ABLE TO STUFF YOUR GULLET AND PUT A ROOF OVER YOUR HEADS!
EVEN TRAVEL AROUND THE COUNTRY IF YOU WANT!
WE CAN'T PASS UP AN OPPORTUNITY LIKE THIS!!
BALTIMORE AND OHIO R.R. CO.
SOMEONE HAD PUT HIM ON TO A BIG DEAL THAT WAS GOING DOWN IN THE NEIGHBORHOOD. A VERY BIG DEAL, AND OUR SERVICES WERE NEEDED.
BUT THOUGH I HAD NO PROBLEM PLAYING DELIVERY BOY FOR A LOCAL LIKE FRANKIE, THERE WAS NO WAY I WAS GETTING MIXED UP IN THIS JOB.
AND YES, IT MEANS WORKING FOR THE GERMANS AND THE RUSSIANS FROM THE JEWISH MOB... AND FOR THE SICILIANS AT THE DOCKS, TOO!
I SIGNED US UP, WE GOTTA DO IT TOGETHER!!
IT'S NOT MY PROBLEM.
LISTEN, YOU STUBBORN MULE, I KNOW WHERE I COME FROM, AND I WANT TO GET AS FAR AWAY FROM THIS CESSPOOL AS I CAN!
EVEN IF IT MEANS EATING FROM THE SAME BOWL AS THOSE DOGS!!
SO ASK YOURSELF WHAT YOU REALLY WANT, AL CHRYSLER!
WHAT I WANT, "FINGER" JOE, IS FOR YOU TO STOP ACTING LIKE YOU'RE THE BOSS!
ALSO, STOP PUTTING ON AIRS AND USING WORDS THAT NOBODY UNDERSTANDS!!
IT DOESN'T WORK ON ME!!
38

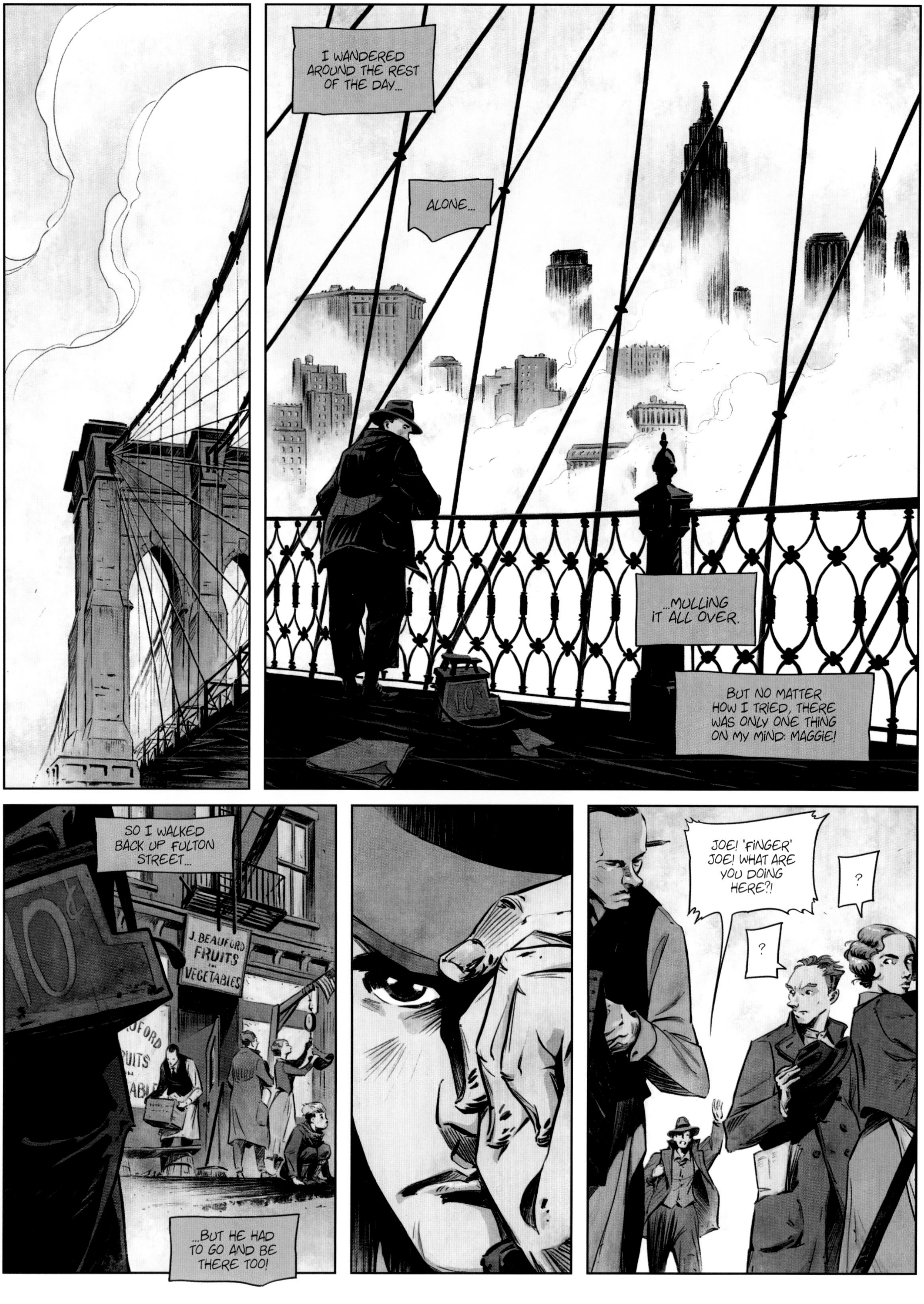

I WANDERED AROUND THE REST OF THE DAY...
ALONE...
...MULLING IT ALL OVER.
BUT NO MATTER HOW I TRIED, THERE WAS ONLY ONE THING ON MY MIND: MAGGIE!
10¢
SO I WALKED BACK UP FULTON STREET...
J. BEAUFORD FRUITS VEGETABLES
...BUT HE HAD TO GO AND BE THERE TOO!
JOE! "FINGER" JOE! WHAT ARE YOU DOING HERE?!
?
?

39

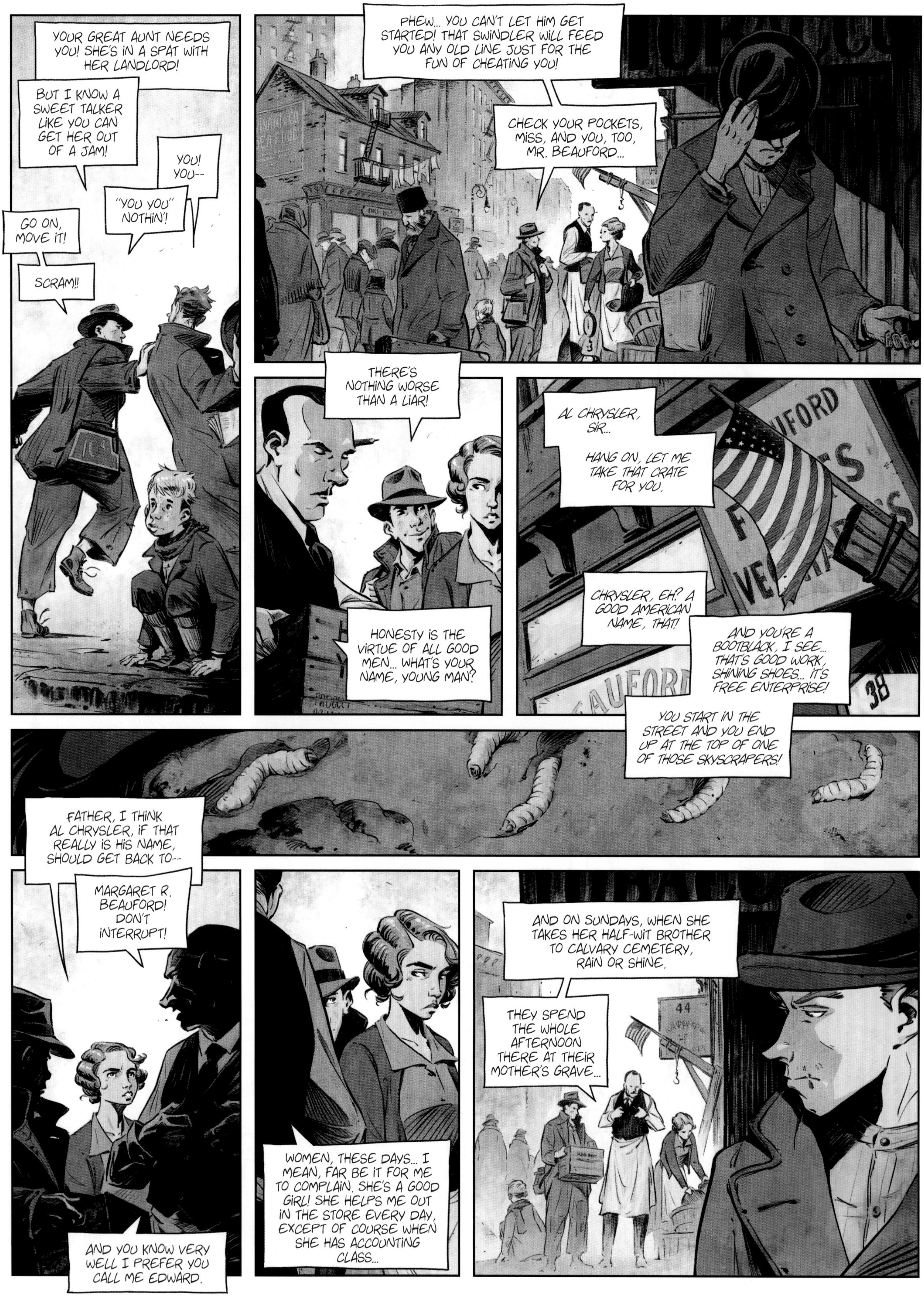
YOUR GREAT AUNT NEEDS YOU! SHE'S IN A SPAT WITH HER LANDLORD!
BUT I KNOW A SWEET TALKER LIKE YOU CAN GET HER OUT OF A JAM!
YOU! YOU--
"YOU YOU" NOTHIN'!
GO ON, MOVE IT!
SCRAM!!
PHEW... YOU CAN'T LET HIM GET STARTED! THAT SWINDLER WILL FEED YOU ANY OLD LINE JUST FOR THE FUN OF CHEATING YOU!
CHECK YOUR POCKETS, MISS, AND YOU, TOO, MR. BEAUFORD...
THERE'S NOTHING WORSE THAN A LIAR!
HONESTY IS THE VIRTUE OF ALL GOOD MEN... WHAT'S YOUR NAME, YOUNG MAN?
AL CHRYSLER, SIR...
HANG ON, LET ME TAKE THAT CRATE FOR YOU.
CHRYSLER, EH? A GOOD AMERICAN NAME, THAT!
AND YOU'RE A BOOTBLACK, I SEE... THAT'S GOOD WORK, SHINING SHOES... IT'S FREE ENTERPRISE!
YOU START IN THE STREET AND YOU END UP AT THE TOP OF ONE OF THOSE SKYSCRAPERS!
FATHER, I THINK AL CHRYSLER, IF THAT REALLY IS HIS NAME, SHOULD GET BACK TO--
MARGARET R. BEAUFORD! DON'T INTERRUPT!
AND YOU KNOW VERY WELL I PREFER YOU CALL ME EDWARD.
WOMEN, THESE DAYS... I MEAN, FAR BE IT FOR ME TO COMPLAIN. SHE'S A GOOD GIRL! SHE HELPS ME OUT IN THE STORE EVERY DAY, EXCEPT OF COURSE WHEN SHE HAS ACCOUNTING CLASS...
AND ON SUNDAYS, WHEN SHE TAKES HER HALF-WIT BROTHER TO CALVARY CEMETERY, RAIN OR SHINE.
THEY SPEND THE WHOLE AFTERNOON THERE AT THEIR MOTHER'S GRAVE...
40

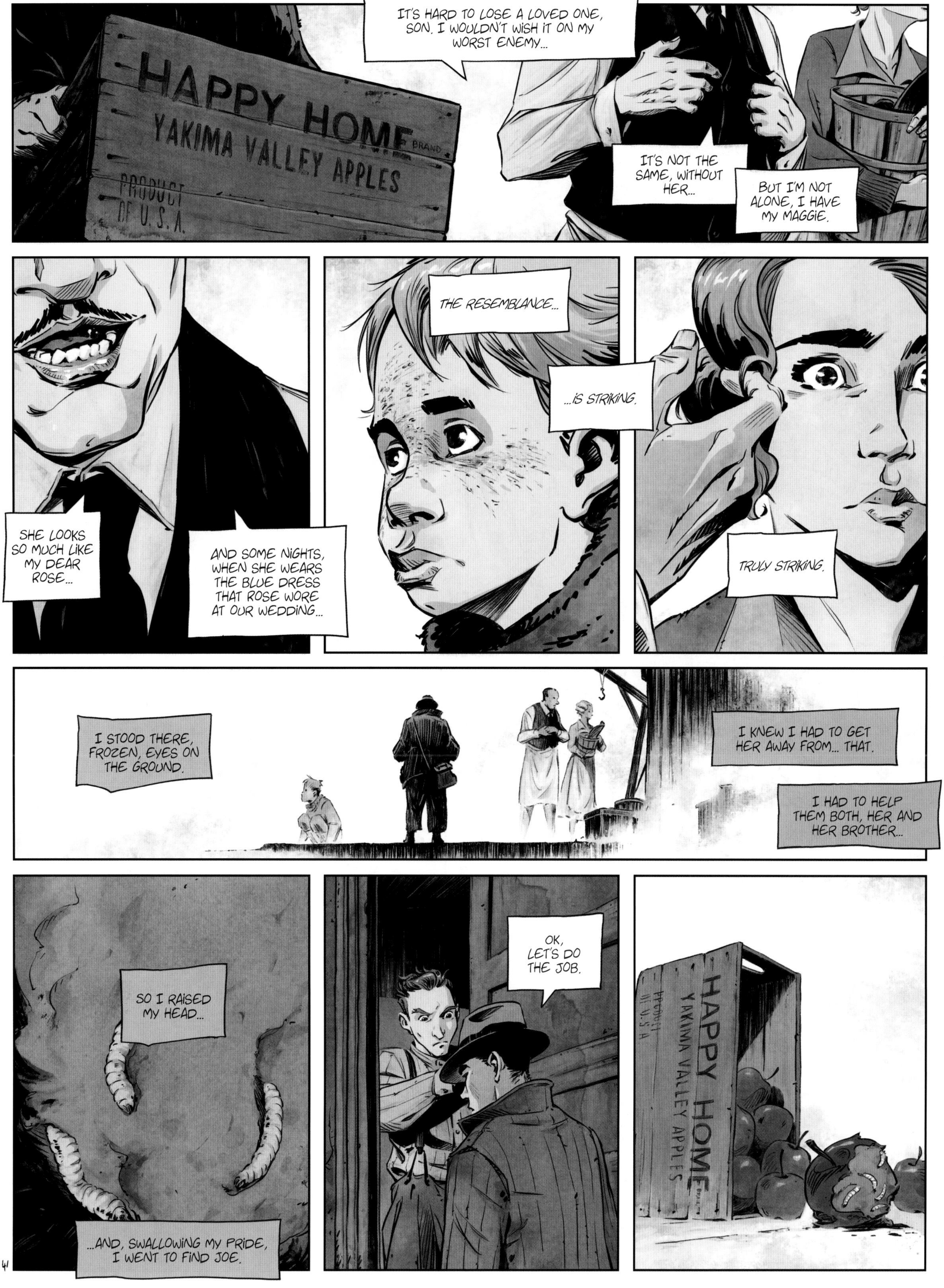
HAPPY HOME
YAKIMA VALLEY APPLES
PRODUCT OF U.S.A.
IT'S HARD TO LOSE A LOVED ONE, SON. I WOULDN'T WISH IT ON MY WORST ENEMY...
IT'S NOT THE SAME, WITHOUT HER...
BUT I'M NOT ALONE, I HAVE MY MAGGIE.
SHE LOOKS SO MUCH LIKE MY DEAR ROSE...
AND SOME NIGHTS, WHEN SHE WEARS THE BLUE DRESS THAT ROSE WORE AT OUR WEDDING...
THE RESEMBLANCE...
...IS STRIKING.
TRULY STRIKING.
I STOOD THERE, FROZEN, EYES ON THE GROUND.
I KNEW I HAD TO GET HER AWAY FROM... THAT.
I HAD TO HELP THEM BOTH, HER AND HER BROTHER...
SO I RAISED MY HEAD...
...AND, SWALLOWING MY PRIDE, I WENT TO FIND JOE.
OK, LET'S DO THE JOB.
HAPPY HOME
YAKIMA VALLEY APPLES
PRODUCT OF U.S.A.

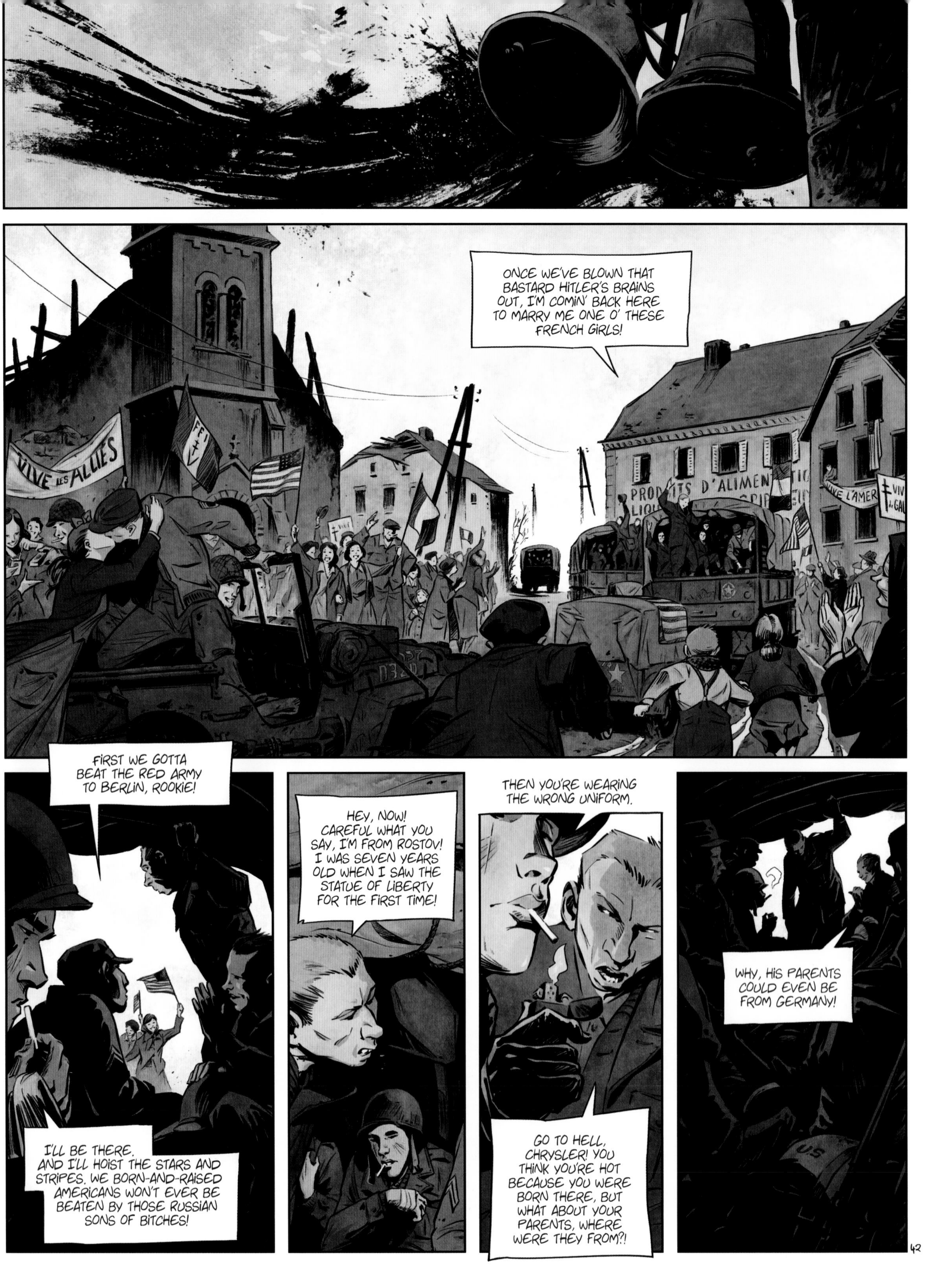
VIVE LES ALLIES
ONCE WE'VE BLOWN THAT BASTARD HITLER'S BRAINS OUT, I'M COMIN' BACK HERE TO MARRY ME ONE O' THESE FRENCH GIRLS!
FIRST WE GOTTA BEAT THE RED ARMY TO BERLIN, ROOKIE!
I'LL BE THERE. AND I'LL HOIST THE STARS AND STRIPES. WE BORN-AND-RAISED AMERICANS WON'T EVER BE BEATEN BY THOSE RUSSIAN SONS OF BITCHES!
HEY, NOW! CAREFUL WHAT YOU SAY, I'M FROM ROSTOV! I WAS SEVEN YEARS OLD WHEN I SAW THE STATUE OF LIBERTY FOR THE FIRST TIME!
THEN YOU'RE WEARING THE WRONG UNIFORM.
GO TO HELL, CHRYSLER! YOU THINK YOU'RE HOT BECAUSE YOU WERE BORN THERE, BUT WHAT ABOUT YOUR PARENTS, WHERE WERE THEY FROM?!
WHY, HIS PARENTS COULD EVEN BE FROM GERMANY!
US
42

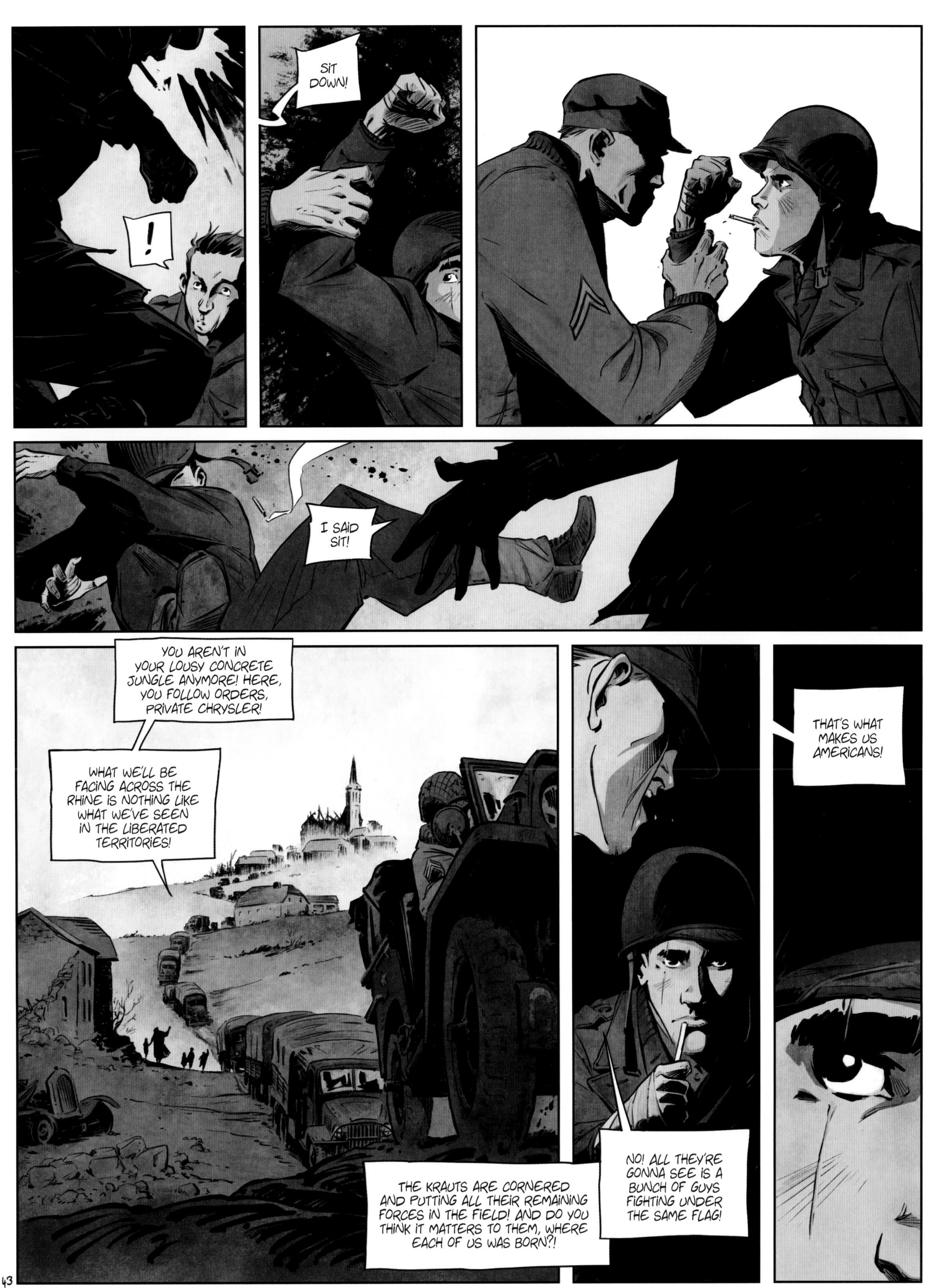
!
SIT DOWN!
I SAID SIT!
YOU AREN'T IN YOUR LOUSY CONCRETE JUNGLE ANYMORE! HERE, YOU FOLLOW ORDERS, PRIVATE CHRYSLER!
WHAT WE'LL BE FACING ACROSS THE RHINE IS NOTHING LIKE WHAT WE'VE SEEN IN THE LIBERATED TERRITORIES!
THE KRAUTS ARE CORNERED AND PUTTING ALL THEIR REMAINING FORCES IN THE FIELD! AND DO YOU THINK IT MATTERS TO THEM, WHERE EACH OF US WAS BORN?!
NO! ALL THEY'RE GONNA SEE IS A BUNCH OF GUYS FIGHTING UNDER THE SAME FLAG!
THAT'S WHAT MAKES US AMERICANS!
43

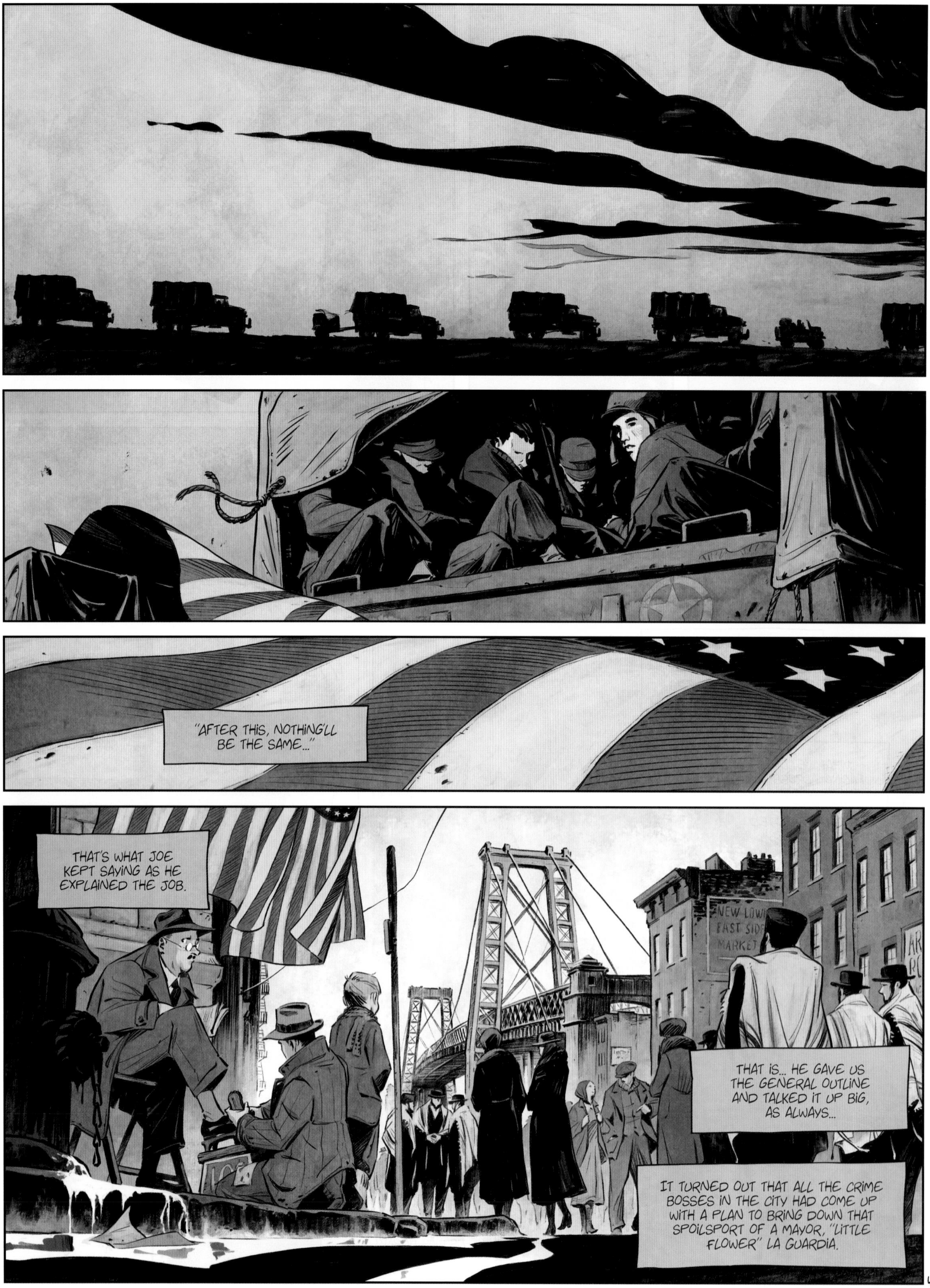
"AFTER THIS, NOTHING'LL BE THE SAME..."
THAT'S WHAT JOE KEPT SAYING AS HE EXPLAINED THE JOB.
NEW LOWER EAST SIDE MARKET
THAT IS... HE GAVE US THE GENERAL OUTLINE AND TALKED IT UP BIG, AS ALWAYS...
IT TURNED OUT THAT ALL THE CRIME BOSSES IN THE CITY HAD COME UP WITH A PLAN TO BRING DOWN THAT SPOILSPORT OF A MAYOR, "LITTLE FLOWER" LA GUARDIA.
44

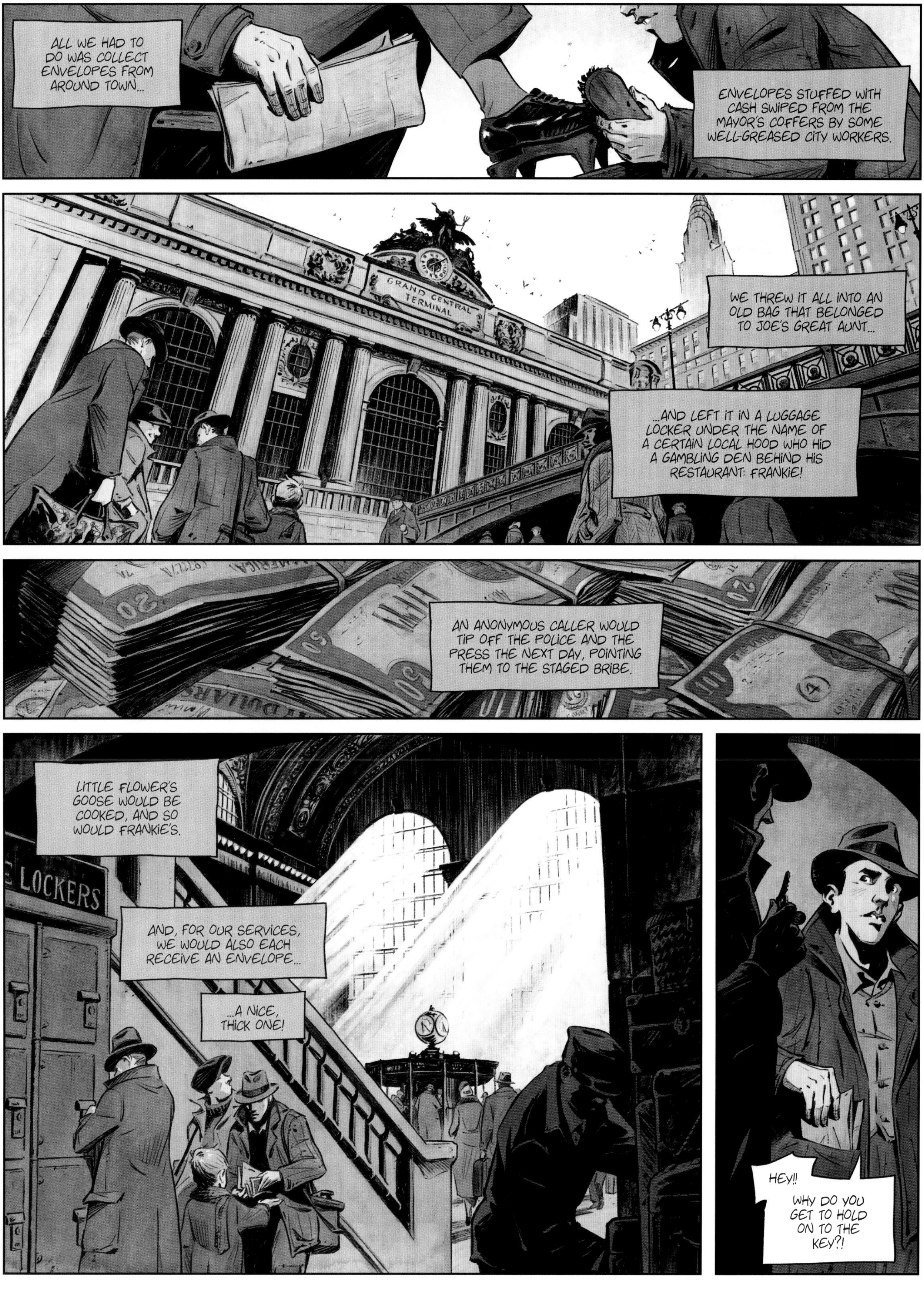
ALL WE HAD TO DO WAS COLLECT ENVELOPES FROM AROUND TOWN...
ENVELOPES STUFFED WITH CASH SWIPED FROM THE MAYOR'S COFFERS BY SOME WELL-GREASED CITY WORKERS.
GRAND CENTRAL TERMINAL
WE THREW IT ALL INTO AN OLD BAG THAT BELONGED TO JOE'S GREAT AUNT...
...AND LEFT IT IN A LUGGAGE LOCKER UNDER THE NAME OF A CERTAIN LOCAL HOOD WHO HID A GAMBLING DEN BEHIND HIS RESTAURANT: FRANKIE!
AN ANONYMOUS CALLER WOULD TIP OFF THE POLICE AND THE PRESS THE NEXT DAY, POINTING THEM TO THE STAGED BRIBE.
LITTLE FLOWER'S GOOSE WOULD BE COOKED, AND SO WOULD FRANKIE'S.
LOCKERS
AND, FOR OUR SERVICES, WE WOULD ALSO EACH RECEIVE AN ENVELOPE...
...A NICE, THICK ONE!
HEY!!
WHY DO YOU GET TO HOLD ON TO THE KEY?!

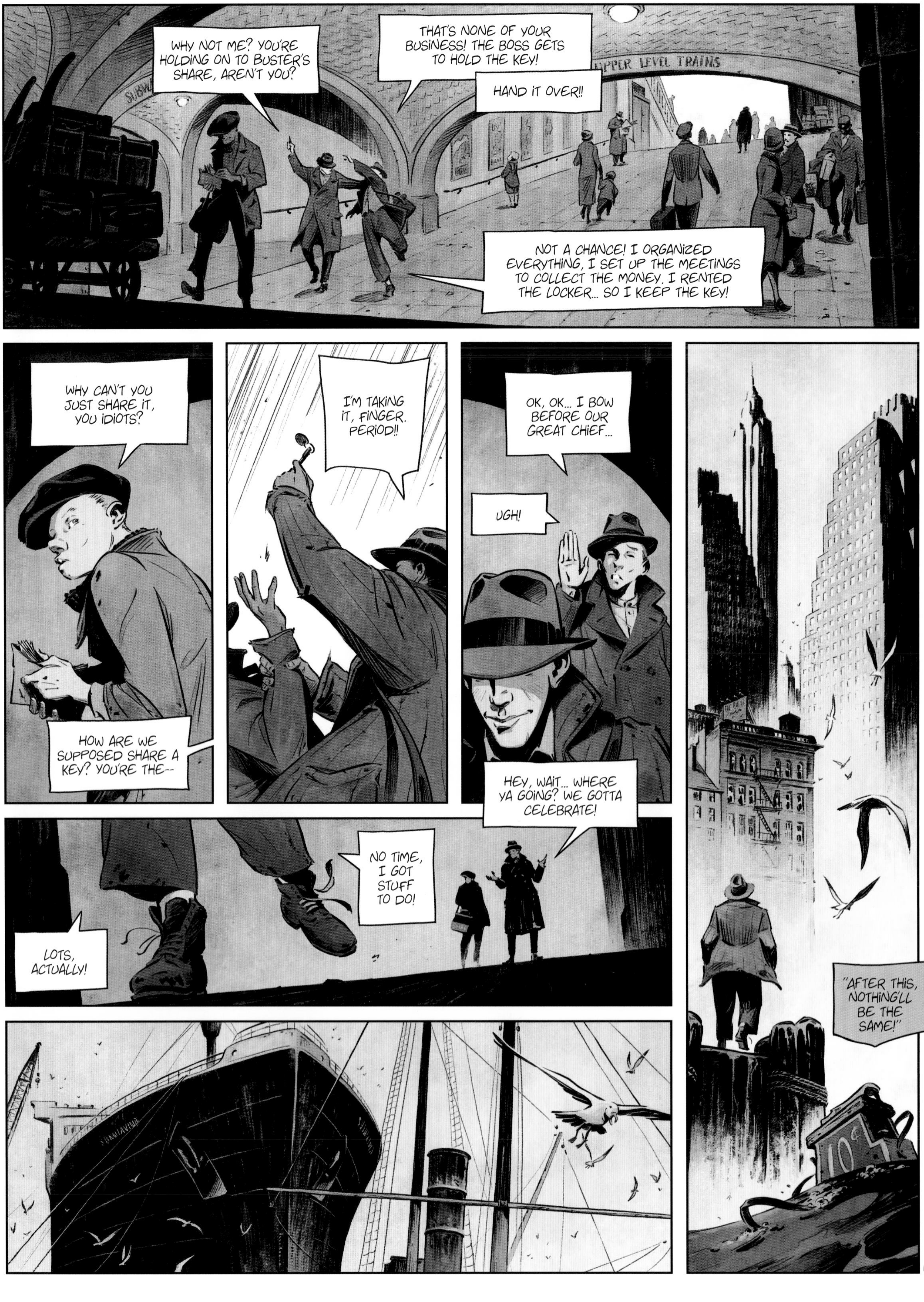
WHY NOT ME? YOU'RE HOLDING ON TO BUSTER'S SHARE, AREN'T YOU?
THAT'S NONE OF YOUR BUSINESS! THE BOSS GETS TO HOLD THE KEY!
HAND IT OVER!!
UPPER LEVEL TRAINS
NOT A CHANCE! I ORGANIZED EVERYTHING, I SET UP THE MEETINGS TO COLLECT THE MONEY. I RENTED THE LOCKER... SO I KEEP THE KEY!
WHY CAN'T YOU JUST SHARE IT, YOU IDIOTS?
HOW ARE WE SUPPOSED SHARE A KEY? YOU'RE THE--
I'M TAKING IT, FINGER. PERIOD!!
OK, OK... I BOW BEFORE OUR GREAT CHIEF...
UGH!
HEY, WAIT... WHERE YA GOING? WE GOTTA CELEBRATE!
NO TIME, I GOT STUFF TO DO!
LOTS, ACTUALLY!
"AFTER THIS, NOTHING'LL BE THE SAME!"
10¢
46

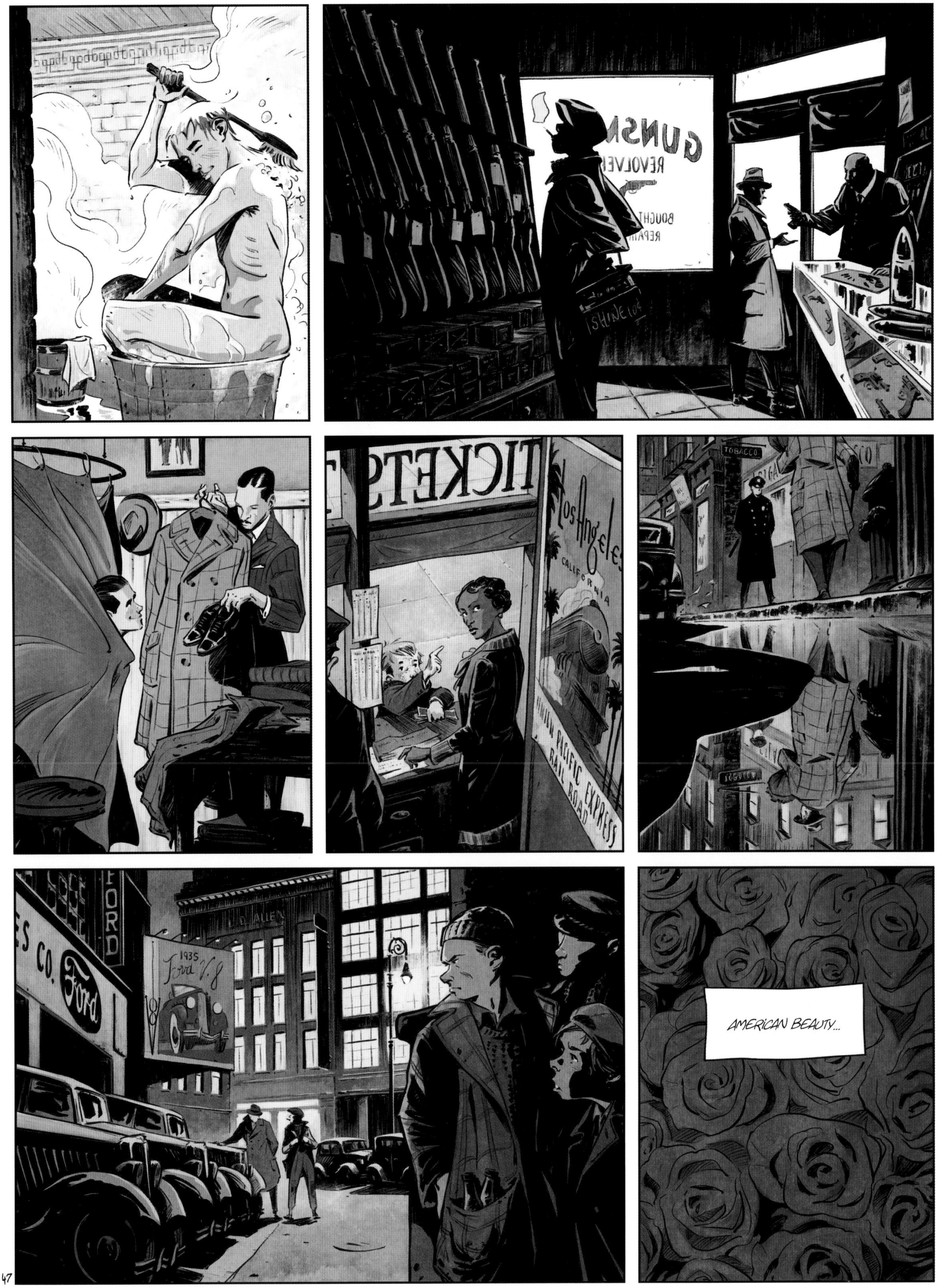
GUNS
REVOLVER
BOUGHT
REPAIR
SHINE
TICKETS
Los Angeles
CALIFORNIA
PACIFIC EXPRESS
RAIL ROAD
TOBACCO
FORD
Ford
1935
Ford V-8
AMERICAN BEAUTY...

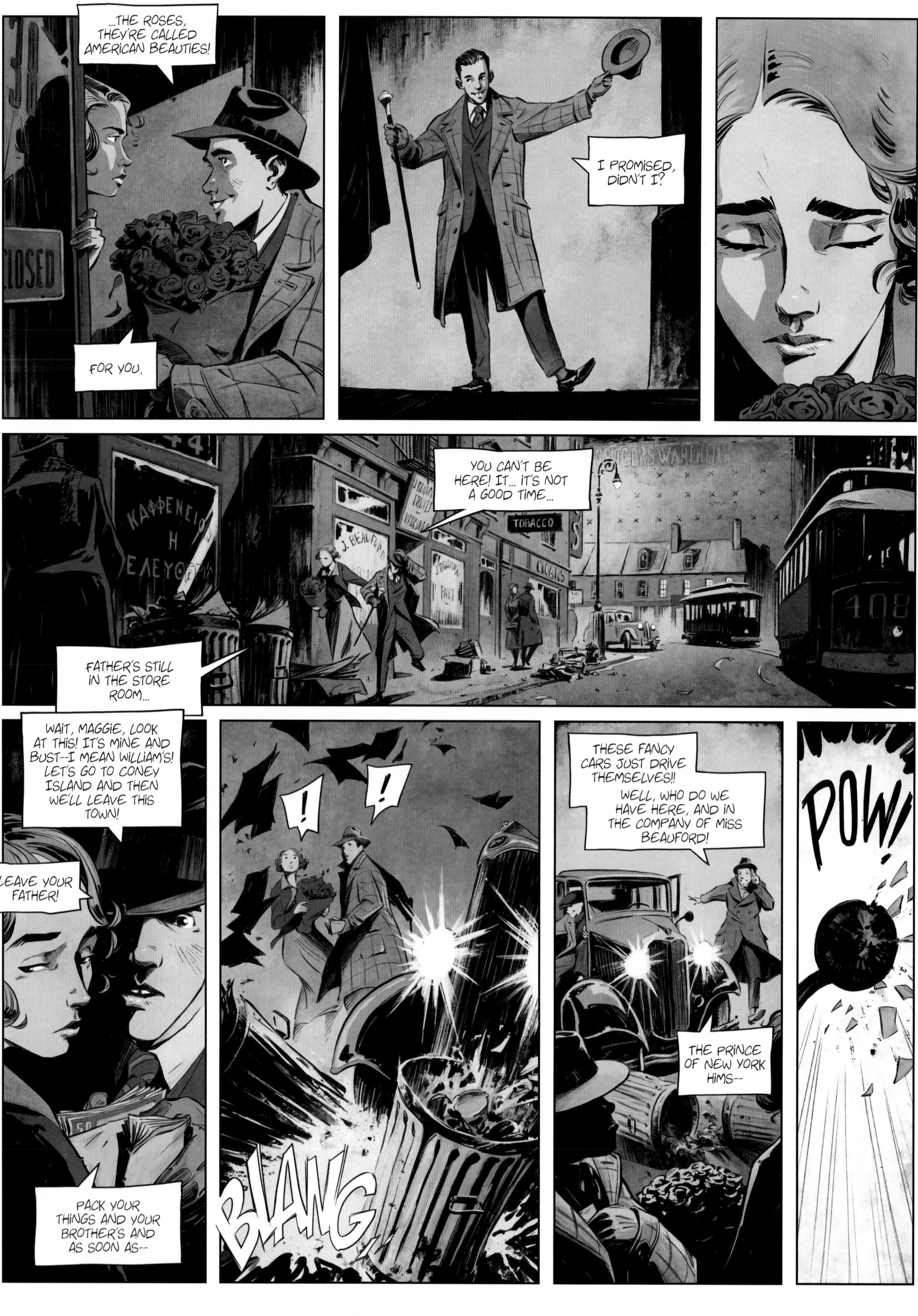
...THE ROSES, THEY'RE CALLED AMERICAN BEAUTIES!
CLOSED
FOR YOU.
I PROMISED, DIDN'T I?
YOU CAN'T BE HERE! IT... IT'S NOT A GOOD TIME...
TOBACCO
CIGARS
J. BEAUFORD
408
FATHER'S STILL IN THE STORE ROOM...
WAIT, MAGGIE, LOOK AT THIS! IT'S MINE AND BUST--I MEAN WILLIAM'S! LET'S GO TO CONEY ISLAND AND THEN WE'LL LEAVE THIS TOWN!
LEAVE YOUR FATHER!
PACK YOUR THINGS AND YOUR BROTHER'S AND AS SOON AS--
!
!
BLANG
THESE FANCY CARS JUST DRIVE THEMSELVES!!
WELL, WHO DO WE HAVE HERE, AND IN THE COMPANY OF MISS BEAUFORD!
THE PRINCE OF NEW YORK HIMS--
POW!

48

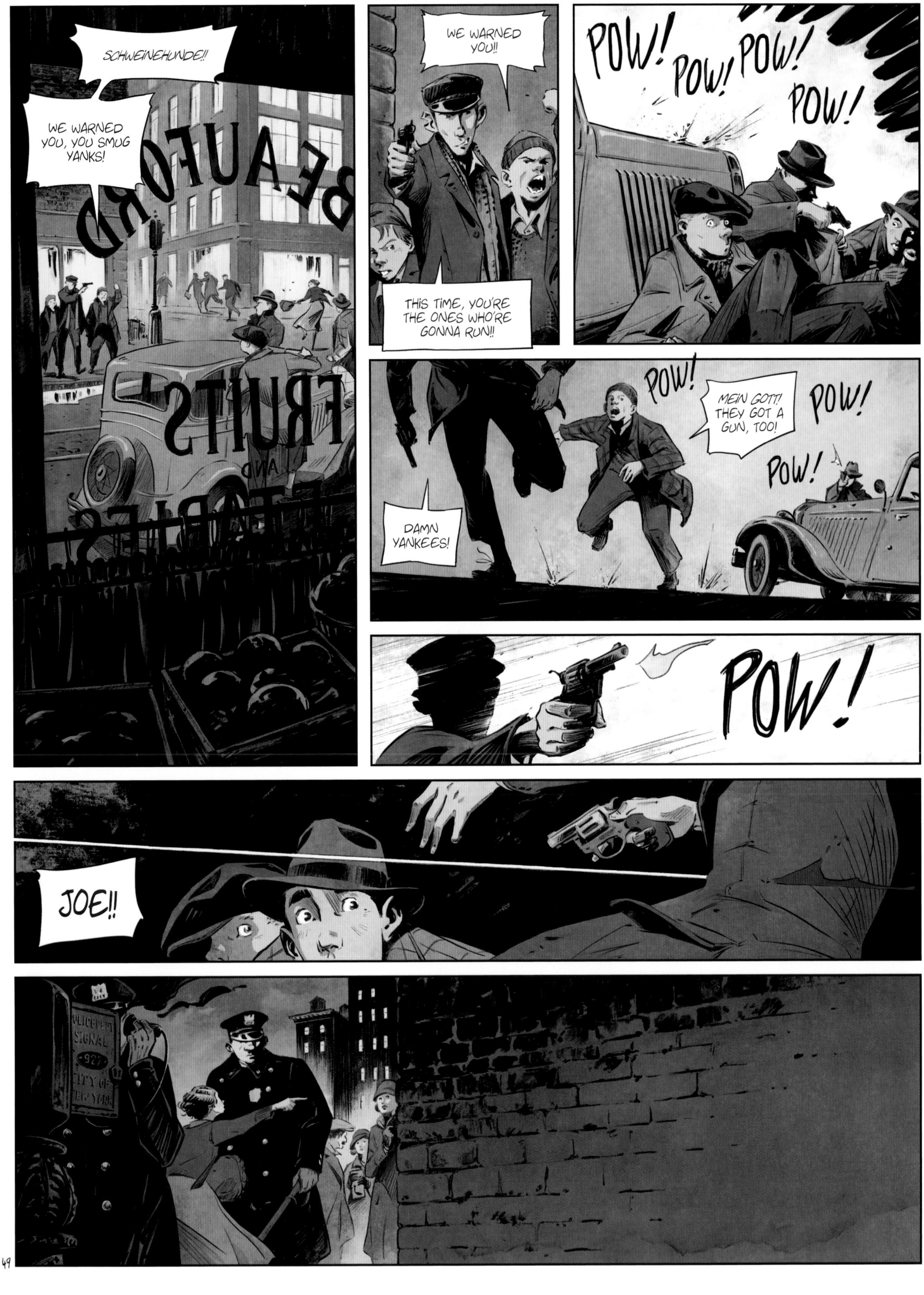
SCHWEINEHUNDE!!
WE WARNED YOU, YOU SMUG YANKS!
BEAUFORD
FRUITS
AND
VEGETABLES
WE WARNED YOU!!
THIS TIME, YOU'RE THE ONES WHO'RE GONNA RUN!!
POW! POW! POW! POW!
POW!
MEIN GOTT! THEY GOT A GUN, TOO!
POW!
POW!
DAMN YANKEES!
POW!
JOE!!
POLICE DEPT SIGNAL
927
CITY OF NEW YORK
49

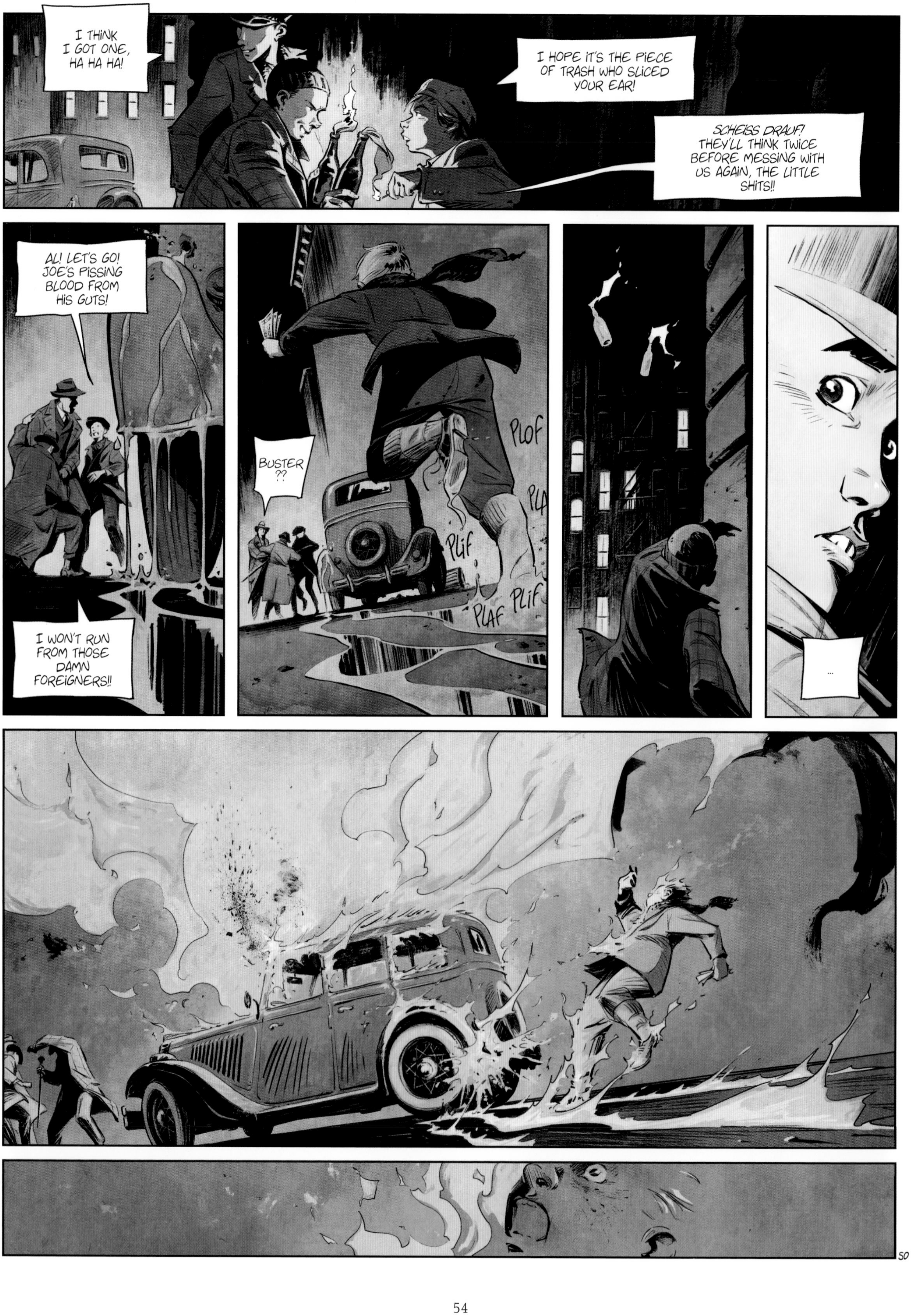
I THINK I GOT ONE, HA HA HA!
I HOPE IT'S THE PIECE OF TRASH WHO SLICED YOUR EAR!
SCHEISS DRAUF! THEY'LL THINK TWICE BEFORE MESSING WITH US AGAIN, THE LITTLE SHITS!!
AL! LET'S GO! JOE'S PISSING BLOOD FROM HIS GUTS!
I WON'T RUN FROM THOSE DAMN FOREIGNERS!!
BUSTER ??
PLOF
PLIF
PLAF
PLIF
...
50

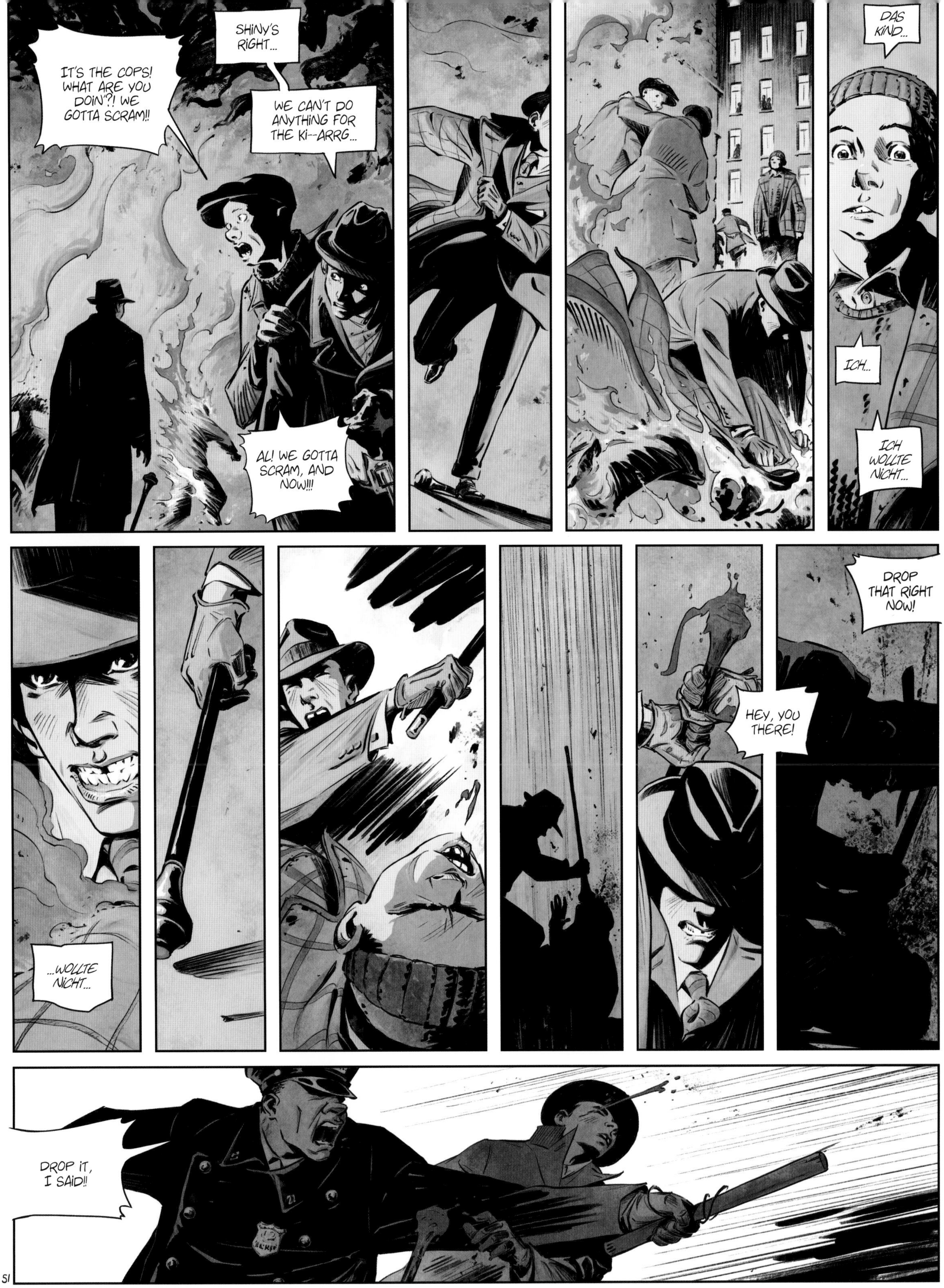
IT'S THE COPS! WHAT ARE YOU DOIN'?! WE GOTTA SCRAM!!
SHINY'S RIGHT...
WE CAN'T DO ANYTHING FOR THE KI--ARRG...
AL! WE GOTTA SCRAM, AND NOW!!!
DAS KIND...
ICH...
ICH WOLLTE NICHT...
...WOLLTE NICHT...
HEY, YOU THERE!
DROP THAT RIGHT NOW!
DROP IT, I SAID!!

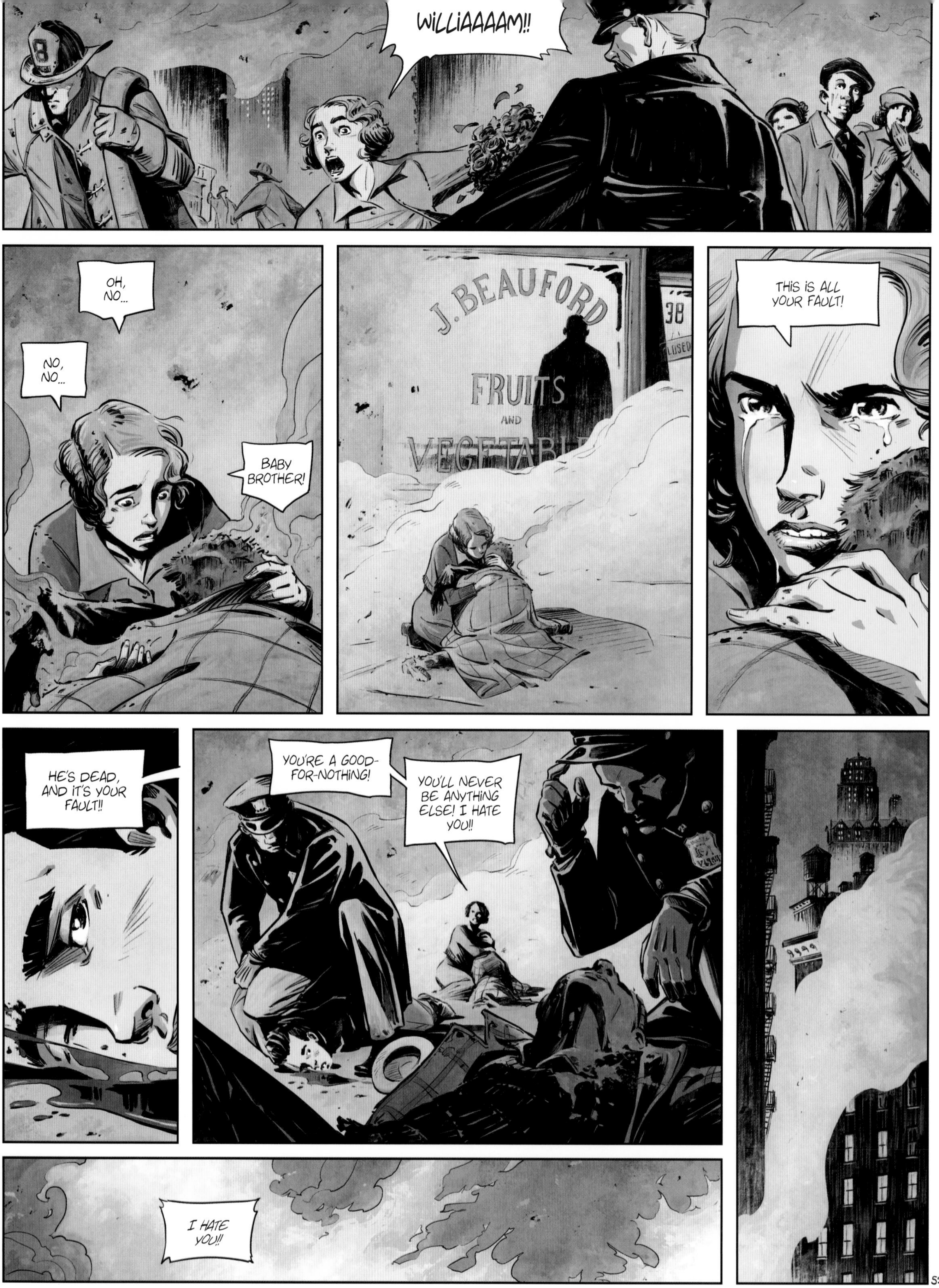
WILLIAAAAM!!
OH, NO...
NO, NO...
BABY BROTHER!
J. BEAUFORD
FRUITS AND VEGETABLES
38
CLOSED
THIS IS ALL YOUR FAULT!
HE'S DEAD, AND IT'S YOUR FAULT!!
YOU'RE A GOOD-FOR-NOTHING!
YOU'LL NEVER BE ANYTHING ELSE! I HATE YOU!!
I HATE YOU!!

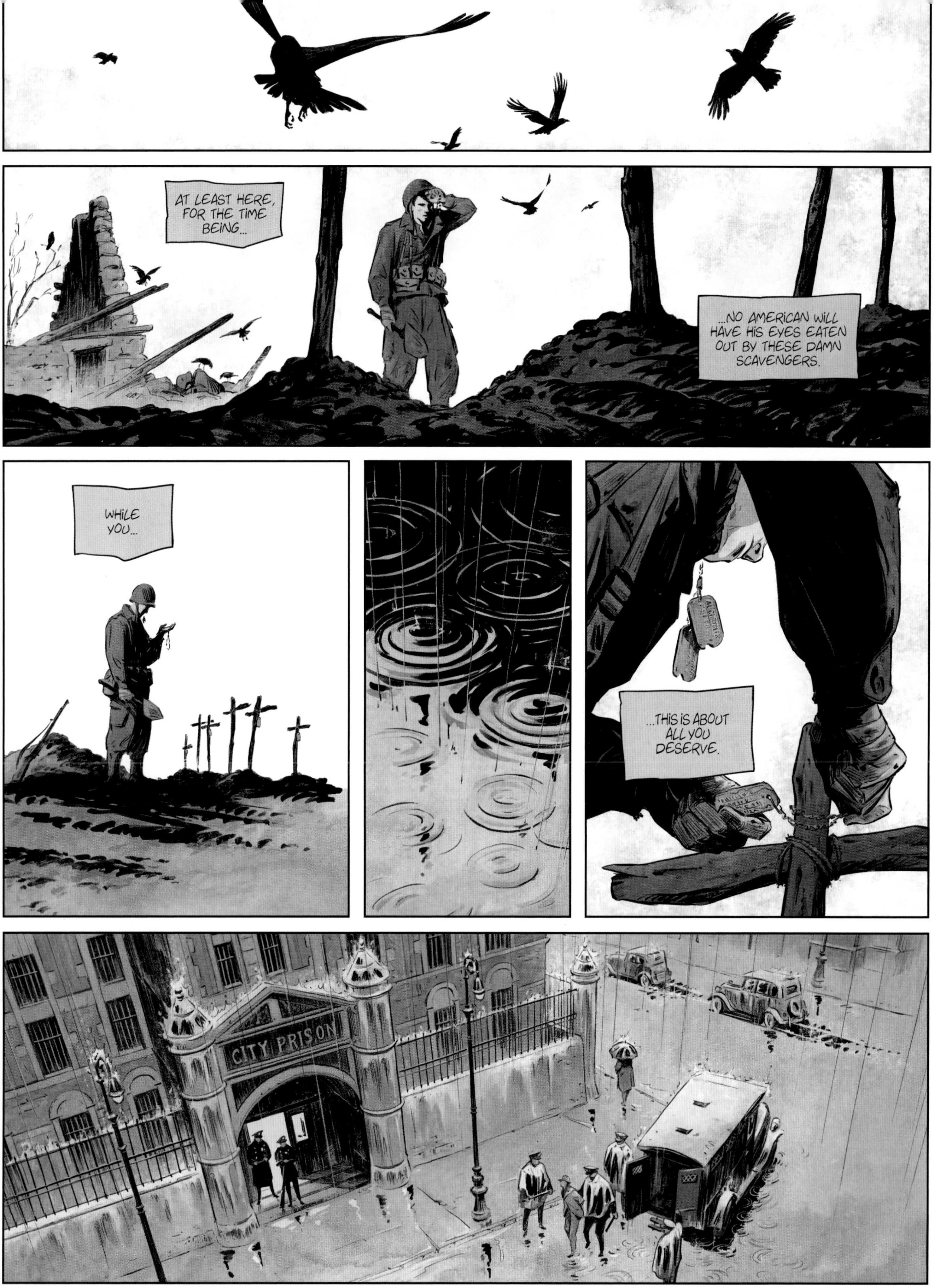
AT LEAST HERE, FOR THE TIME BEING...
...NO AMERICAN WILL HAVE HIS EYES EATEN OUT BY THESE DAMN SCAVENGERS.
WHILE YOU...
...THIS IS ABOUT ALL YOU DESERVE.
CITY PRISON

53

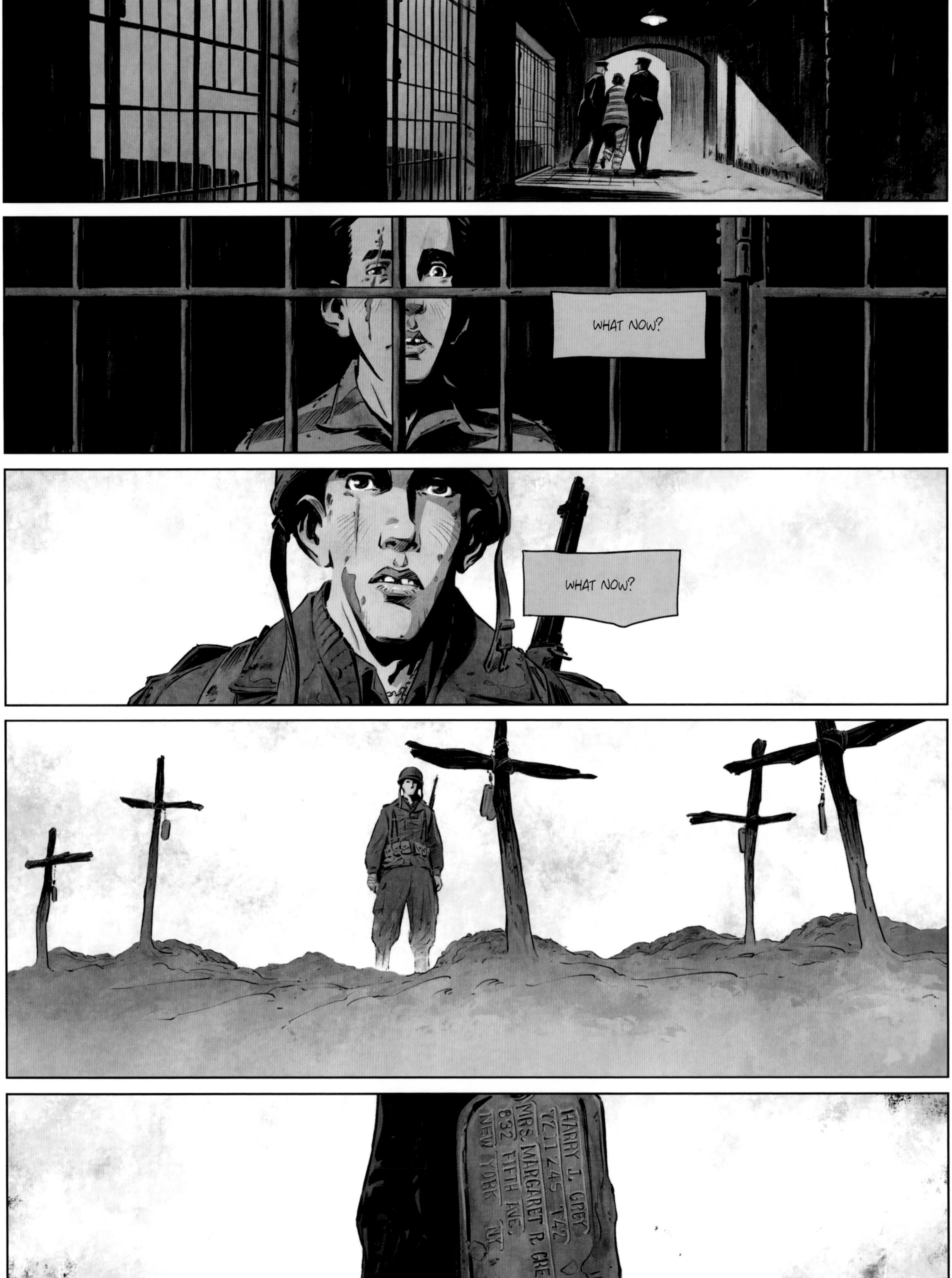
WHAT NOW?
WHAT NOW?
HARRY J. GREY
12112245 T42
MRS. MARGARET R. GREY
832 FIFTH AVE.
NEW YORK N.Y.

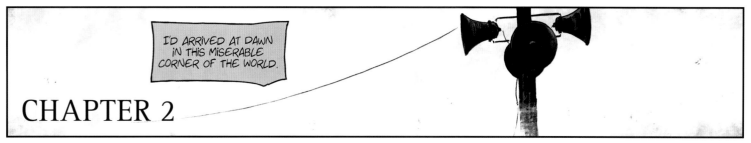

I'D ARRIVED AT DAWN IN THIS MISERABLE CORNER OF THE WORLD.

CHAPTER 2

AND THINGS WERE ALREADY GOING SOUR.

THAT'S NOT MY PROBLEM, ROOKIE!

BUT I WAS SUPPOSED TO HEAD NORTH!

I WAS SUPPOSED TO JOIN THE 3RD ARMY AND MARCH ON BERLIN TO RAISE THE STARS AND STRIPES!!

I GOT NO BUSINESS BEING ON THE SOUTHERN FRONT!

HANG ON, WHAT'RE YOU GOIN' ON ABOUT?

THIS IS GERMANY! THE FRONT IS EVERYWHERE! WE'RE SURROUNDED BY KRAUTS, ISN'T THAT RIGHT, KENTUCKY?

YEP.

EVEN IF MOST OF 'EM ARE SURRENDERING AT THIS POINT, SOME ARE STILL RESISTING. AND BELIEVE ME, ROOKIE, THOSE ONES ARE THE WORST!

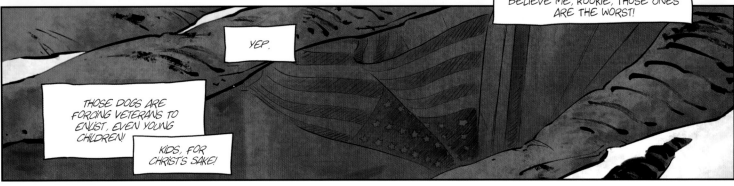

YEP.

THOSE DOGS ARE FORCING VETERANS TO ENLIST, EVEN YOUNG CHILDREN!

KIDS, FOR CHRIST'S SAKE!

YEP.

PIECE OF SHIT NAZIS!

BU-URP!

SO IF YER NOT HAPPY TO BE HERE WITH US, GO TAKE IT UP WITH THE COMMAND SERGEANT MAJOR UNDER THAT TENT OVER THERE NEXT TO THE MESS.

IT'S GOTTA BE A MISTAKE.

U.S. ARMY FIELD RATION C ERATIONS WT

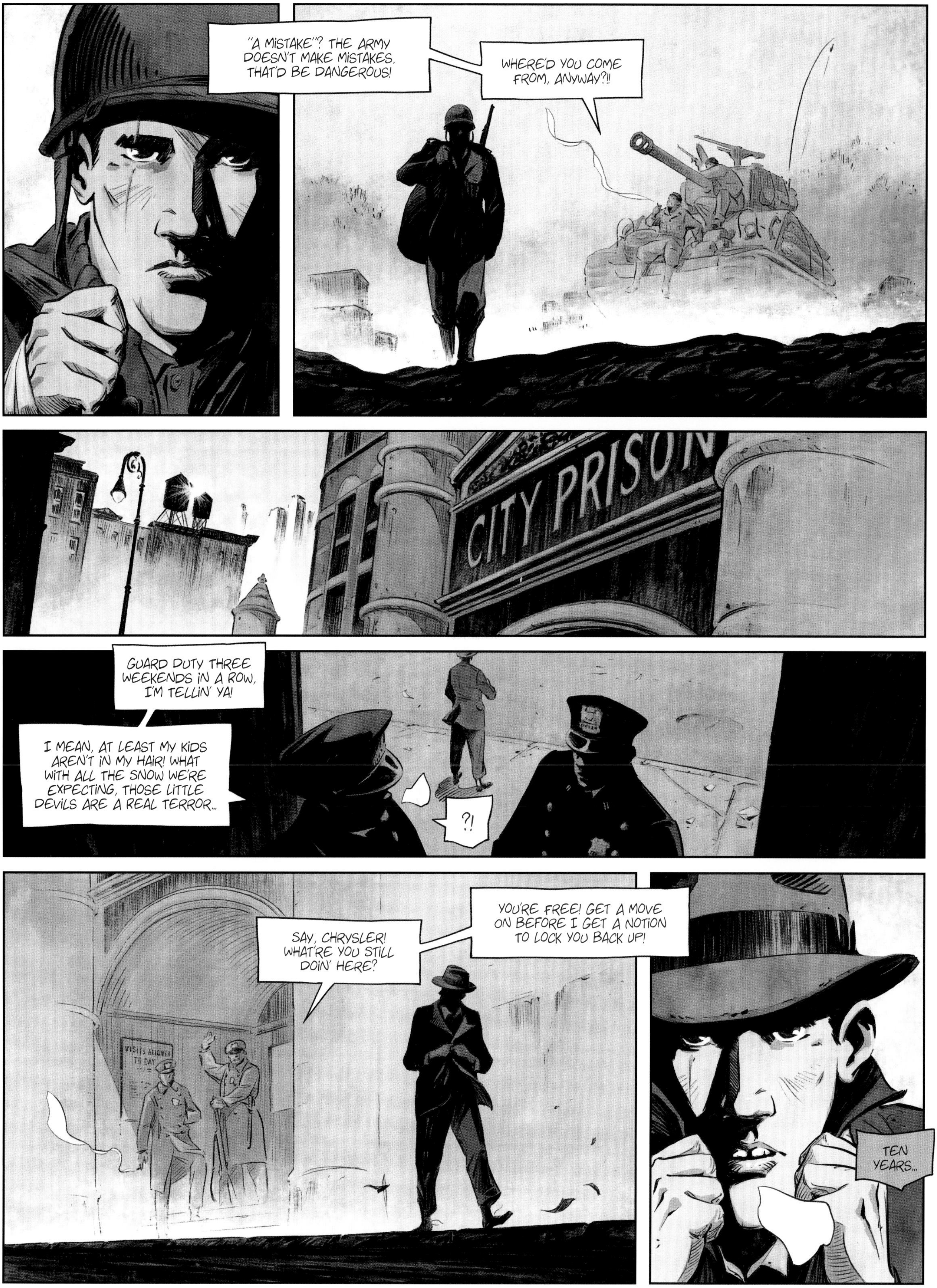
"A MISTAKE"? THE ARMY DOESN'T MAKE MISTAKES. THAT'D BE DANGEROUS!
WHERE'D YOU COME FROM, ANYWAY?!!
CITY PRISON
GUARD DUTY THREE WEEKENDS IN A ROW, I'M TELLIN' YA!
I MEAN, AT LEAST MY KIDS AREN'T IN MY HAIR! WHAT WITH ALL THE SNOW WE'RE EXPECTING, THOSE LITTLE DEVILS ARE A REAL TERROR...
?!
SAY, CHRYSLER! WHAT'RE YOU STILL DOIN' HERE?
YOU'RE FREE! GET A MOVE ON BEFORE I GET A NOTION TO LOCK YOU BACK UP!
VISITS ALLOWED TO DAY
TEN YEARS...
3

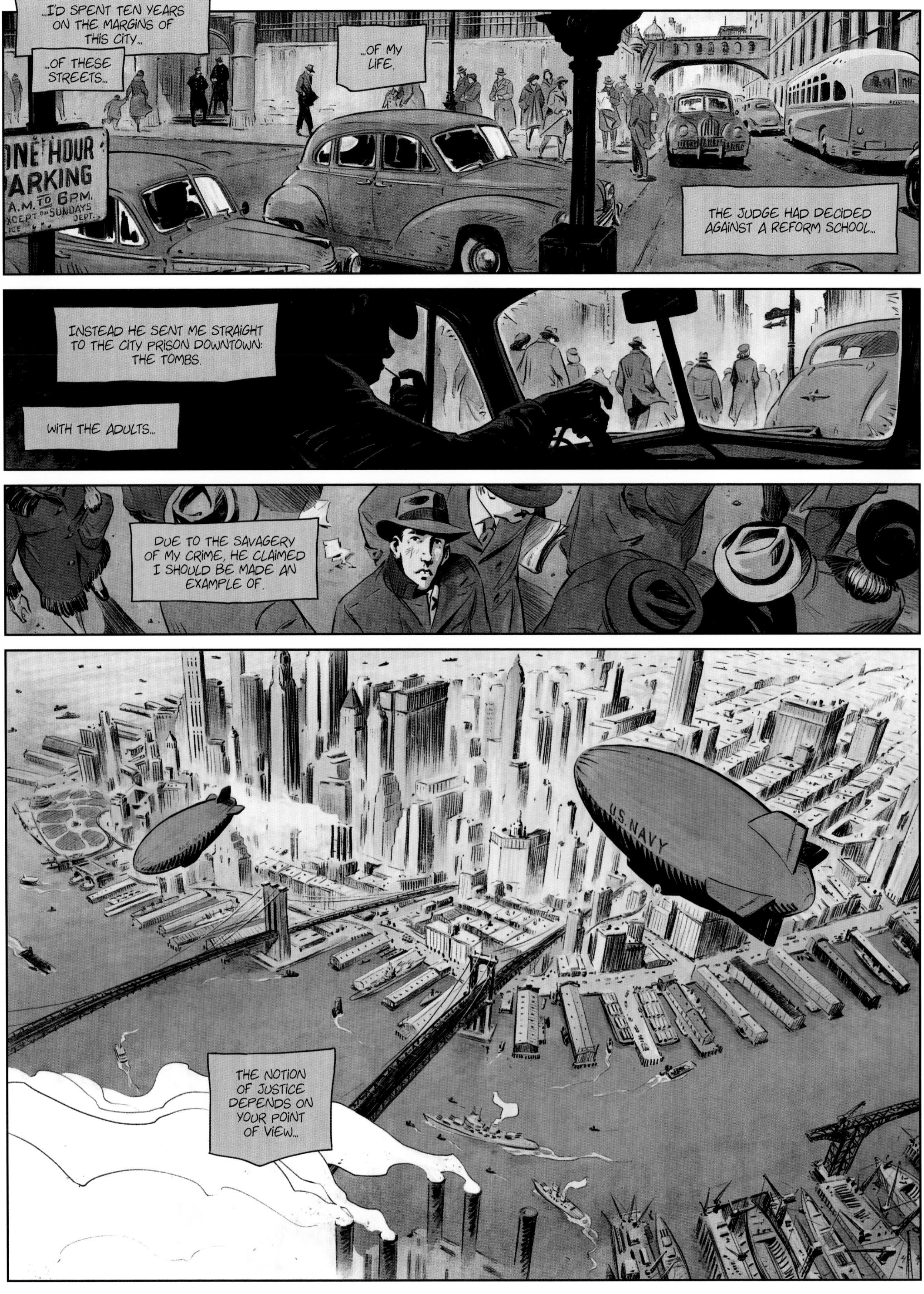

...I'D SPENT TEN YEARS ON THE MARGINS OF THIS CITY...
...OF THESE STREETS...
...OF MY LIFE.
PARKING
THE JUDGE HAD DECIDED AGAINST A REFORM SCHOOL...
INSTEAD HE SENT ME STRAIGHT TO THE CITY PRISON DOWNTOWN: THE TOMBS.
WITH THE ADULTS...
DUE TO THE SAVAGERY OF MY CRIME, HE CLAIMED I SHOULD BE MADE AN EXAMPLE OF.
U.S. NAVY
THE NOTION OF JUSTICE DEPENDS ON YOUR POINT OF VIEW...

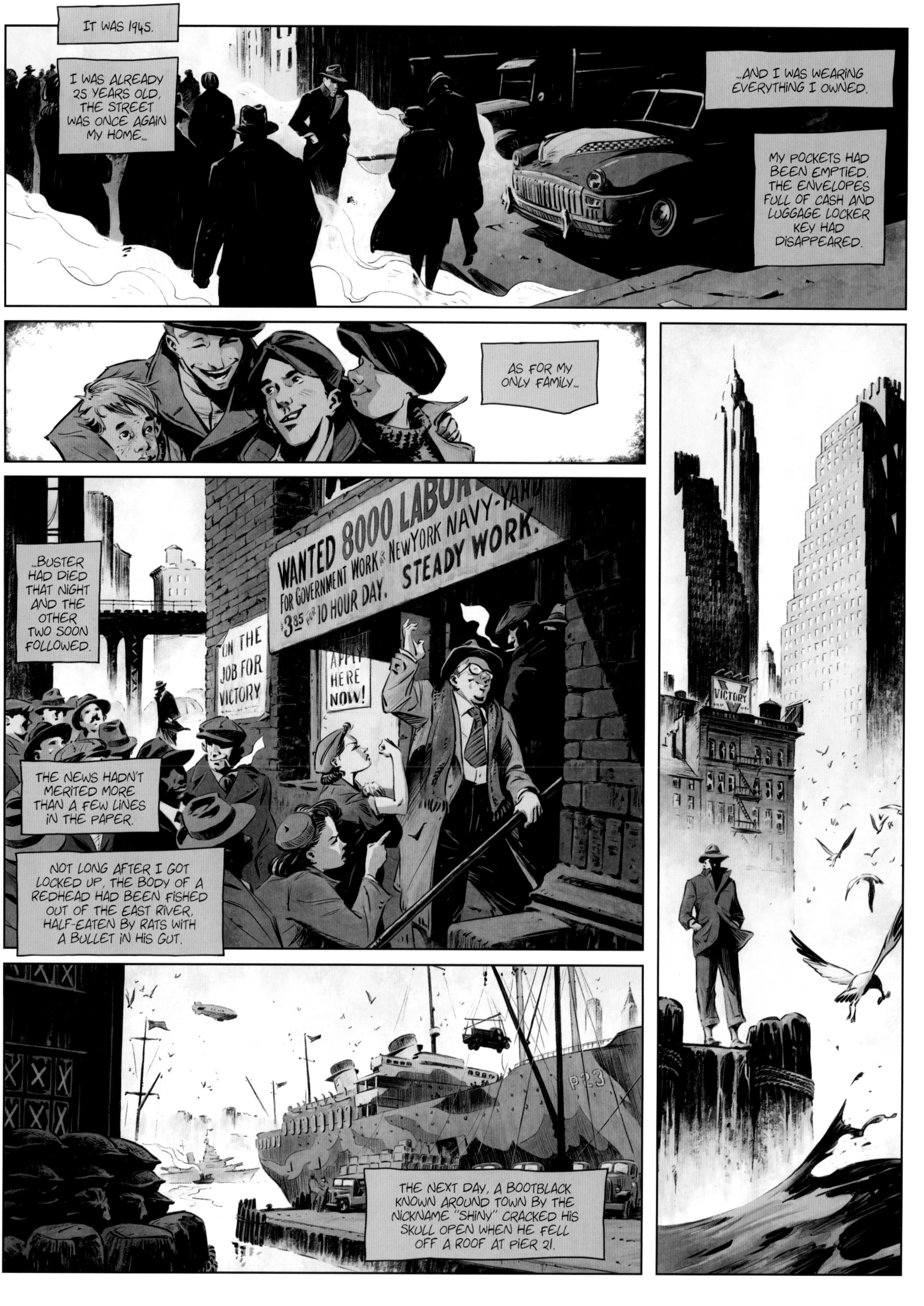
IT WAS 1945.
I WAS ALREADY 25 YEARS OLD, THE STREET WAS ONCE AGAIN MY HOME...
...AND I WAS WEARING EVERYTHING I OWNED.
MY POCKETS HAD BEEN EMPTIED. THE ENVELOPES FULL OF CASH AND LUGGAGE LOCKER KEY HAD DISAPPEARED.
AS FOR MY ONLY FAMILY...
...BUSTER HAD DIED THAT NIGHT AND THE OTHER TWO SOON FOLLOWED.
WANTED 8000 LABOR
FOR GOVERNMENT WORK AT NEW YORK NAVY-YARD
$3.85 FOR 10 HOUR DAY. STEADY WORK.
ON THE JOB FOR VICTORY
APPLY HERE NOW!
THE NEWS HADN'T MERITED MORE THAN A FEW LINES IN THE PAPER.
NOT LONG AFTER I GOT LOCKED UP, THE BODY OF A REDHEAD HAD BEEN FISHED OUT OF THE EAST RIVER, HALF-EATEN BY RATS WITH A BULLET IN HIS GUT.
VICTORY
P23
THE NEXT DAY, A BOOTBLACK KNOWN AROUND TOWN BY THE NICKNAME "SHINY" CRACKED HIS SKULL OPEN WHEN HE FELL OFF A ROOF AT PIER 21.
5

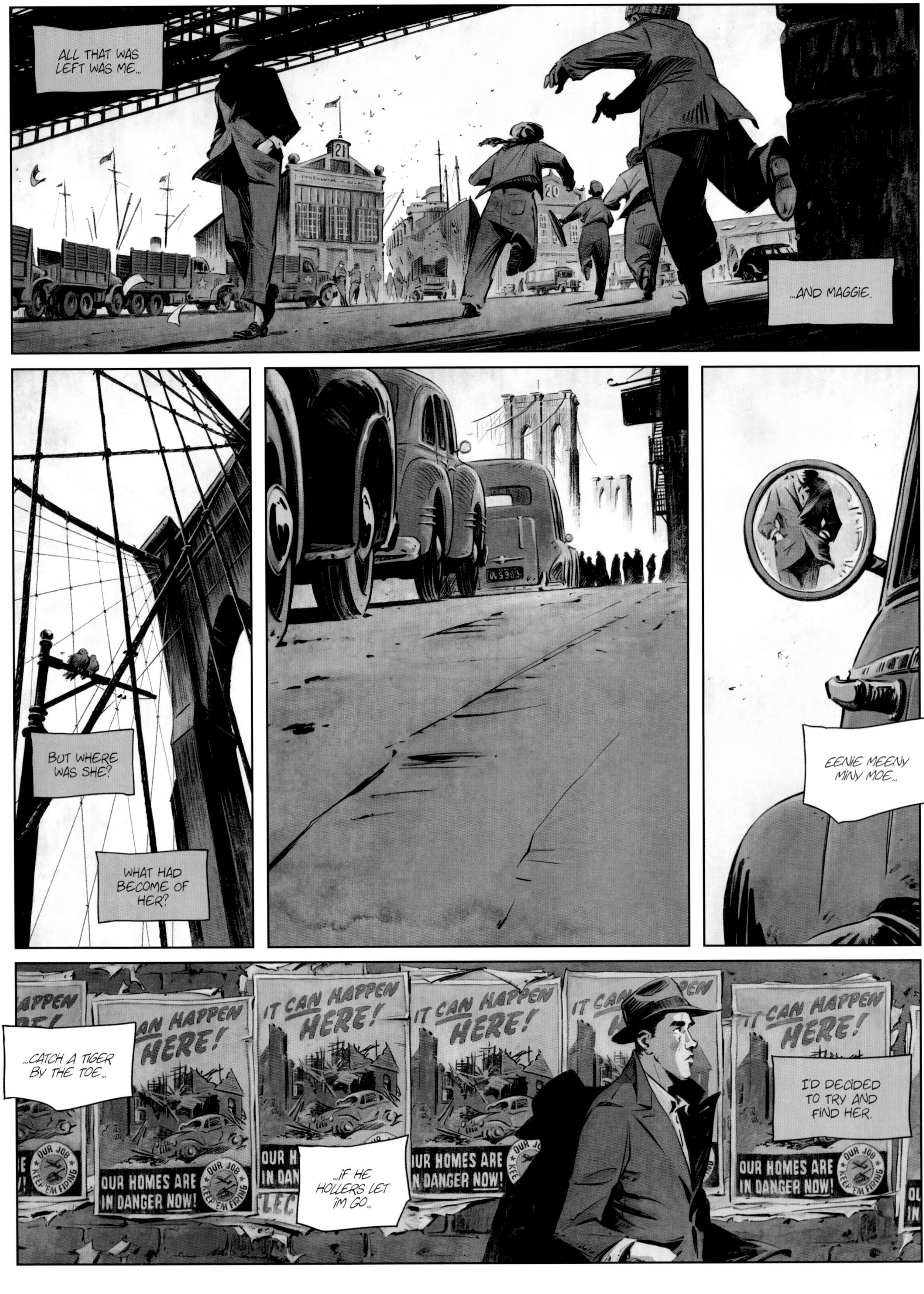
ALL THAT WAS LEFT WAS ME...
...AND MAGGIE.
BUT WHERE WAS SHE?
WHAT HAD BECOME OF HER?
EENIE MEENY MINY MOE...
...CATCH A TIGER BY THE TOE...
IT CAN HAPPEN HERE!
OUR HOMES ARE IN DANGER NOW!
OUR JOB KEEP 'EM FIRING
...IF HE HOLLERS LET 'IM GO...
I'D DECIDED TO TRY AND FIND HER.
6

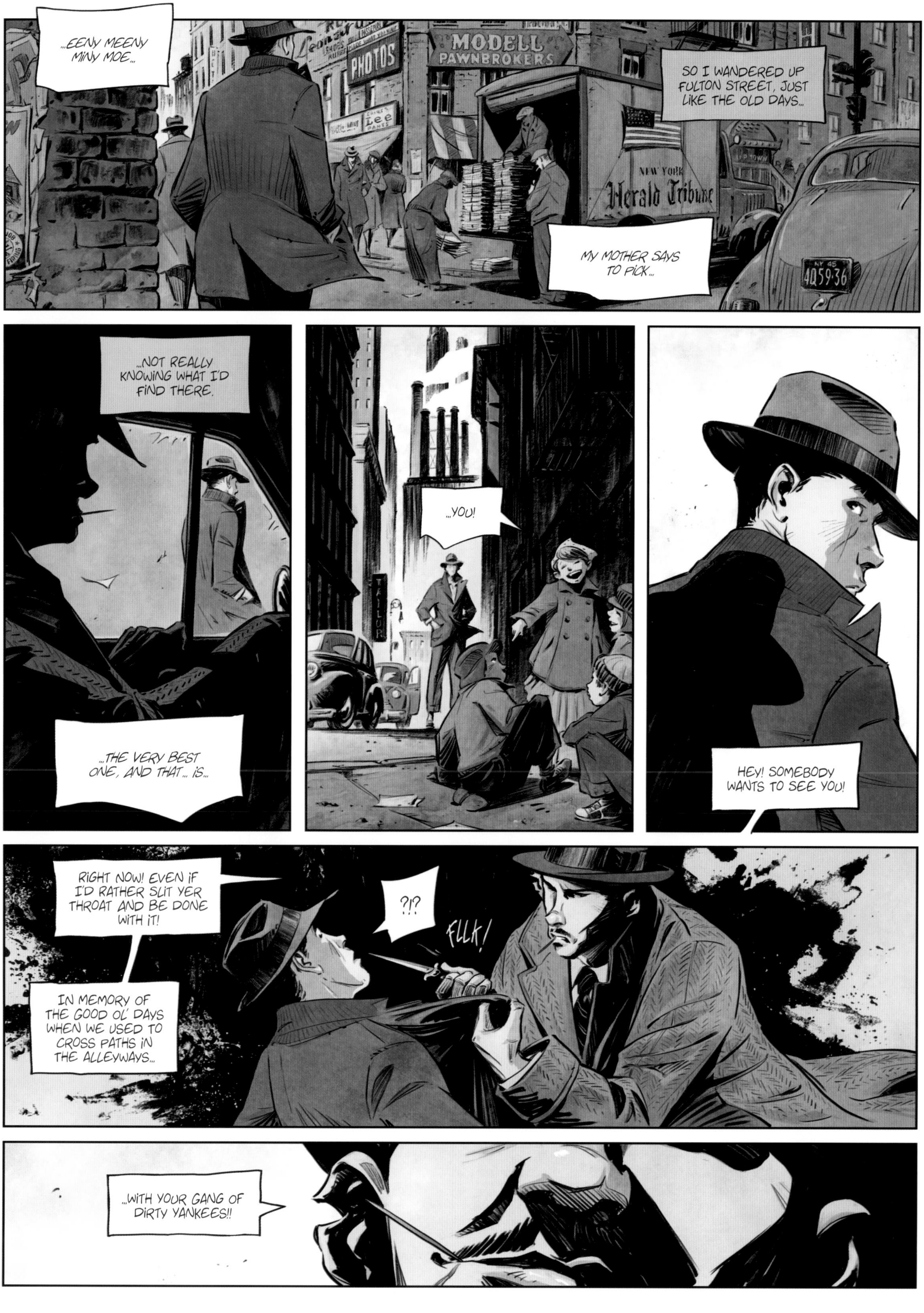
...EENY MEENY MINY MOE...
MODELL PAWNBROKERS
PHOTOS
SO I WANDERED UP FULTON STREET, JUST LIKE THE OLD DAYS...
NEW YORK Herald Tribune
MY MOTHER SAYS TO PICK...
...NOT REALLY KNOWING WHAT I'D FIND THERE.
...THE VERY BEST ONE, AND THAT... IS...
...YOU!
TAILOR
HEY! SOMEBODY WANTS TO SEE YOU!
RIGHT NOW! EVEN IF I'D RATHER SLIT YER THROAT AND BE DONE WITH IT!
?!?
FLLK!
IN MEMORY OF THE GOOD OL' DAYS WHEN WE USED TO CROSS PATHS IN THE ALLEYWAYS...
...WITH YOUR GANG OF DIRTY YANKEES!!
7

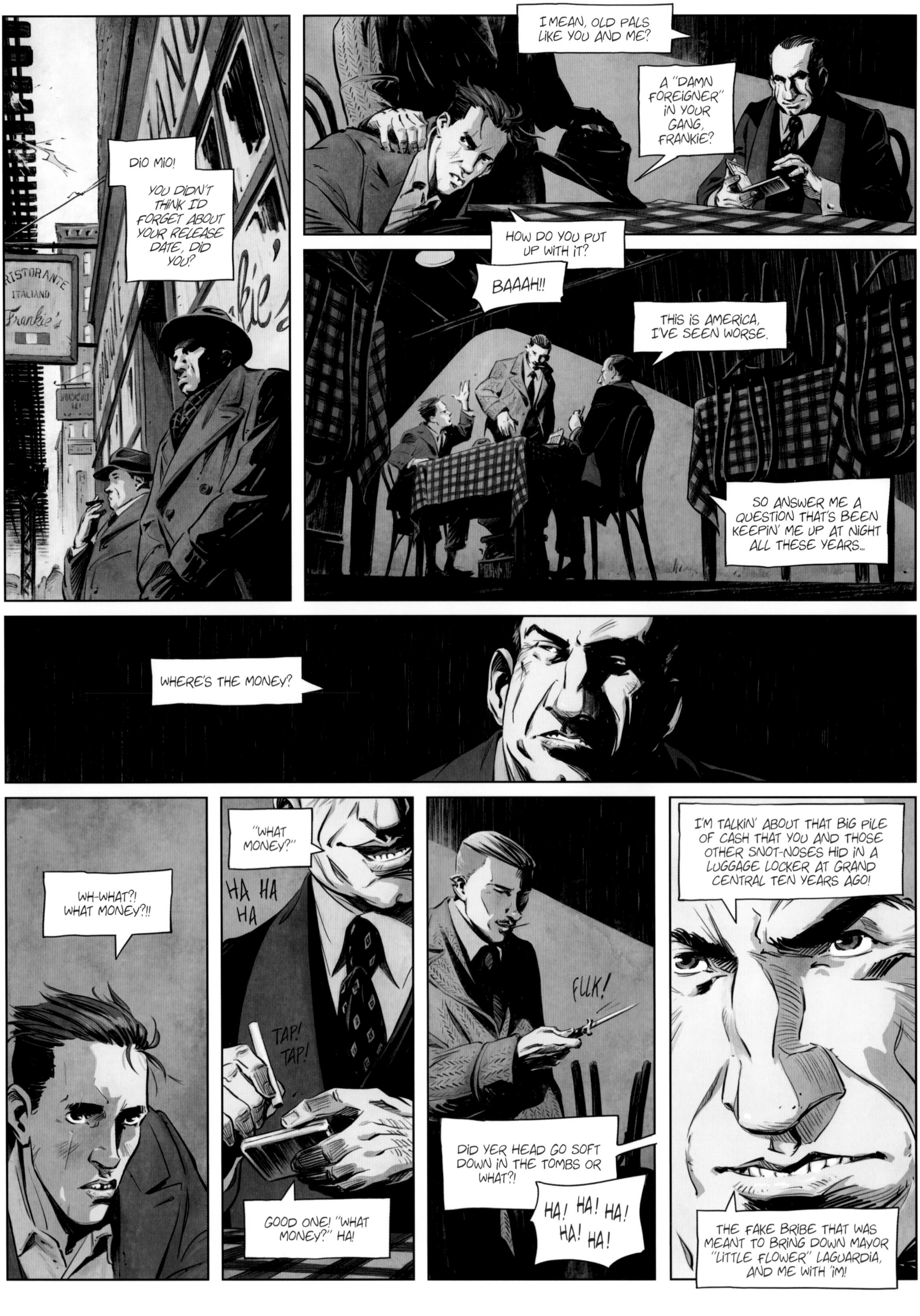
DIO MIO!
YOU DIDN'T THINK I'D FORGET ABOUT YOUR RELEASE DATE, DID YOU?
RISTORANTE ITALIANO Frankie's
I MEAN, OLD PALS LIKE YOU AND ME?
A "DAMN FOREIGNER" IN YOUR GANG, FRANKIE?
HOW DO YOU PUT UP WITH IT?
BAAAH!!
THIS IS AMERICA, I'VE SEEN WORSE.
SO ANSWER ME A QUESTION THAT'S BEEN KEEPIN' ME UP AT NIGHT ALL THESE YEARS...
WHERE'S THE MONEY?
WH-WHAT?! WHAT MONEY?!!
"WHAT MONEY?"
HA HA HA
TAP! TAP!
GOOD ONE! "WHAT MONEY?" HA!
FLIK!
DID YER HEAD GO SOFT DOWN IN THE TOMBS OR WHAT?!
HA! HA! HA! HA! HA!
I'M TALKIN' ABOUT THAT BIG PILE OF CASH THAT YOU AND THOSE OTHER SNOT-NOSES HID IN A LUGGAGE LOCKER AT GRAND CENTRAL TEN YEARS AGO!
THE FAKE BRIBE THAT WAS MEANT TO BRING DOWN MAYOR "LITTLE FLOWER" LAGUARDIA, AND ME WITH 'IM!

8

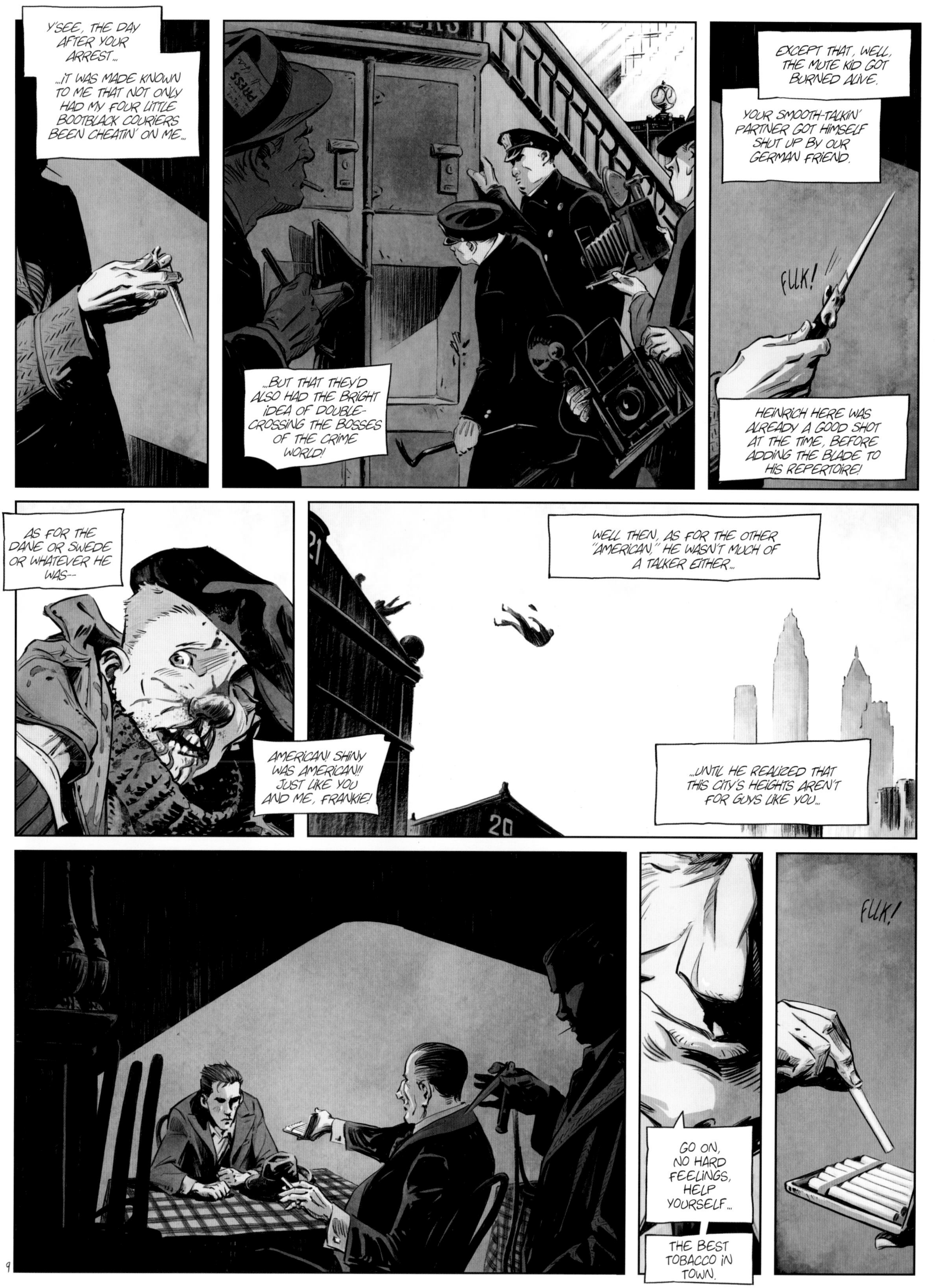

Y'SEE, THE DAY AFTER YOUR ARREST...
...IT WAS MADE KNOWN TO ME THAT NOT ONLY HAD MY FOUR LITTLE BOOTBLACK COURIERS BEEN CHEATIN' ON ME...
PRESS
...BUT THAT THEY'D ALSO HAD THE BRIGHT IDEA OF DOUBLE-CROSSING THE BOSSES OF THE CRIME WORLD!
EXCEPT THAT, WELL, THE MUTE KID GOT BURNED ALIVE.
YOUR SMOOTH-TALKIN' PARTNER GOT HIMSELF SHUT UP BY OUR GERMAN FRIEND.
FLIK!
HEINRICH HERE WAS ALREADY A GOOD SHOT AT THE TIME, BEFORE ADDING THE BLADE TO HIS REPERTOIRE!
AS FOR THE DANE OR SWEDE OR WHATEVER HE WAS--
AMERICAN! SHINY WAS AMERICAN!! JUST LIKE YOU AND ME, FRANKIE!
WELL THEN, AS FOR THE OTHER "AMERICAN," HE WASN'T MUCH OF A TALKER EITHER...
21
...UNTIL HE REALIZED THAT THIS CITY'S HEIGHTS AREN'T FOR GUYS LIKE YOU...
20
9
GO ON, NO HARD FEELINGS, HELP YOURSELF...
THE BEST TOBACCO IN TOWN.
FLIK!

RIGHT.

LET'S NOT WASTE OUR TIME... GO ON, SPIT IT OUT!

YOU KNOW, WHEN IT COMES DOWN TO IT, IF THAT LOCKER HADN'T BEEN EMPTIED, I WOULDA GONE TO JAIL!

AND WHEN THE MAYOR FOUND OUT WHAT THE CITY CRIME BOSSES HAD COOKED UP, HE SET THE DOGS LOOSE ON 'EM!

HE WENT AFTER THE BIG FISH!

BUT ONLY THE BIGGEST!

WHAT WERE THOSE SICILIAN WHARF RATS THINKIN', ANYWAY? THAT JUST CUZ I'M NOT A KING FROM THE OLD WORLD THEY COULD GET RID OF ME THAT EASY?

WELL THEY WERE WRONG, ALL RIGHT!

ALL I HAD TO DO WAS COME IN AND TAKE OVER THE FREE TURF WHEN THE DUST SETTLED...

...AND NOW I CONTROL THE LONGSHORE-MEN, ALL THE GAMBLING ON THE EAST SIDE, AND EVEN THE NUMBERS RACKET RUN BY THE DAMN COLOREDS UP IN HARLEM! AND WHO'S TO THANK?

AMERICA, MY FAIRY GODMOTHER!

SO, BACK TO THAT MONEY THAT WAS STOLEN ON MY TURF! WHERE IS IT?

IT DIDN'T JUST GROW WINGS. SOMEBODY TOOK IT.

SOMEBODY WITH THE KEY TO THAT DAMN LOCKER!

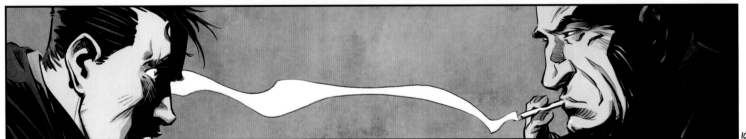

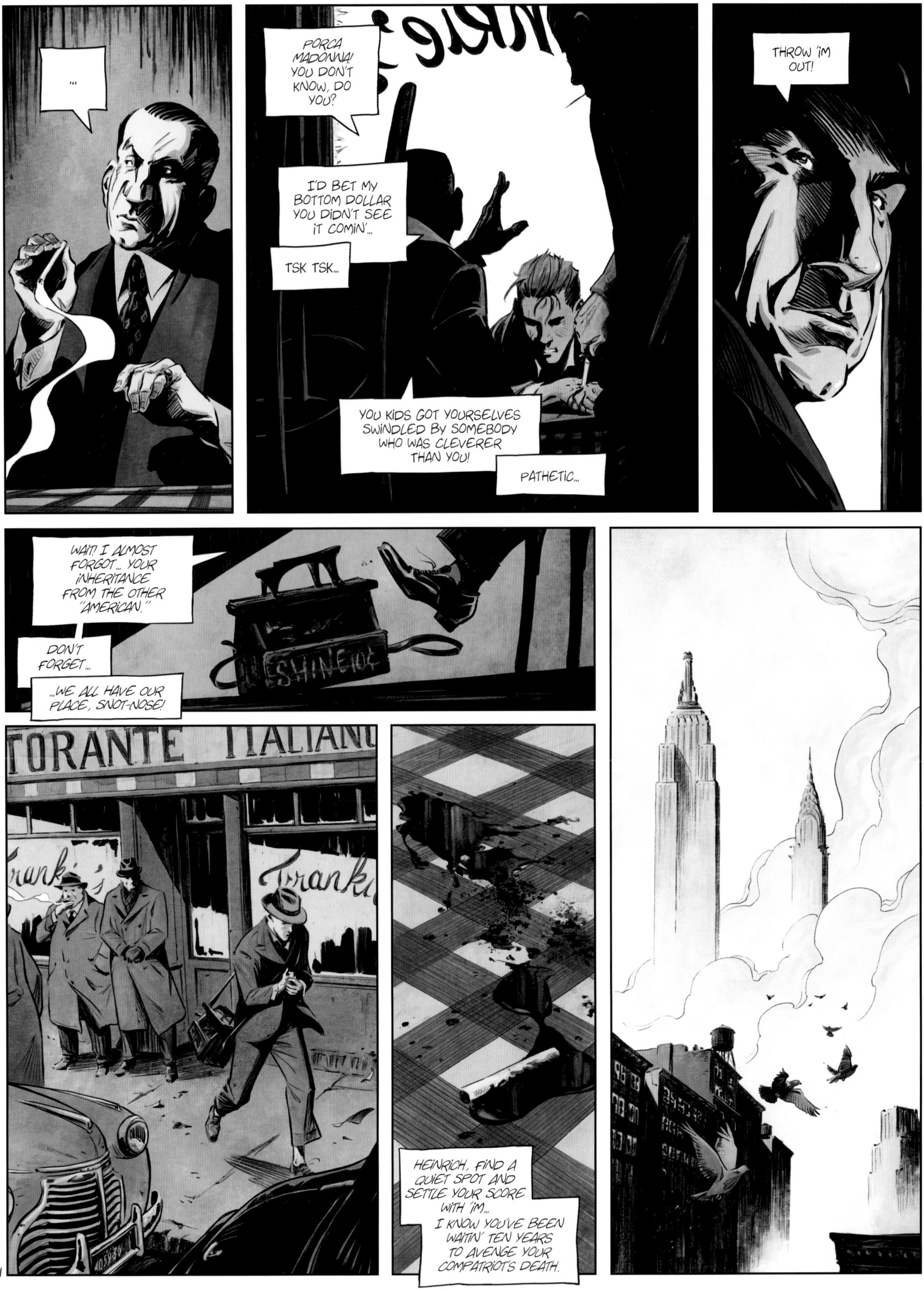
...
PORCA MADONNA! YOU DON'T KNOW, DO YOU?
I'D BET MY BOTTOM DOLLAR YOU DIDN'T SEE IT COMIN'...
TSK TSK...
YOU KIDS GOT YOURSELVES SWINDLED BY SOMEBODY WHO WAS CLEVERER THAN YOU!
PATHETIC...
THROW 'IM OUT!
WAIT! I ALMOST FORGOT... YOUR INHERITANCE FROM THE OTHER "AMERICAN."
DON'T FORGET...
...WE ALL HAVE OUR PLACE, SNOT-NOSE!
TORANTE ITALIAN
HEINRICH, FIND A QUIET SPOT AND SETTLE YOUR SCORE WITH 'IM...
I KNOW YOU'VE BEEN WAITIN' TEN YEARS TO AVENGE YOUR COMPATRIOT'S DEATH.

11

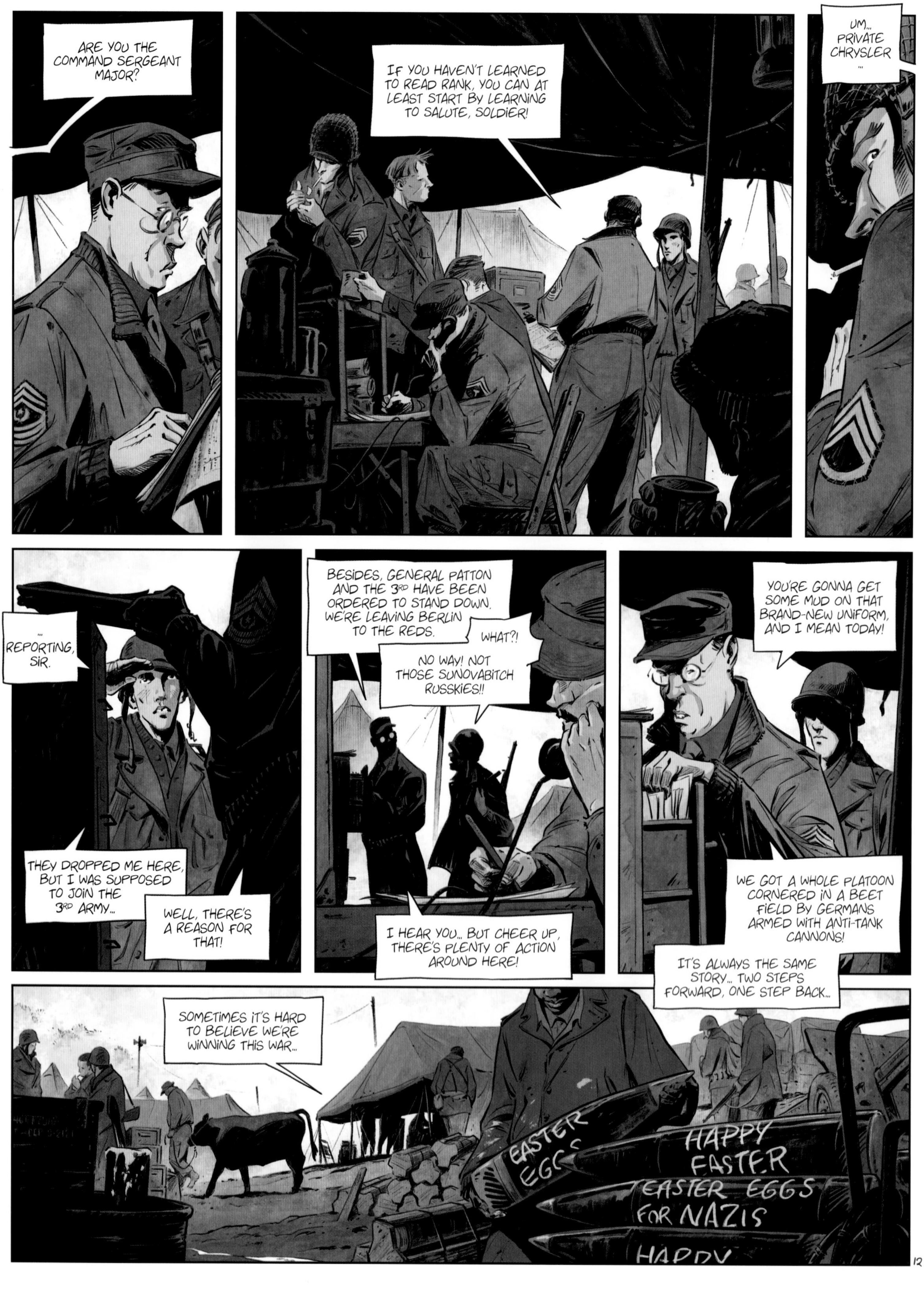
ARE YOU THE COMMAND SERGEANT MAJOR?
IF YOU HAVEN'T LEARNED TO READ RANK, YOU CAN AT LEAST START BY LEARNING TO SALUTE, SOLDIER!
UM... PRIVATE CHRYSLER ...
... REPORTING, SIR.
THEY DROPPED ME HERE, BUT I WAS SUPPOSED TO JOIN THE 3RD ARMY...
WELL, THERE'S A REASON FOR THAT!
BESIDES, GENERAL PATTON AND THE 3RD HAVE BEEN ORDERED TO STAND DOWN. WE'RE LEAVING BERLIN TO THE REDS.
WHAT?!
NO WAY! NOT THOSE SUNOVABITCH RUSSKIES!!
I HEAR YOU... BUT CHEER UP, THERE'S PLENTY OF ACTION AROUND HERE!
YOU'RE GONNA GET SOME MUD ON THAT BRAND-NEW UNIFORM, AND I MEAN TODAY!
WE GOT A WHOLE PLATOON CORNERED IN A BEET FIELD BY GERMANS ARMED WITH ANTI-TANK CANNONS!
IT'S ALWAYS THE SAME STORY... TWO STEPS FORWARD, ONE STEP BACK...
SOMETIMES IT'S HARD TO BELIEVE WE'RE WINNING THIS WAR...
EASTER EGGS
HAPPY EASTER
EASTER EGGS FOR NAZIS
12

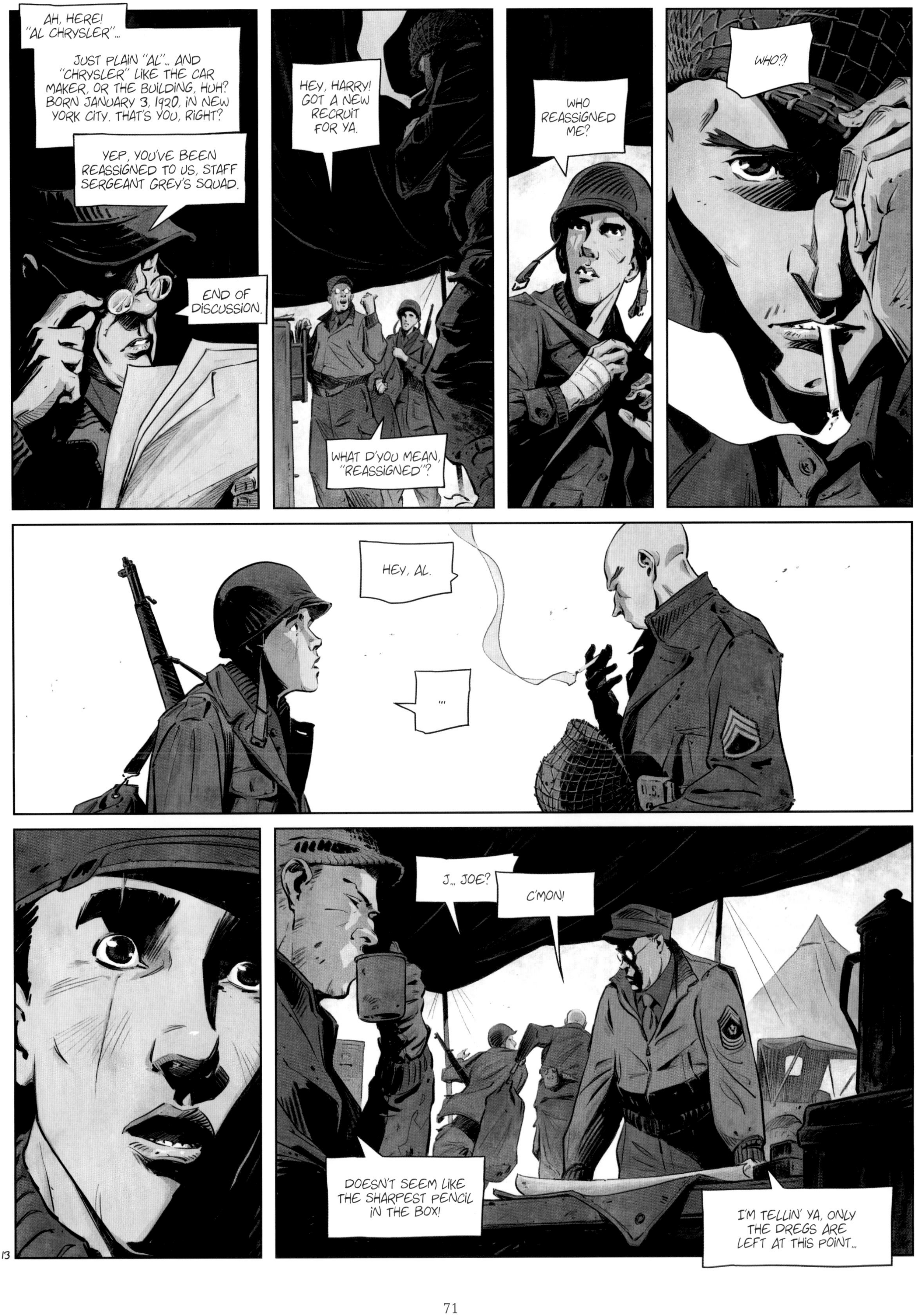
AH, HERE! "AL CHRYSLER"...
JUST PLAIN "AL"... AND "CHRYSLER" LIKE THE CAR MAKER, OR THE BUILDING, HUH? BORN JANUARY 3, 1920, IN NEW YORK CITY. THAT'S YOU, RIGHT?
YEP, YOU'VE BEEN REASSIGNED TO US, STAFF SERGEANT GREY'S SQUAD.
END OF DISCUSSION.
HEY, HARRY! GOT A NEW RECRUIT FOR YA.
WHAT D'YOU MEAN, "REASSIGNED"?
WHO REASSIGNED ME?
WHO?!
HEY, AL.
...
J... JOE?
C'MON!
DOESN'T SEEM LIKE THE SHARPEST PENCIL IN THE BOX!
I'M TELLIN' YA, ONLY THE DREGS ARE LEFT AT THIS POINT...
13

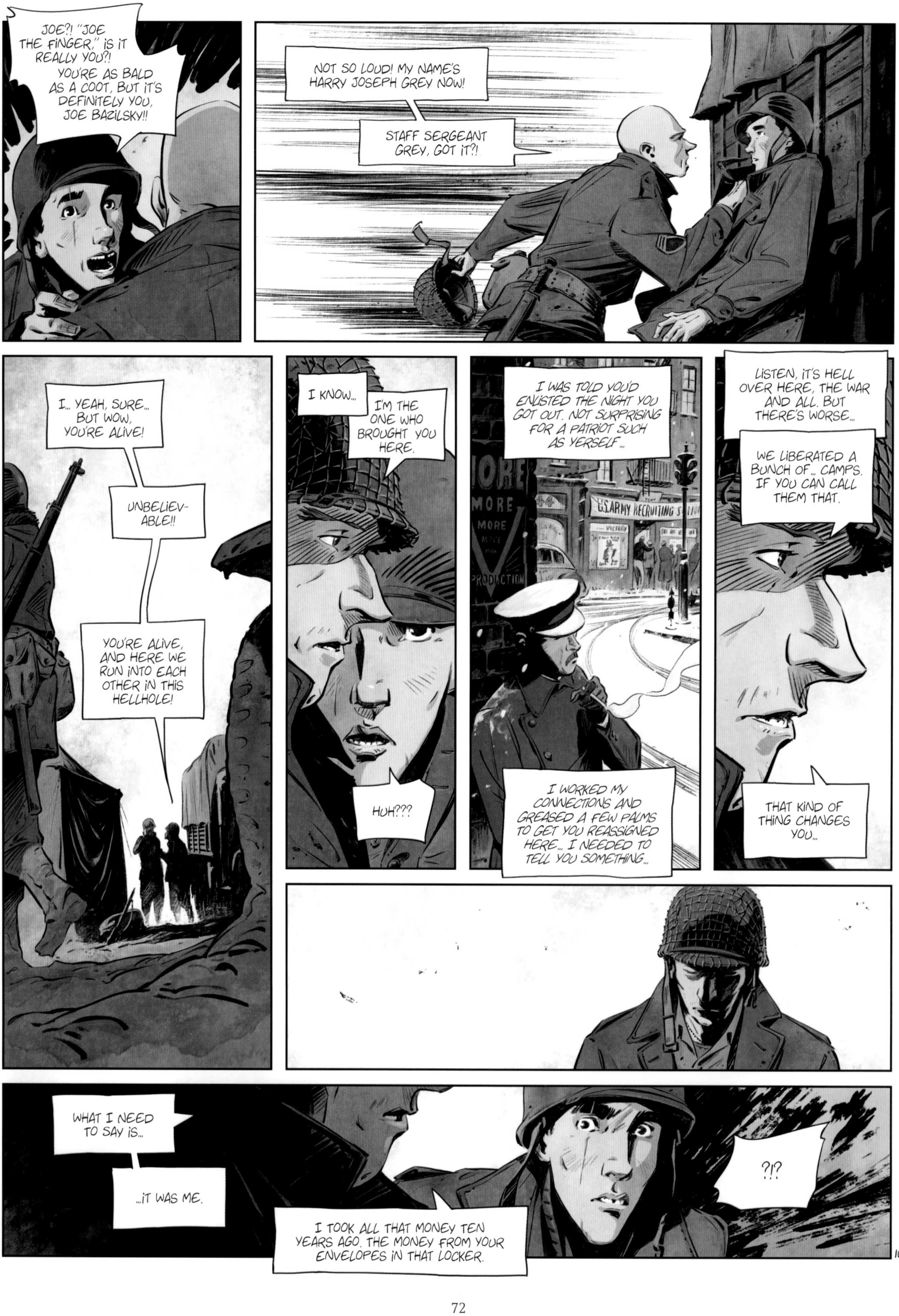

JOE?! "JOE THE FINGER," IS IT REALLY YOU?! YOU'RE AS BALD AS A COOT, BUT IT'S DEFINITELY YOU, JOE BAZILSKY!!
NOT SO LOUD! MY NAME'S HARRY JOSEPH GREY NOW!
STAFF SERGEANT GREY, GOT IT?!
I... YEAH, SURE... BUT WOW, YOU'RE ALIVE!
UNBELIEV-ABLE!!
YOU'RE ALIVE, AND HERE WE RUN INTO EACH OTHER IN THIS HELLHOLE!
I KNOW...
I'M THE ONE WHO BROUGHT YOU HERE.
HUH???
I WAS TOLD YOU'D ENLISTED THE NIGHT YOU GOT OUT. NOT SURPRISING FOR A PATRIOT SUCH AS YERSELF...
U.S. ARMY RECRUITING S
I WORKED MY CONNECTIONS AND GREASED A FEW PALMS TO GET YOU REASSIGNED HERE... I NEEDED TO TELL YOU SOMETHING...
LISTEN, IT'S HELL OVER HERE, THE WAR AND ALL. BUT THERE'S WORSE...
WE LIBERATED A BUNCH OF... CAMPS. IF YOU CAN CALL THEM THAT.
THAT KIND OF THING CHANGES YOU...
WHAT I NEED TO SAY IS...
...IT WAS ME.
I TOOK ALL THAT MONEY TEN YEARS AGO. THE MONEY FROM YOUR ENVELOPES IN THAT LOCKER.
?!?
14

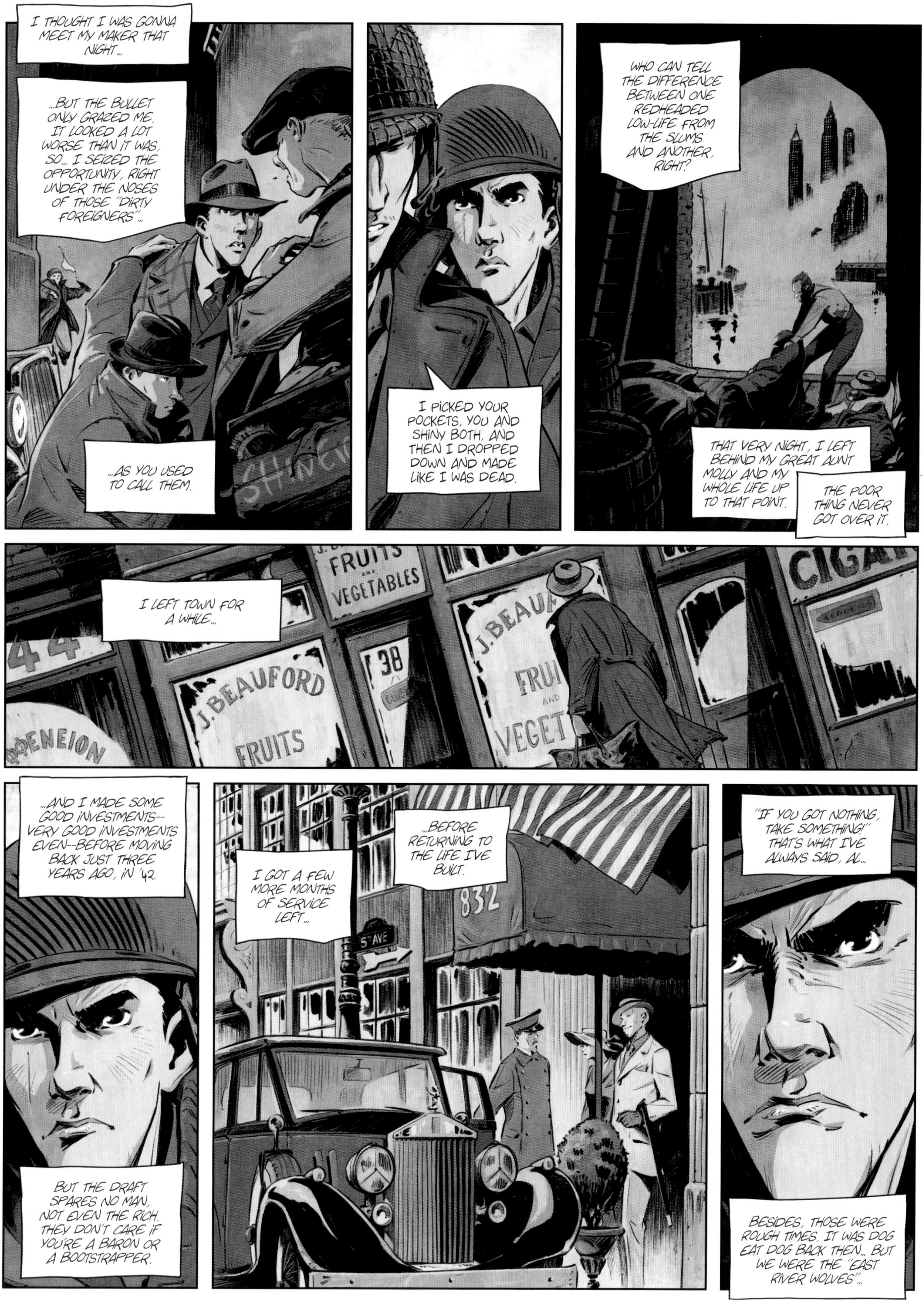
I THOUGHT I WAS GONNA MEET MY MAKER THAT NIGHT...
...BUT THE BULLET ONLY GRAZED ME. IT LOOKED A LOT WORSE THAN IT WAS, SO... I SEIZED THE OPPORTUNITY, RIGHT UNDER THE NOSES OF THOSE "DIRTY FOREIGNERS"...
...AS YOU USED TO CALL THEM.
I PICKED YOUR POCKETS, YOU AND SHINY BOTH, AND THEN I DROPPED DOWN AND MADE LIKE I WAS DEAD.
WHO CAN TELL THE DIFFERENCE BETWEEN ONE REDHEADED LOW-LIFE FROM THE SLUMS AND ANOTHER, RIGHT?
THAT VERY NIGHT, I LEFT BEHIND MY GREAT AUNT MOLLY AND MY WHOLE LIFE UP TO THAT POINT.
THE POOR THING NEVER GOT OVER IT.
I LEFT TOWN FOR A WHILE...
FRUITS AND VEGETABLES
J. BEAUFORD FRUITS
CIGA
...AND I MADE SOME GOOD INVESTMENTS-- VERY GOOD INVESTMENTS EVEN--BEFORE MOVING BACK JUST THREE YEARS AGO, IN '42.
BUT THE DRAFT SPARES NO MAN, NOT EVEN THE RICH. THEY DON'T CARE IF YOU'RE A BARON OR A BOOTSTRAPPER.
I GOT A FEW MORE MONTHS OF SERVICE LEFT...
...BEFORE RETURNING TO THE LIFE I'VE BUILT.
832
5th AVE
"IF YOU GOT NOTHING, TAKE SOMETHING!" THAT'S WHAT I'VE ALWAYS SAID, AL...
BESIDES, THOSE WERE ROUGH TIMES. IT WAS DOG EAT DOG BACK THEN... BUT WE WERE THE "EAST RIVER WOLVES"...
15

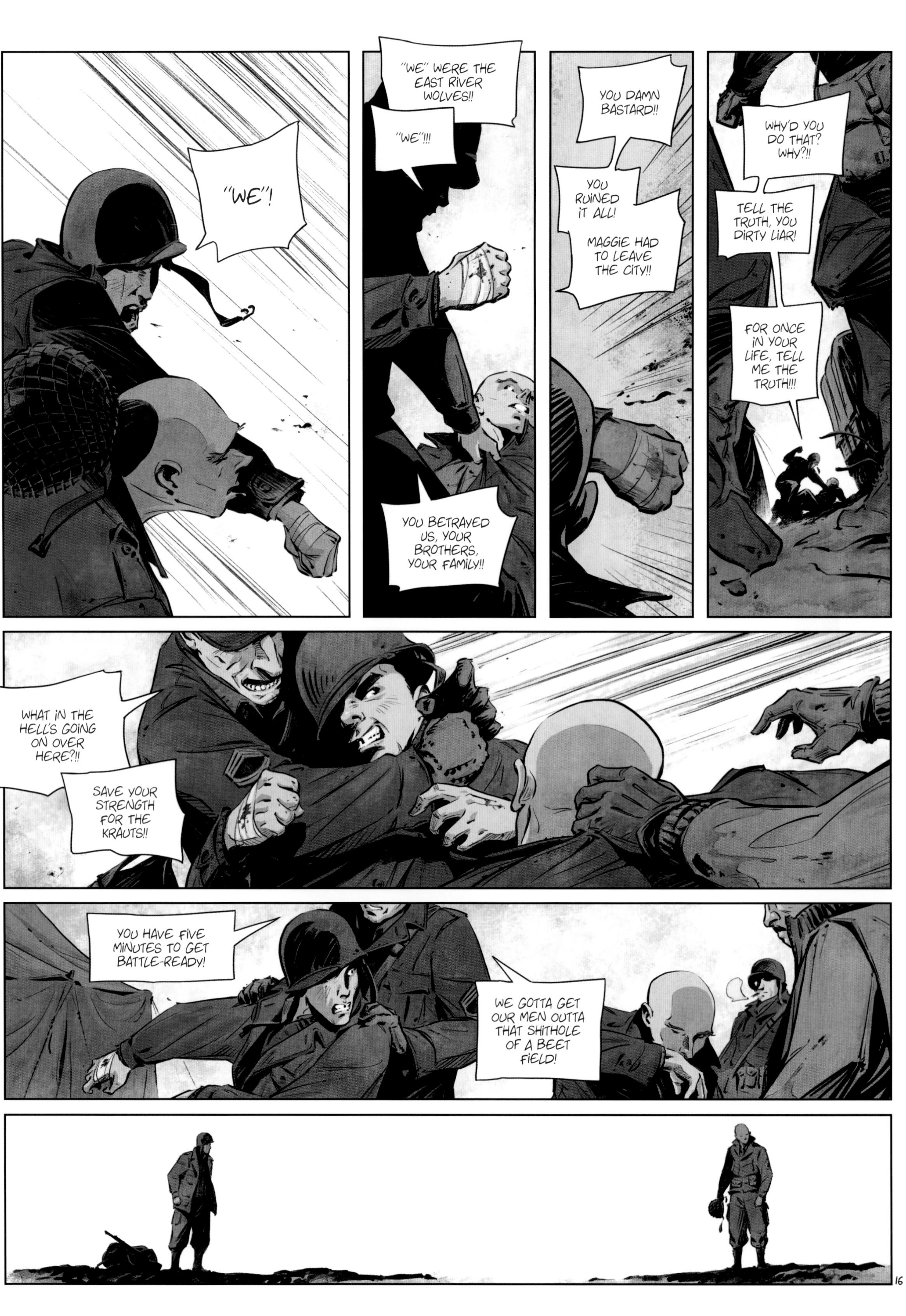
"WE"!
"WE" WERE THE EAST RIVER WOLVES!!
"WE"!!!
YOU BETRAYED US, YOUR BROTHERS, YOUR FAMILY!!
YOU DAMN BASTARD!!
YOU RUINED IT ALL!
MAGGIE HAD TO LEAVE THE CITY!!
WHY'D YOU DO THAT? WHY?!!
TELL THE TRUTH, YOU DIRTY LIAR!
FOR ONCE IN YOUR LIFE, TELL ME THE TRUTH!!!
WHAT IN THE HELL'S GOING ON OVER HERE?!!
SAVE YOUR STRENGTH FOR THE KRAUTS!!
YOU HAVE FIVE MINUTES TO GET BATTLE-READY!
WE GOTTA GET OUR MEN OUTTA THAT SHITHOLE OF A BEET FIELD!
16

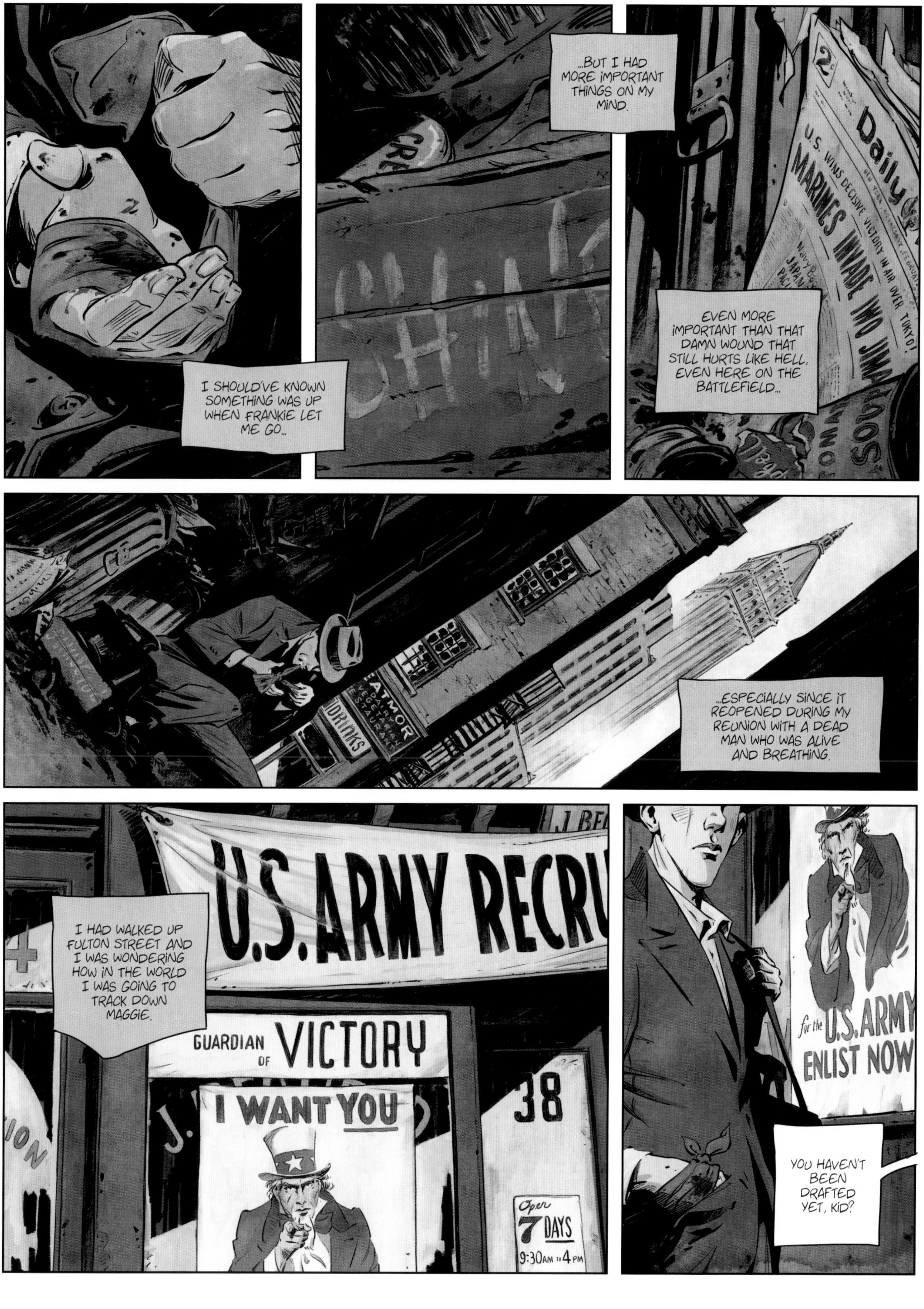
I SHOULD'VE KNOWN SOMETHING WAS UP WHEN FRANKIE LET ME GO...
...BUT I HAD MORE IMPORTANT THINGS ON MY MIND.
2¢
Daily
U.S. WINS DECISIVE VICTORY IN AIR OVER TOKYO!
MARINES INVADE IWO JIMA
EVEN MORE IMPORTANT THAN THAT DAMN WOUND THAT STILL HURTS LIKE HELL, EVEN HERE ON THE BATTLEFIELD...
DRINKS
...ESPECIALLY SINCE IT REOPENED DURING MY REUNION WITH A DEAD MAN WHO WAS ALIVE AND BREATHING.
U.S. ARMY RECRU
I HAD WALKED UP FULTON STREET AND I WAS WONDERING HOW IN THE WORLD I WAS GOING TO TRACK DOWN MAGGIE.
GUARDIAN OF VICTORY
I WANT YOU
38
Open 7 DAYS 9:30AM to 4PM
for the U.S. ARMY
ENLIST NOW
YOU HAVEN'T BEEN DRAFTED YET, KID?

17

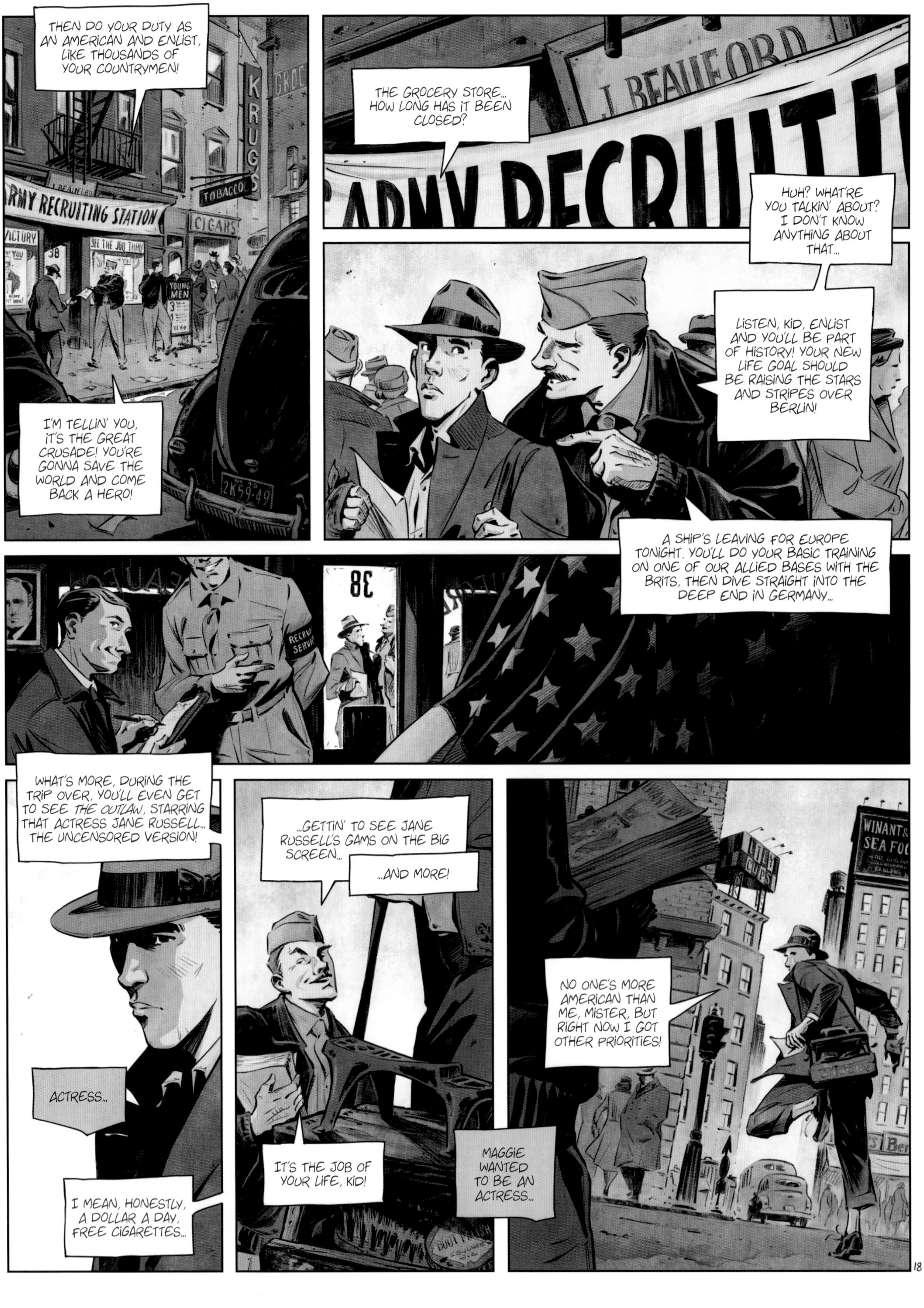

THEN DO YOUR DUTY AS AN AMERICAN AND ENLIST, LIKE THOUSANDS OF YOUR COUNTRYMEN!
KRUG'S
TOBACCO
ARMY RECRUITING STATION
CIGARS
I'M TELLIN' YOU, IT'S THE GREAT CRUSADE! YOU'RE GONNA SAVE THE WORLD AND COME BACK A HERO!
THE GROCERY STORE... HOW LONG HAS IT BEEN CLOSED?
HUH? WHAT'RE YOU TALKIN' ABOUT? I DON'T KNOW ANYTHING ABOUT THAT...
LISTEN, KID, ENLIST AND YOU'LL BE PART OF HISTORY! YOUR NEW LIFE GOAL SHOULD BE RAISING THE STARS AND STRIPES OVER BERLIN!
A SHIP'S LEAVING FOR EUROPE TONIGHT. YOU'LL DO YOUR BASIC TRAINING ON ONE OF OUR ALLIED BASES WITH THE BRITS, THEN DIVE STRAIGHT INTO THE DEEP END IN GERMANY...
WHAT'S MORE, DURING THE TRIP OVER, YOU'LL EVEN GET TO SEE *THE OUTLAW*, STARRING THAT ACTRESS JANE RUSSELL... THE UNCENSORED VERSION!
ACTRESS...
I MEAN, HONESTLY, A DOLLAR A DAY, FREE CIGARETTES...
...GETTIN' TO SEE JANE RUSSELL'S GAMS ON THE BIG SCREEN...
...AND MORE!
IT'S THE JOB OF YOUR LIFE, KID!
MAGGIE WANTED TO BE AN ACTRESS...
NO ONE'S MORE AMERICAN THAN ME, MISTER, BUT RIGHT NOW I GOT OTHER PRIORITIES!
18

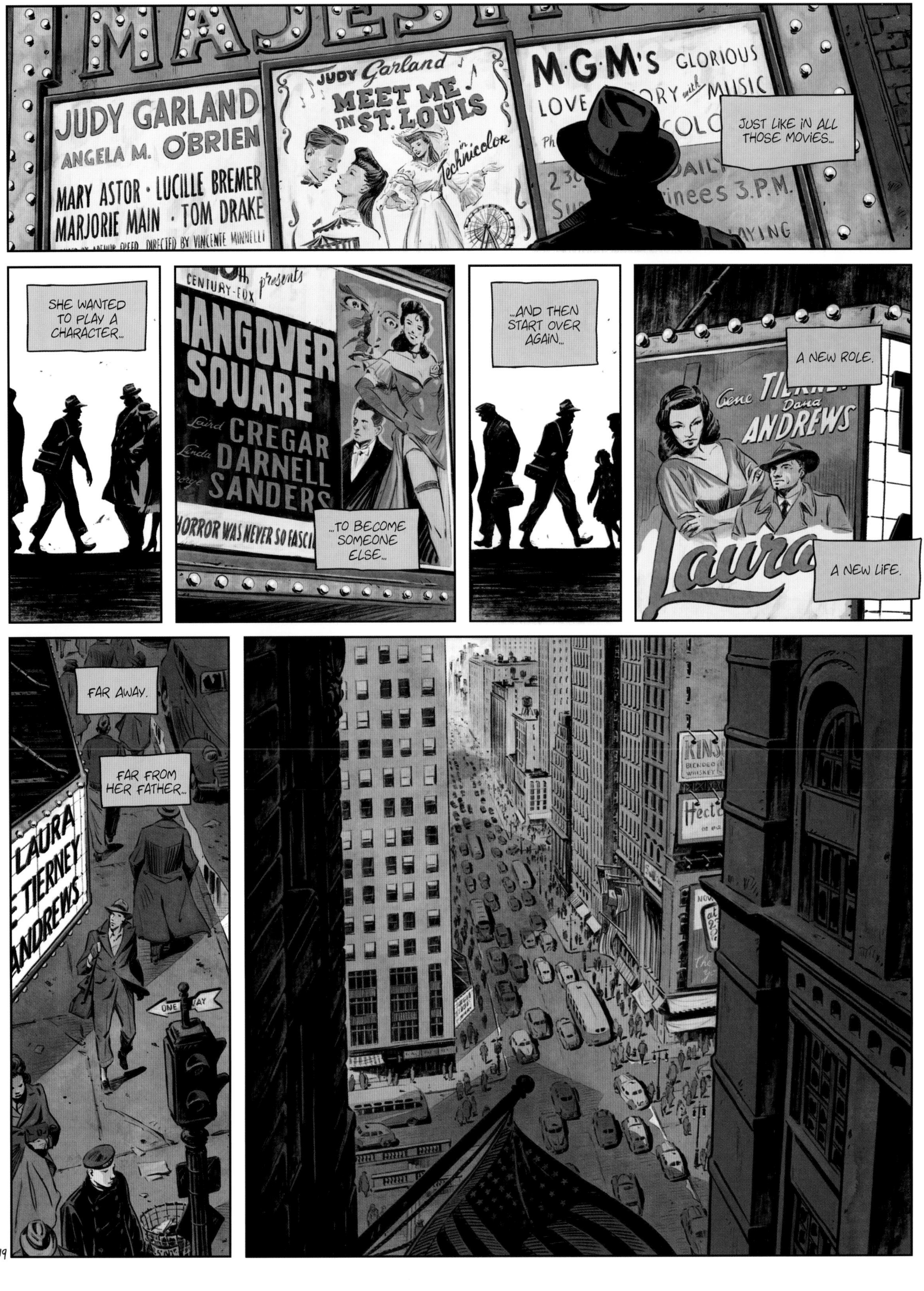
JUDY GARLAND
ANGELA M. O'BRIEN
MARY ASTOR · LUCILLE BREMER
MARJORIE MAIN · TOM DRAKE
JUDY Garland
MEET ME IN ST. LOUIS
in Technicolor
M·G·M's GLORIOUS
JUST LIKE IN ALL THOSE MOVIES...
SHE WANTED TO PLAY A CHARACTER...
presents
HANGOVER SQUARE
Laird CREGAR
Linda DARNELL
SANDERS
...TO BECOME SOMEONE ELSE...
...AND THEN START OVER AGAIN...
A NEW ROLE.
Gene
Dana ANDREWS
A NEW LIFE.
FAR AWAY.
FAR FROM HER FATHER...
LAURA
TIERNEY
ANDREWS
BLENDED WHISKEY

19

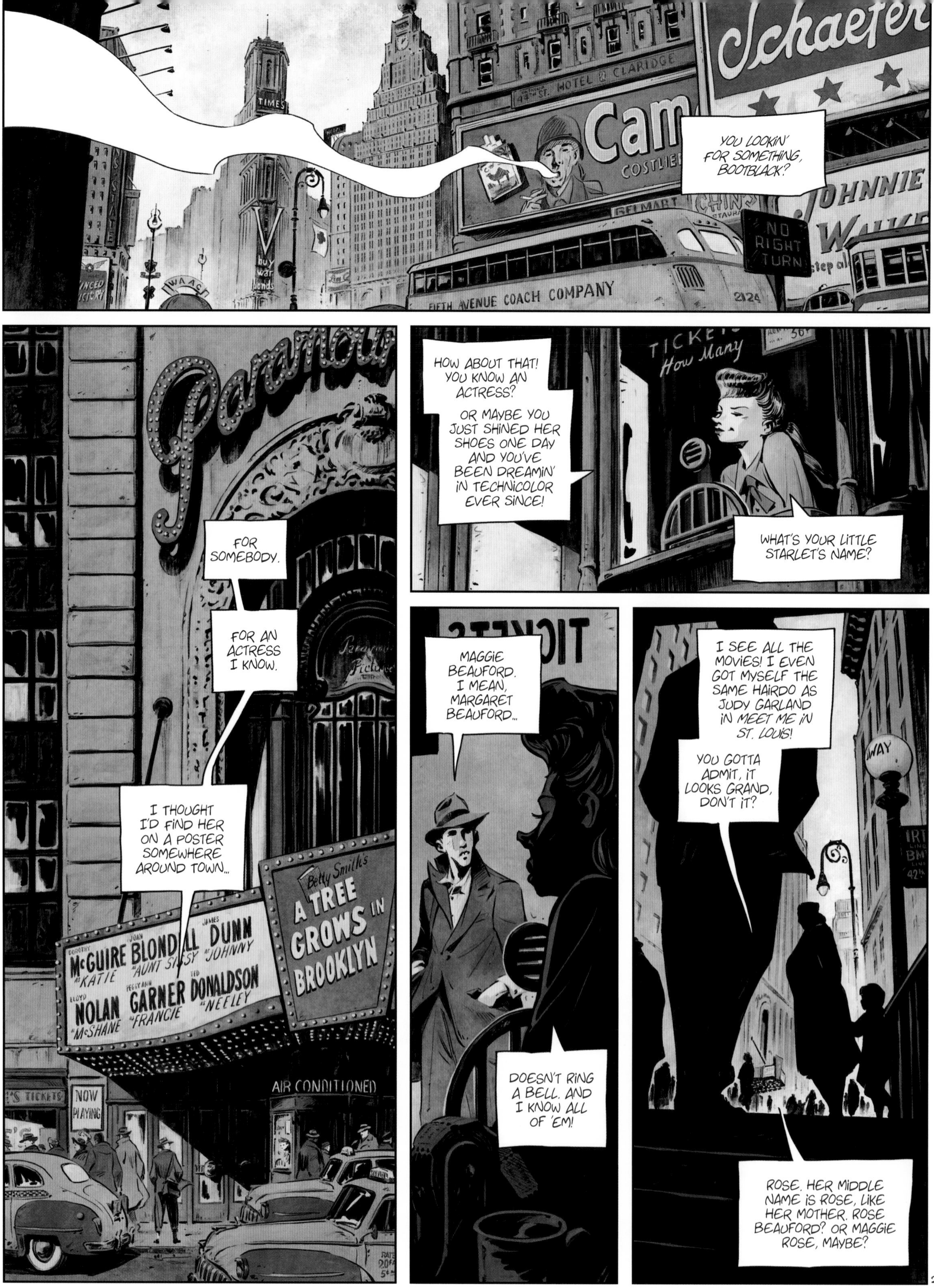

YOU LOOKIN' FOR SOMETHING, BOOTBLACK?
NO RIGHT TURN
FIFTH AVENUE COACH COMPANY
FOR SOMEBODY.
FOR AN ACTRESS I KNOW.
I THOUGHT I'D FIND HER ON A POSTER SOMEWHERE AROUND TOWN...
A TREE GROWS IN BROOKLYN
AIR CONDITIONED
NOW PLAYING
HOW ABOUT THAT! YOU KNOW AN ACTRESS?
OR MAYBE YOU JUST SHINED HER SHOES ONE DAY AND YOU'VE BEEN DREAMIN' IN TECHNICOLOR EVER SINCE!
WHAT'S YOUR LITTLE STARLET'S NAME?
MAGGIE BEAUFORD. I MEAN, MARGARET BEAUFORD...
DOESN'T RING A BELL. AND I KNOW ALL OF 'EM!
I SEE ALL THE MOVIES! I EVEN GOT MYSELF THE SAME HAIRDO AS JUDY GARLAND IN MEET ME IN ST. LOUIS!
YOU GOTTA ADMIT, IT LOOKS GRAND, DON'T IT?
ROSE. HER MIDDLE NAME IS ROSE, LIKE HER MOTHER. ROSE BEAUFORD? OR MAGGIE ROSE, MAYBE?

20

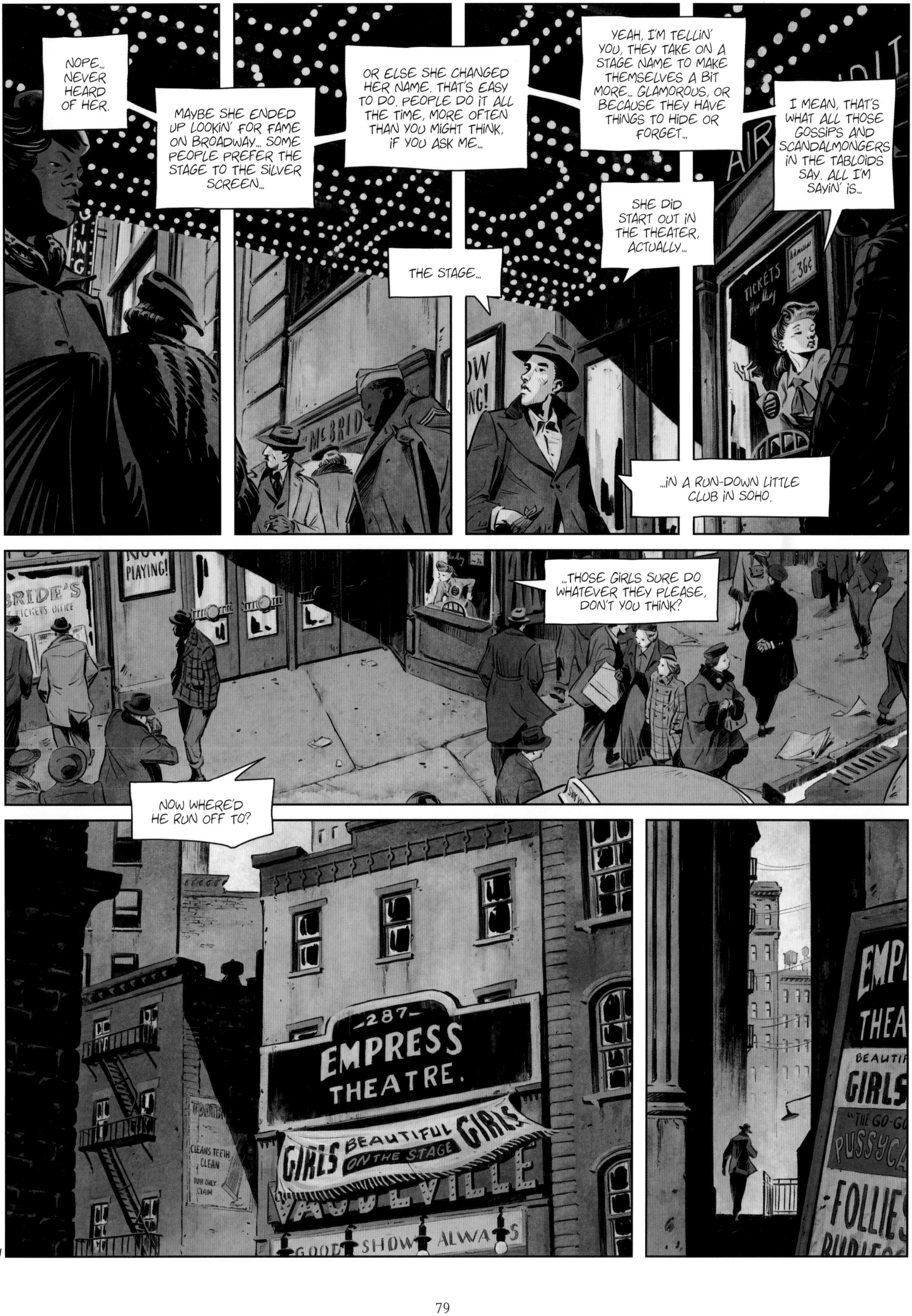
NOPE... NEVER HEARD OF HER.
MAYBE SHE ENDED UP LOOKIN' FOR FAME ON BROADWAY... SOME PEOPLE PREFER THE STAGE TO THE SILVER SCREEN...
OR ELSE SHE CHANGED HER NAME. THAT'S EASY TO DO. PEOPLE DO IT ALL THE TIME, MORE OFTEN THAN YOU MIGHT THINK, IF YOU ASK ME...
THE STAGE...
YEAH, I'M TELLIN' YOU, THEY TAKE ON A STAGE NAME TO MAKE THEMSELVES A BIT MORE... GLAMOROUS, OR BECAUSE THEY HAVE THINGS TO HIDE OR FORGET...
SHE DID START OUT IN THE THEATER, ACTUALLY...
I MEAN, THAT'S WHAT ALL THOSE GOSSIPS AND SCANDALMONGERS IN THE TABLOIDS SAY. ALL I'M SAYIN' IS...
...IN A RUN-DOWN LITTLE CLUB IN SOHO.
TICKETS
...THOSE GIRLS SURE DO WHATEVER THEY PLEASE, DON'T YOU THINK?
NOW PLAYING!
NOW WHERE'D HE RUN OFF TO?
287
EMPRESS THEATRE.
GIRLS BEAUTIFUL ON THE STAGE GIRLS
GOOD SHOW ALWAYS
CLEANS TEETH CLEAN
21

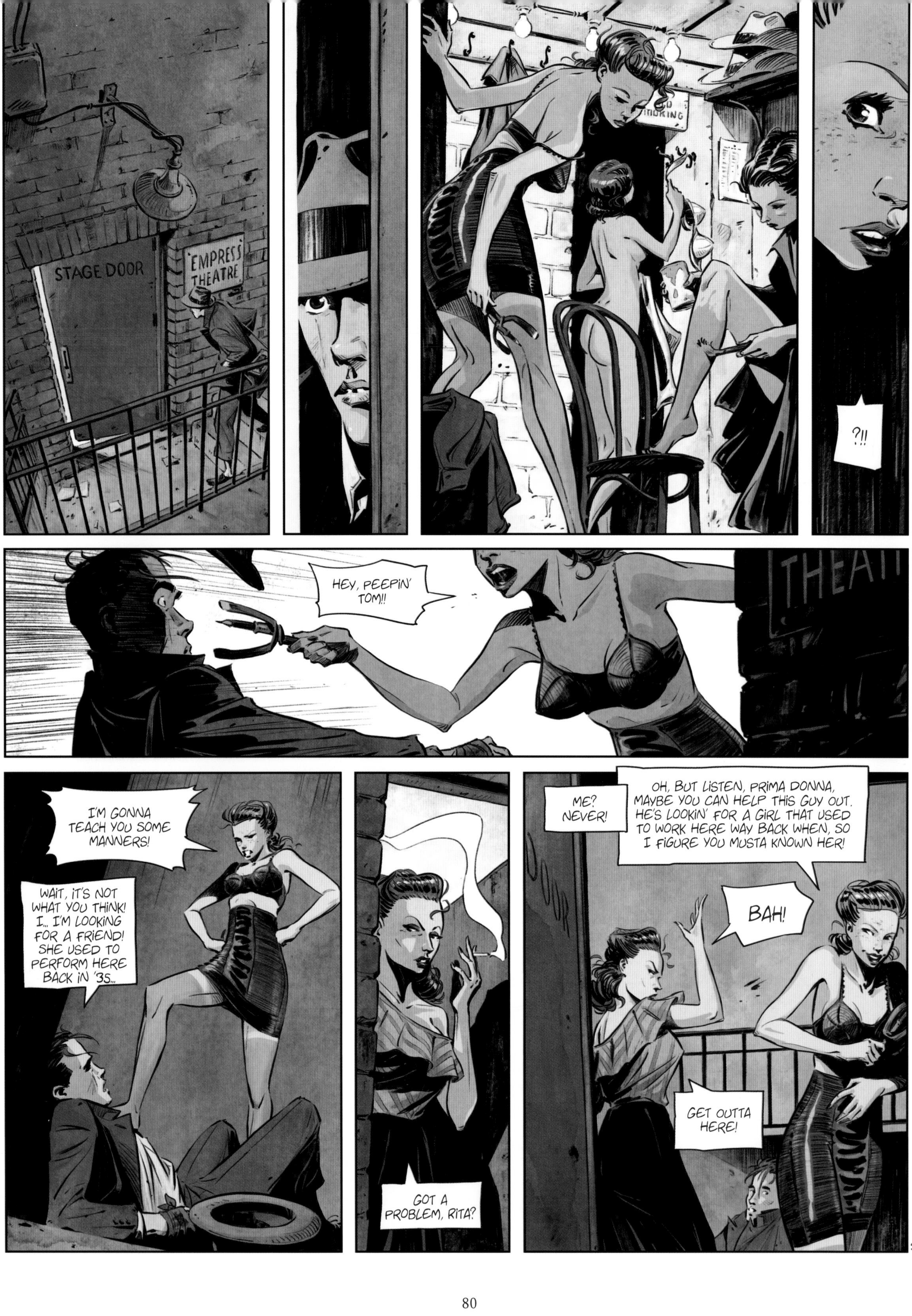
STAGE DOOR
EMPRESS THEATRE
?!!
HEY, PEEPIN' TOM!!
I'M GONNA TEACH YOU SOME MANNERS!
WAIT, IT'S NOT WHAT YOU THINK! I... I'M LOOKING FOR A FRIEND! SHE USED TO PERFORM HERE BACK IN '35...
GOT A PROBLEM, RITA?
ME? NEVER!
OH, BUT LISTEN, PRIMA DONNA, MAYBE YOU CAN HELP THIS GUY OUT. HE'S LOOKIN' FOR A GIRL THAT USED TO WORK HERE WAY BACK WHEN, SO I FIGURE YOU MUSTA KNOWN HER!
BAH!
GET OUTTA HERE!
22

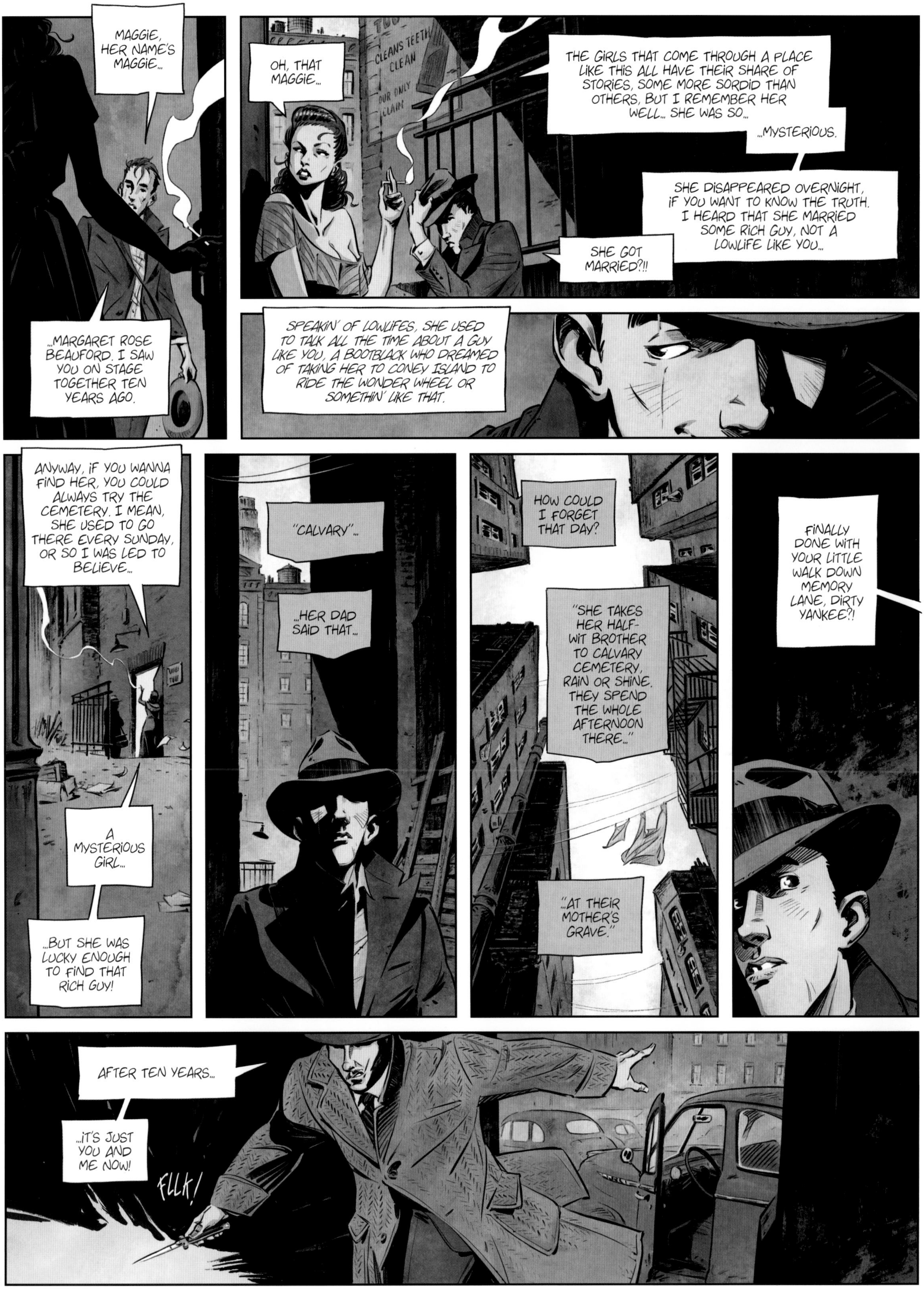
MAGGIE, HER NAME'S MAGGIE...
OH, THAT MAGGIE...
CLEANS TEETH CLEAN
OUR ONLY CLAIM
THE GIRLS THAT COME THROUGH A PLACE LIKE THIS ALL HAVE THEIR SHARE OF STORIES, SOME MORE SORDID THAN OTHERS, BUT I REMEMBER HER WELL... SHE WAS SO...
...MYSTERIOUS.
SHE DISAPPEARED OVERNIGHT, IF YOU WANT TO KNOW THE TRUTH. I HEARD THAT SHE MARRIED SOME RICH GUY, NOT A LOWLIFE LIKE YOU...
SHE GOT MARRIED?!!
...MARGARET ROSE BEAUFORD. I SAW YOU ON STAGE TOGETHER TEN YEARS AGO.
SPEAKIN' OF LOWLIFES, SHE USED TO TALK ALL THE TIME ABOUT A GUY LIKE YOU, A BOOTBLACK WHO DREAMED OF TAKING HER TO CONEY ISLAND TO RIDE THE WONDER WHEEL OR SOMETHIN' LIKE THAT.
ANYWAY, IF YOU WANNA FIND HER, YOU COULD ALWAYS TRY THE CEMETERY. I MEAN, SHE USED TO GO THERE EVERY SUNDAY, OR SO I WAS LED TO BELIEVE...
A MYSTERIOUS GIRL...
...BUT SHE WAS LUCKY ENOUGH TO FIND THAT RICH GUY!
"CALVARY"...
...HER DAD SAID THAT...
HOW COULD I FORGET THAT DAY?
"SHE TAKES HER HALF-WIT BROTHER TO CALVARY CEMETERY, RAIN OR SHINE. THEY SPEND THE WHOLE AFTERNOON THERE..."
"...AT THEIR MOTHER'S GRAVE."
FINALLY DONE WITH YOUR LITTLE WALK DOWN MEMORY LANE, DIRTY YANKEE?!
AFTER TEN YEARS...
...IT'S JUST YOU AND ME NOW!
FLLK!
23

FINDING MAGGIE WAS GOING TO HAVE TO WAIT...

...UNTIL I COULD GET RID OF THIS "DAMN FOREIGNER"!

EXIT · ONLY

NEW Y...
ELEVA...
LINE

CITY H...
←1 BL...

BROOKLYN BRIDGE

EXIT

EVEN IF THAT TIME AROUND, I WAS FORCED TO RUN AWAY FROM HIM.

Victory

ELECTRIC
INSULATE
WIRE·

Michel

MY STREET FIGHTING DAYS WERE WELL BEHIND ME...

WE WERE NO LONGER IN THE SAME LEAGUE.

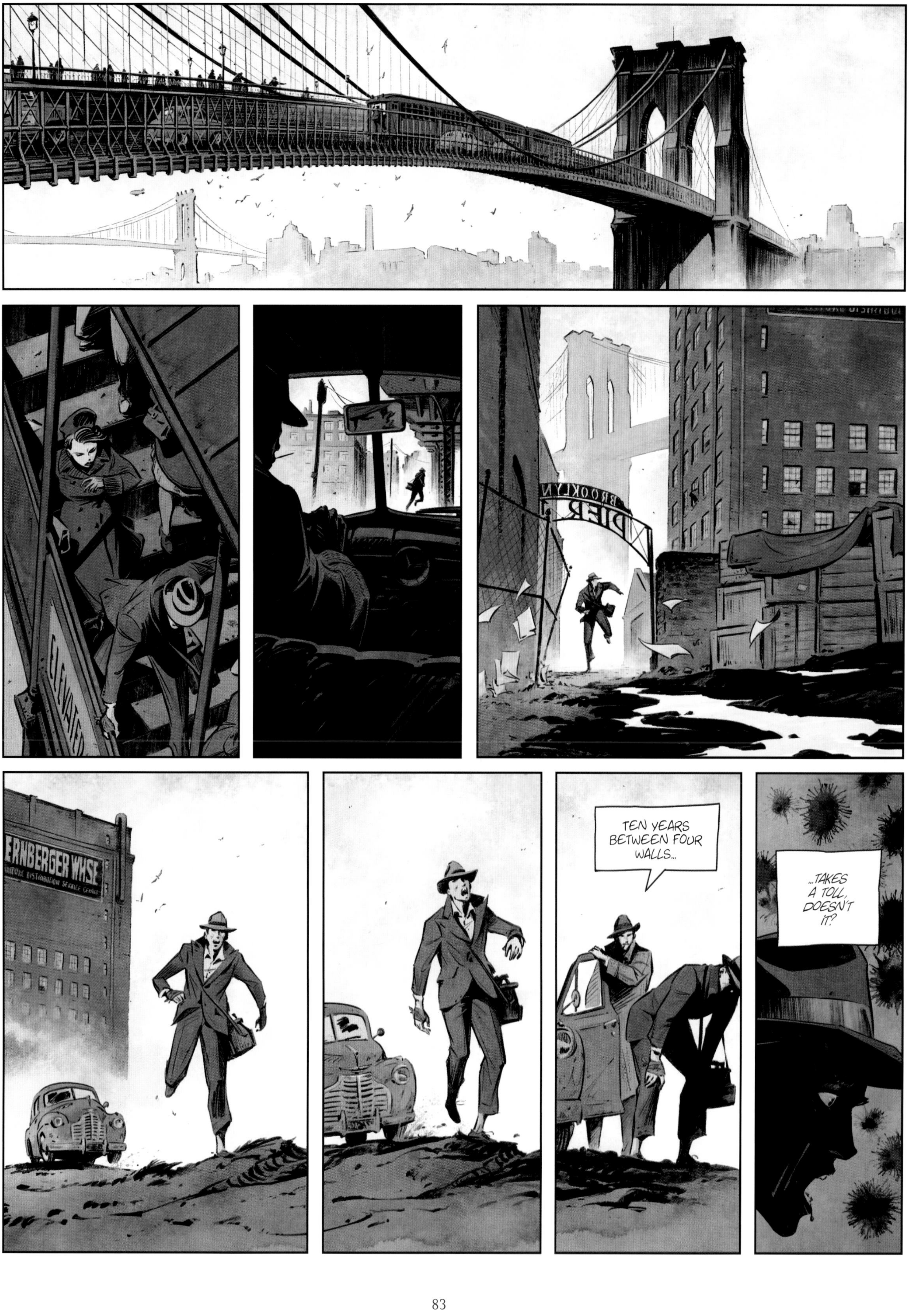
BROOKLYN
PIER
ERNBERGER WHSE
TEN YEARS BETWEEN FOUR WALLS...
...TAKES A TOLL, DOESN'T IT?

25

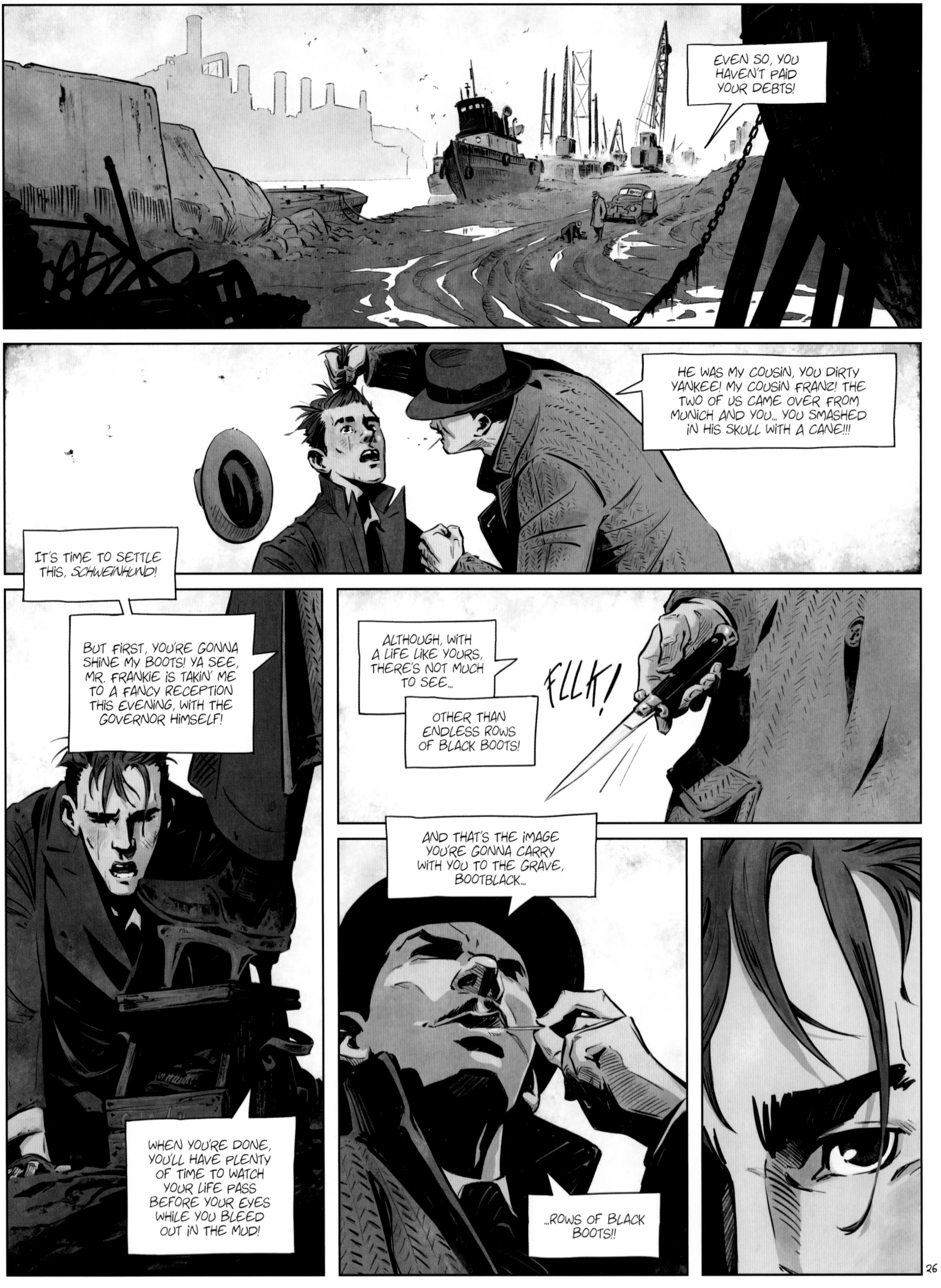
EVEN SO, YOU HAVEN'T PAID YOUR DEBTS!
HE WAS MY COUSIN, YOU DIRTY YANKEE! MY COUSIN FRANZ! THE TWO OF US CAME OVER FROM MUNICH AND YOU... YOU SMASHED IN HIS SKULL WITH A CANE!!!
IT'S TIME TO SETTLE THIS, SCHWEINHUND!
BUT FIRST, YOU'RE GONNA SHINE MY BOOTS! YA SEE, MR. FRANKIE IS TAKIN' ME TO A FANCY RECEPTION THIS EVENING, WITH THE GOVERNOR HIMSELF!
WHEN YOU'RE DONE, YOU'LL HAVE PLENTY OF TIME TO WATCH YOUR LIFE PASS BEFORE YOUR EYES WHILE YOU BLEED OUT IN THE MUD!
ALTHOUGH, WITH A LIFE LIKE YOURS, THERE'S NOT MUCH TO SEE...
OTHER THAN ENDLESS ROWS OF BLACK BOOTS!
FLLK!
AND THAT'S THE IMAGE YOU'RE GONNA CARRY WITH YOU TO THE GRAVE, BOOTBLACK...
...ROWS OF BLACK BOOTS!!
26

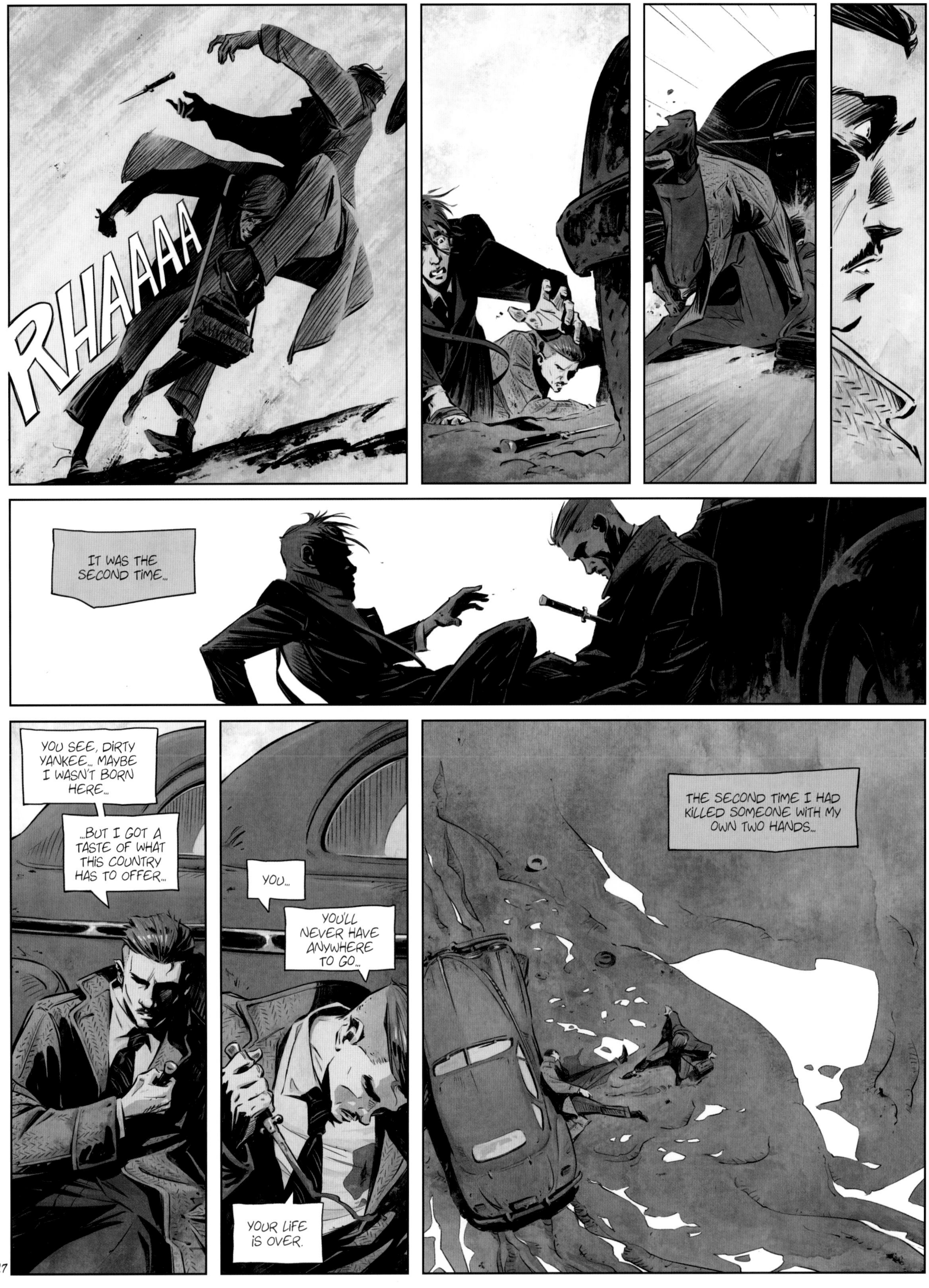
RHAAAA
IT WAS THE SECOND TIME...
YOU SEE, DIRTY YANKEE... MAYBE I WASN'T BORN HERE...
...BUT I GOT A TASTE OF WHAT THIS COUNTRY HAS TO OFFER...
YOU...
YOU'LL NEVER HAVE ANYWHERE TO GO...
YOUR LIFE IS OVER.
THE SECOND TIME I HAD KILLED SOMEONE WITH MY OWN TWO HANDS...
27

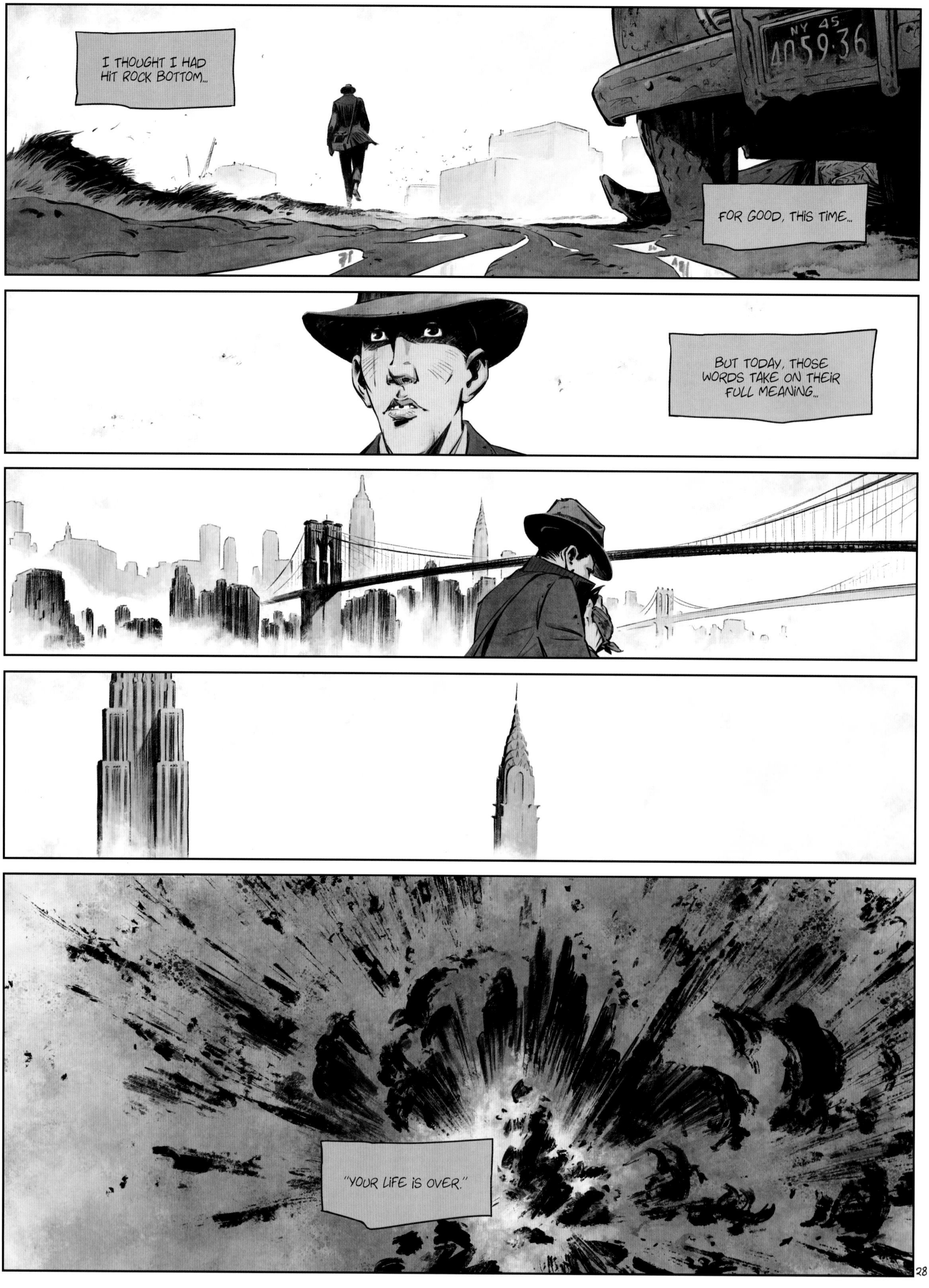
I THOUGHT I HAD HIT ROCK BOTTOM...
NY 45
4059·36
FOR GOOD, THIS TIME...
BUT TODAY, THOSE WORDS TAKE ON THEIR FULL MEANING...
"YOUR LIFE IS OVER."
28

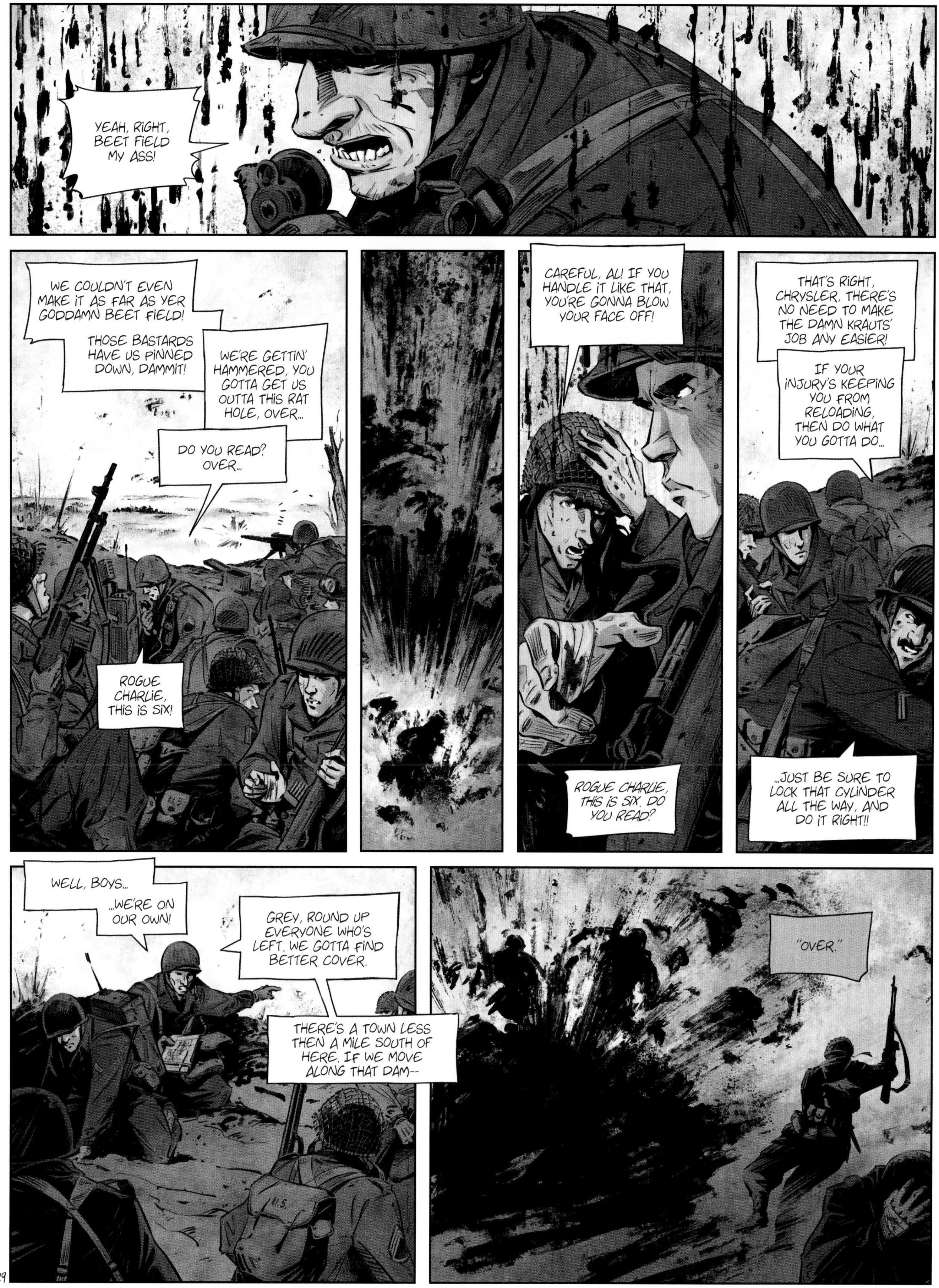
YEAH, RIGHT, BEET FIELD MY ASS!
WE COULDN'T EVEN MAKE IT AS FAR AS YER GODDAMN BEET FIELD!
THOSE BASTARDS HAVE US PINNED DOWN, DAMMIT!
WE'RE GETTIN' HAMMERED, YOU GOTTA GET US OUTTA THIS RAT HOLE, OVER...
DO YOU READ? OVER...
ROGUE CHARLIE, THIS IS SIX!
CAREFUL, AL! IF YOU HANDLE IT LIKE THAT, YOU'RE GONNA BLOW YOUR FACE OFF!
ROGUE CHARLIE, THIS IS SIX. DO YOU READ?
THAT'S RIGHT, CHRYSLER, THERE'S NO NEED TO MAKE THE DAMN KRAUTS' JOB ANY EASIER!
IF YOUR INJURY'S KEEPING YOU FROM RELOADING, THEN DO WHAT YOU GOTTA DO...
...JUST BE SURE TO LOCK THAT CYLINDER ALL THE WAY, AND DO IT RIGHT!!
WELL, BOYS...
...WE'RE ON OUR OWN!
GREY, ROUND UP EVERYONE WHO'S LEFT. WE GOTTA FIND BETTER COVER.
THERE'S A TOWN LESS THEN A MILE SOUTH OF HERE. IF WE MOVE ALONG THAT DAM--
"OVER."
29

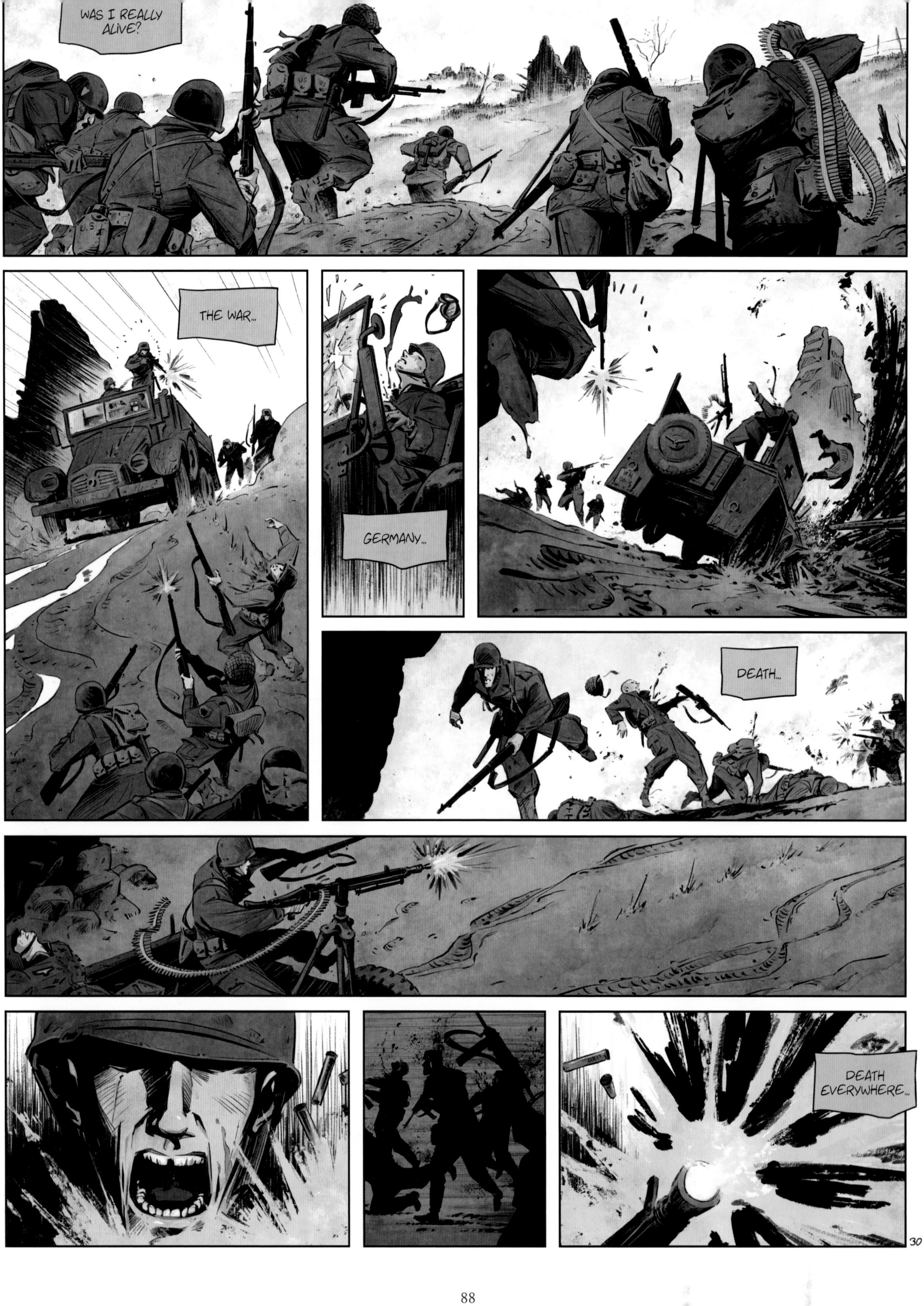
WAS I REALLY ALIVE?
THE WAR...
GERMANY...
DEATH...
DEATH EVERYWHERE...
30

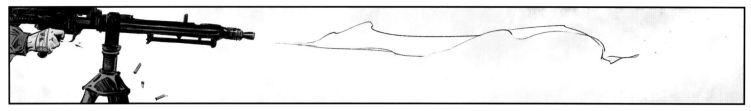

?!

AL! I... I HAVEN'T TOLD YOU EVERYTHING ...

COUGH! COUGH!

YOU KNOW WHY... ARRGH... WHY I CALLED YOU CHRYSLER...

...WHEN WE MET FOR THE FIRST TIME?

COUGH!

NOT TO MENTION JOE, THAT PIECE OF SHIT.

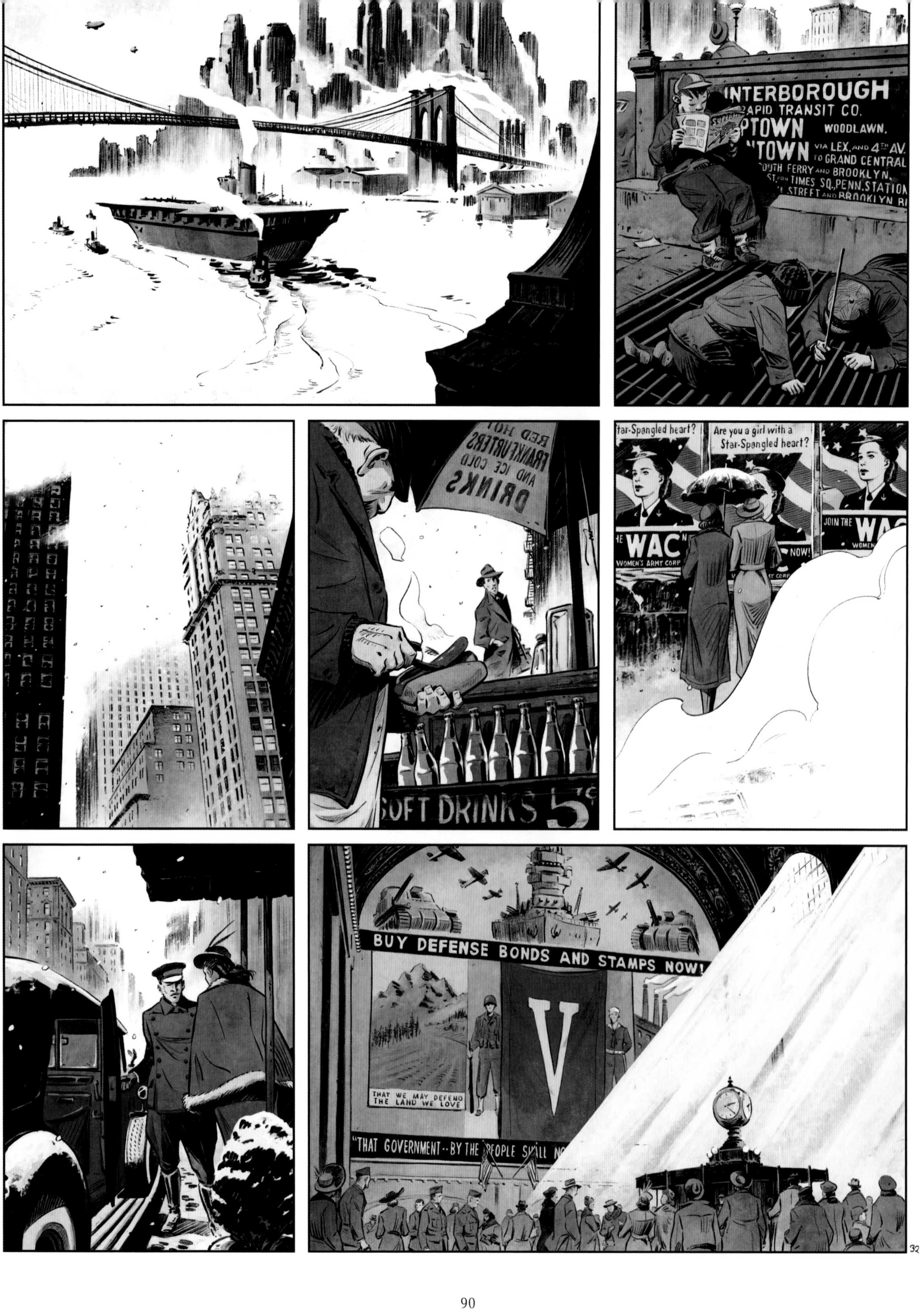
INTERBOROUGH
APID TRANSIT CO.
PTOWN WOODLAWN.
NTOWN VIA LEX. AND 4TH AV. TO GRAND CENTRAL
OUTH FERRY AND BROOKLYN.
ST. FOR TIMES SQ. PENN. STATION
STREET AND BROOKLYN
RED HOT FRANKFURTERS AND ICE COLD DRINKS
SOFT DRINKS 5¢
Star-Spangled heart?
Are you a girl with a Star-Spangled heart?
WAC
WOMEN'S ARMY CORP
NOW!
JOIN THE WAC
BUY DEFENSE BONDS AND STAMPS NOW!
V
THAT WE MAY DEFEND THE LAND WE LOVE
"THAT GOVERNMENT -- BY THE PEOPLE SHALL N
32

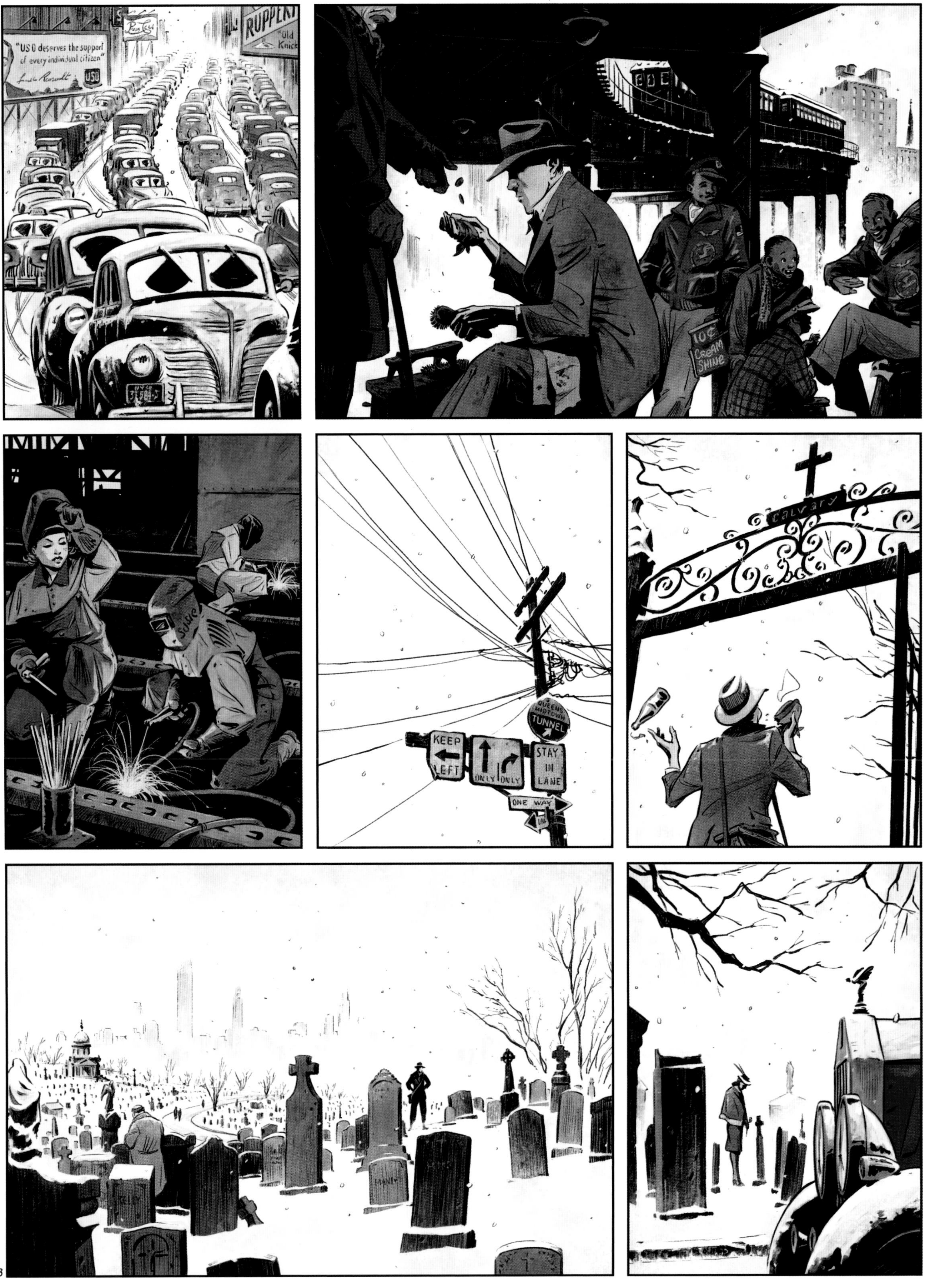
"USO deserves the support of every individual citizen"
RUPPERT
"Old Knick
10¢ CREAM SHINE
QUEENS MIDTOWN TUNNEL
KEEP LEFT
ONLY
ONLY
STAY IN LANE
ONE WAY
CALVARY

33

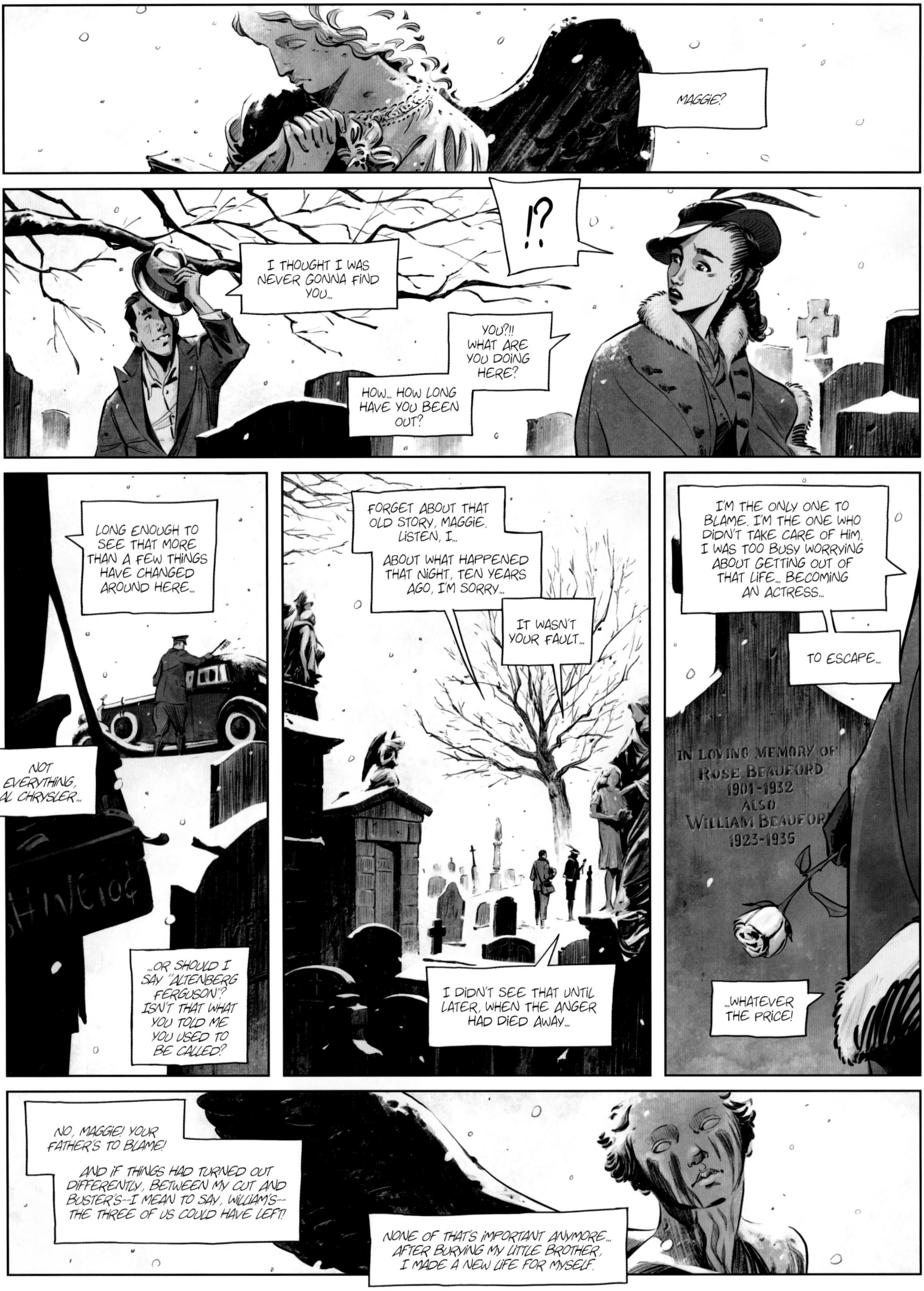

MAGGIE?
I THOUGHT I WAS NEVER GONNA FIND YOU...
!?
YOU?!! WHAT ARE YOU DOING HERE?
HOW... HOW LONG HAVE YOU BEEN OUT?
LONG ENOUGH TO SEE THAT MORE THAN A FEW THINGS HAVE CHANGED AROUND HERE...
NOT EVERYTHING, AL CHRYSLER...
...OR SHOULD I SAY "ALTENBERG FERGUSON"? ISN'T THAT WHAT YOU TOLD ME YOU USED TO BE CALLED?
FORGET ABOUT THAT OLD STORY, MAGGIE. LISTEN, I...
ABOUT WHAT HAPPENED THAT NIGHT, TEN YEARS AGO, I'M SORRY...
IT WASN'T YOUR FAULT...
I DIDN'T SEE THAT UNTIL LATER, WHEN THE ANGER HAD DIED AWAY...
I'M THE ONLY ONE TO BLAME. I'M THE ONE WHO DIDN'T TAKE CARE OF HIM. I WAS TOO BUSY WORRYING ABOUT GETTING OUT OF THAT LIFE... BECOMING AN ACTRESS...
TO ESCAPE...
IN LOVING MEMORY OF
ROSE BEAUFORD
1901-1932
ALSO
WILLIAM BEAUFOR
1923-1935
...WHATEVER THE PRICE!
NO, MAGGIE! YOUR FATHER'S TO BLAME!
AND IF THINGS HAD TURNED OUT DIFFERENTLY, BETWEEN MY CUT AND BUSTER'S--I MEAN TO SAY, WILLIAM'S-- THE THREE OF US COULD HAVE LEFT!
NONE OF THAT'S IMPORTANT ANYMORE... AFTER BURYING MY LITTLE BROTHER, I MADE A NEW LIFE FOR MYSELF.
34

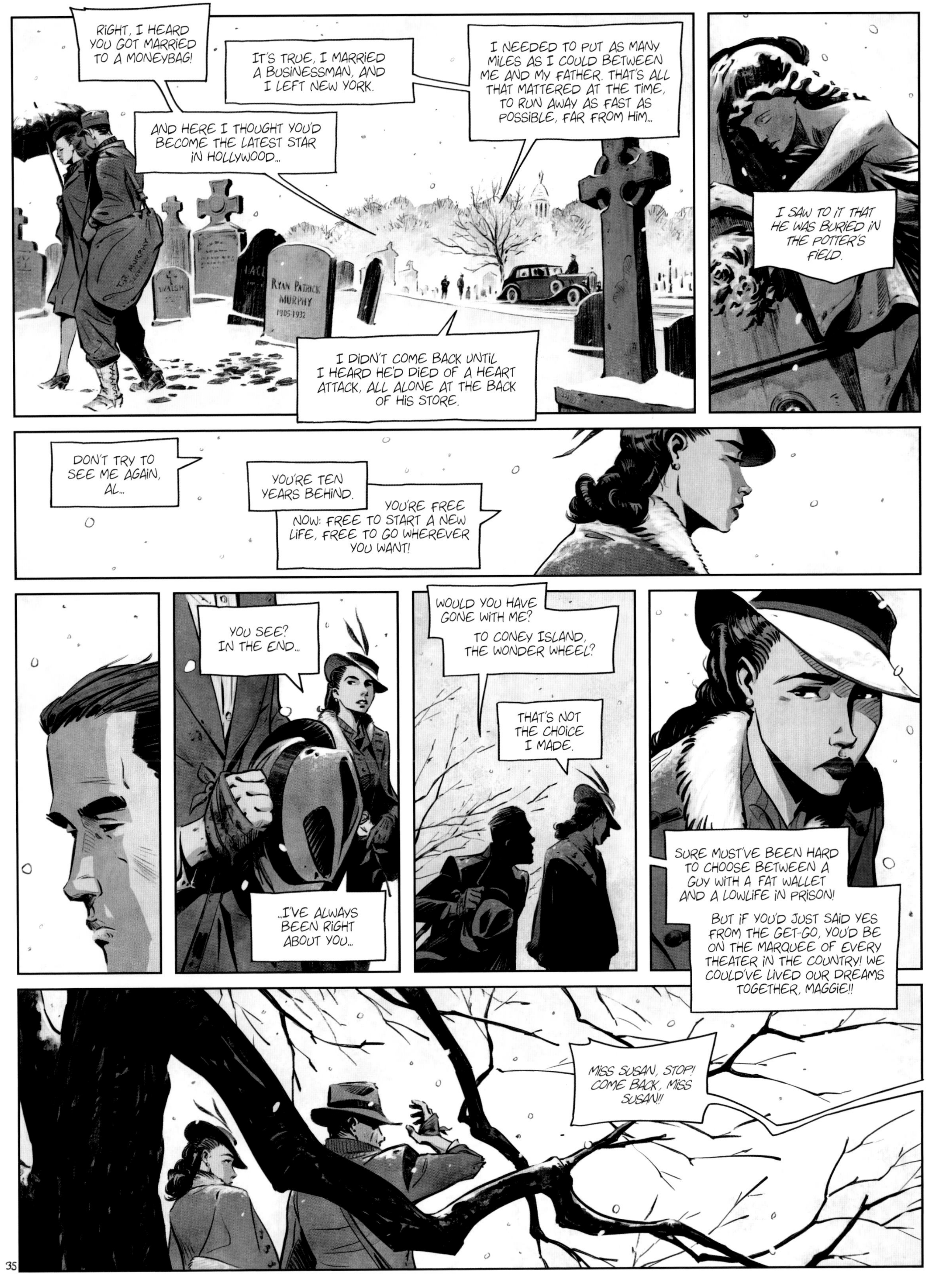

RIGHT, I HEARD YOU GOT MARRIED TO A MONEYBAG!
AND HERE I THOUGHT YOU'D BECOME THE LATEST STAR IN HOLLYWOOD...
IT'S TRUE, I MARRIED A BUSINESSMAN, AND I LEFT NEW YORK.
I NEEDED TO PUT AS MANY MILES AS I COULD BETWEEN ME AND MY FATHER. THAT'S ALL THAT MATTERED AT THE TIME, TO RUN AWAY AS FAST AS POSSIBLE, FAR FROM HIM...
WALSH
RYAN PATRICK MURPHY 1905-1932
I DIDN'T COME BACK UNTIL I HEARD HE'D DIED OF A HEART ATTACK, ALL ALONE AT THE BACK OF HIS STORE.
I SAW TO IT THAT HE WAS BURIED IN THE POTTER'S FIELD.
DON'T TRY TO SEE ME AGAIN, AL...
YOU'RE TEN YEARS BEHIND.
YOU'RE FREE NOW: FREE TO START A NEW LIFE, FREE TO GO WHEREVER YOU WANT!
YOU SEE? IN THE END...
...I'VE ALWAYS BEEN RIGHT ABOUT YOU...
WOULD YOU HAVE GONE WITH ME?
TO CONEY ISLAND, THE WONDER WHEEL?
THAT'S NOT THE CHOICE I MADE.
SURE MUST'VE BEEN HARD TO CHOOSE BETWEEN A GUY WITH A FAT WALLET AND A LOWLIFE IN PRISON!
BUT IF YOU'D JUST SAID YES FROM THE GET-GO, YOU'D BE ON THE MARQUEE OF EVERY THEATER IN THE COUNTRY! WE COULD'VE LIVED OUR DREAMS TOGETHER, MAGGIE!!
MISS SUSAN, STOP! COME BACK, MISS SUSAN!!
35

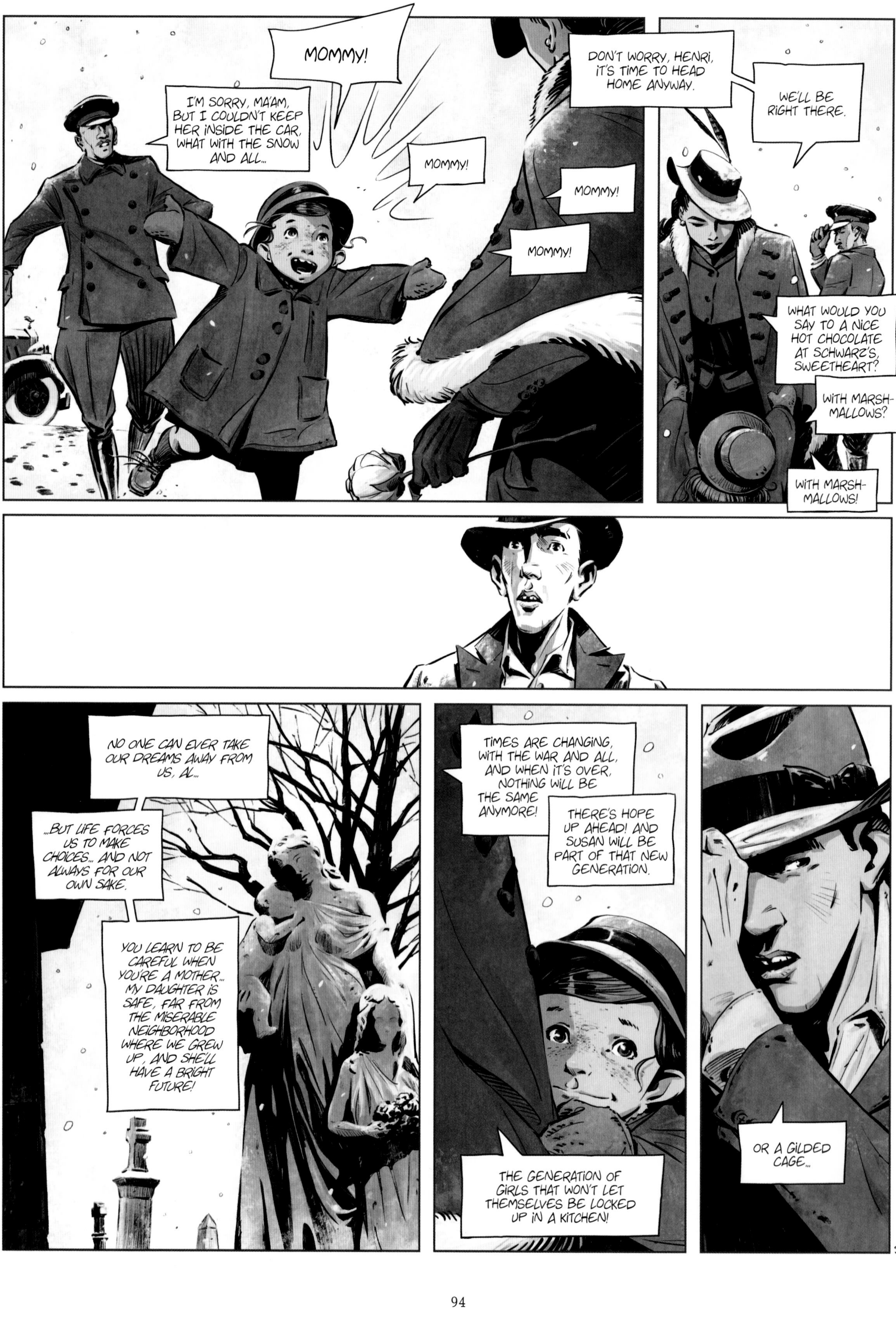
MOMMY!
I'M SORRY, MA'AM, BUT I COULDN'T KEEP HER INSIDE THE CAR, WHAT WITH THE SNOW AND ALL...
MOMMY!
MOMMY!
MOMMY!
DON'T WORRY, HENRI, IT'S TIME TO HEAD HOME ANYWAY.
WE'LL BE RIGHT THERE.
WHAT WOULD YOU SAY TO A NICE HOT CHOCOLATE AT SCHWARZ'S, SWEETHEART?
WITH MARSH-MALLOWS?
WITH MARSH-MALLOWS!
NO ONE CAN EVER TAKE OUR DREAMS AWAY FROM US, AL...
...BUT LIFE FORCES US TO MAKE CHOICES... AND NOT ALWAYS FOR OUR OWN SAKE.
YOU LEARN TO BE CAREFUL WHEN YOU'RE A MOTHER... MY DAUGHTER IS SAFE, FAR FROM THE MISERABLE NEIGHBORHOOD WHERE WE GREW UP, AND SHE'LL HAVE A BRIGHT FUTURE!
TIMES ARE CHANGING, WITH THE WAR AND ALL, AND WHEN IT'S OVER, NOTHING WILL BE THE SAME ANYMORE!
THERE'S HOPE UP AHEAD! AND SUSAN WILL BE PART OF THAT NEW GENERATION.
THE GENERATION OF GIRLS THAT WON'T LET THEMSELVES BE LOCKED UP IN A KITCHEN!
OR A GILDED CAGE...
36

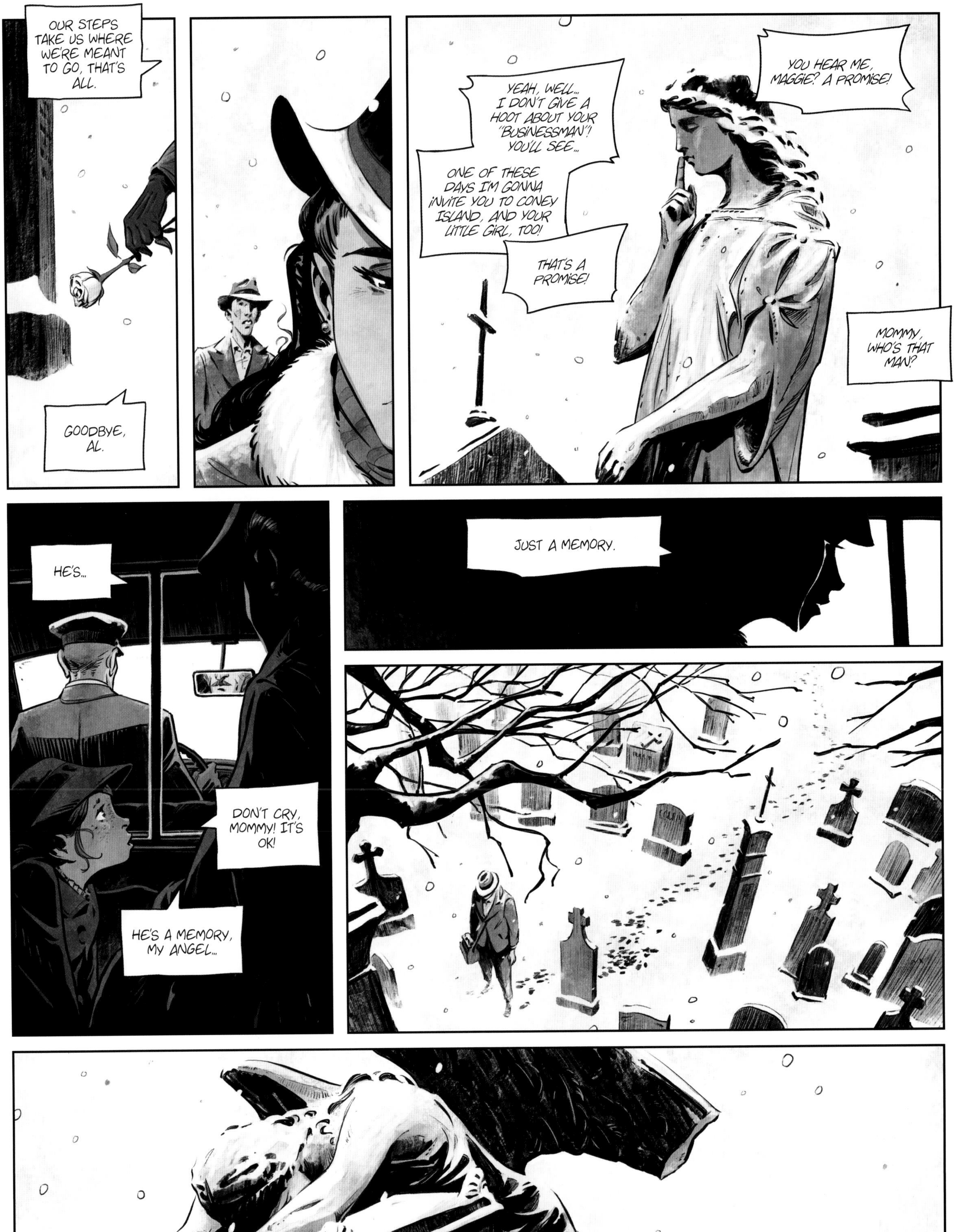
OUR STEPS TAKE US WHERE WE'RE MEANT TO GO, THAT'S ALL.
GOODBYE, AL.
YEAH, WELL... I DON'T GIVE A HOOT ABOUT YOUR "BUSINESSMAN"! YOU'LL SEE...
ONE OF THESE DAYS I'M GONNA INVITE YOU TO CONEY ISLAND, AND YOUR LITTLE GIRL, TOO!
THAT'S A PROMISE!
YOU HEAR ME, MAGGIE? A PROMISE!
MOMMY, WHO'S THAT MAN?
HE'S...
JUST A MEMORY.
DON'T CRY, MOMMY! IT'S OK!
HE'S A MEMORY, MY ANGEL...

37

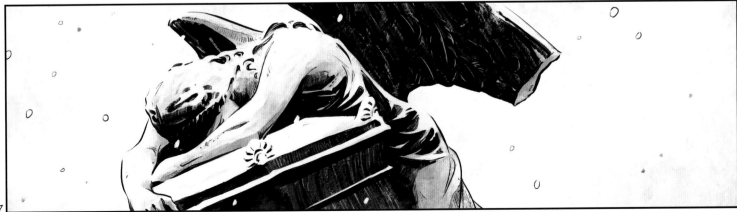

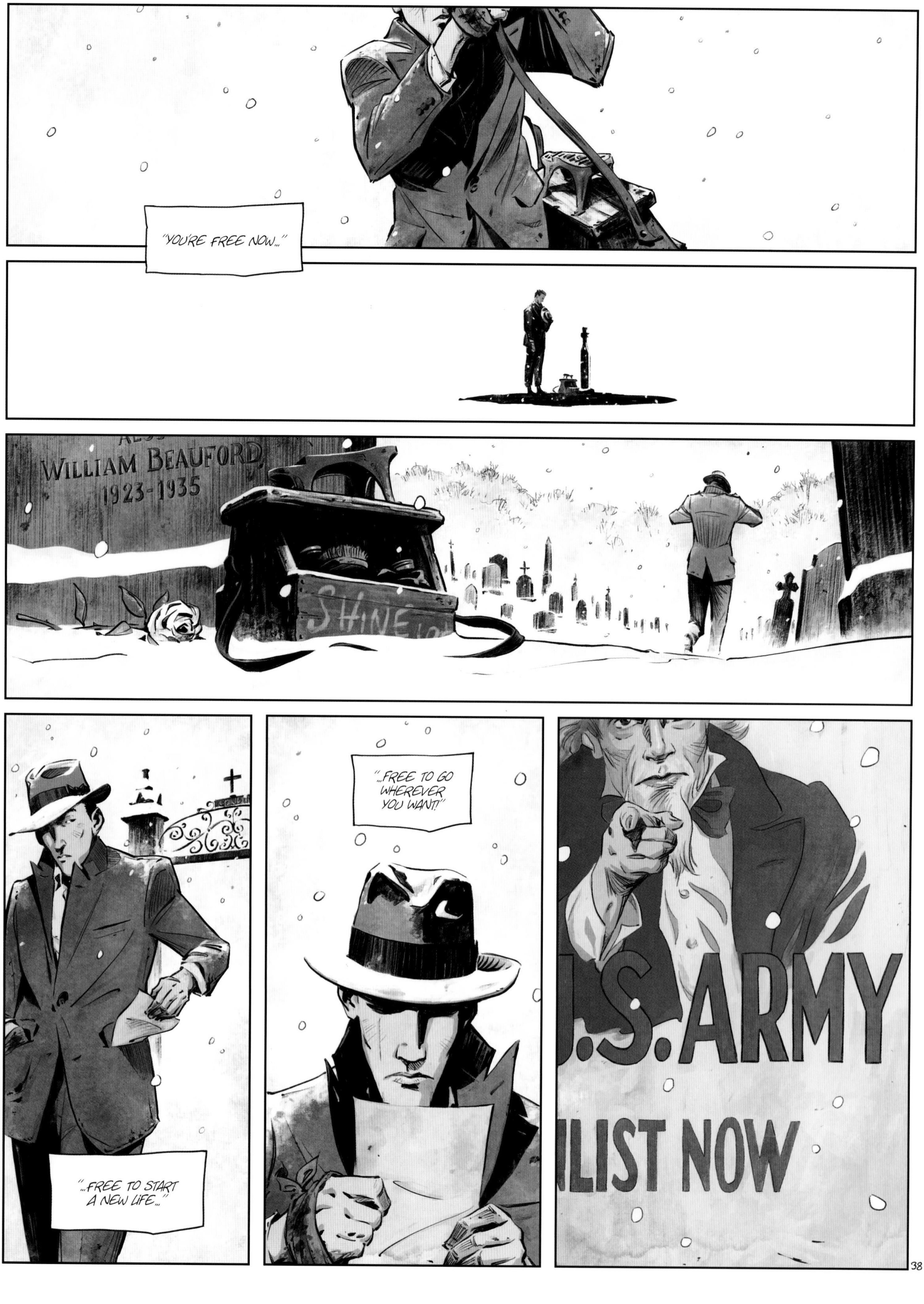
"YOU'RE FREE NOW..."
WILLIAM BEAUFORD
1923-1935
SHINE
"...FREE TO START A NEW LIFE..."
"...FREE TO GO WHEREVER YOU WANT!"
U.S. ARMY
NLIST NOW
38

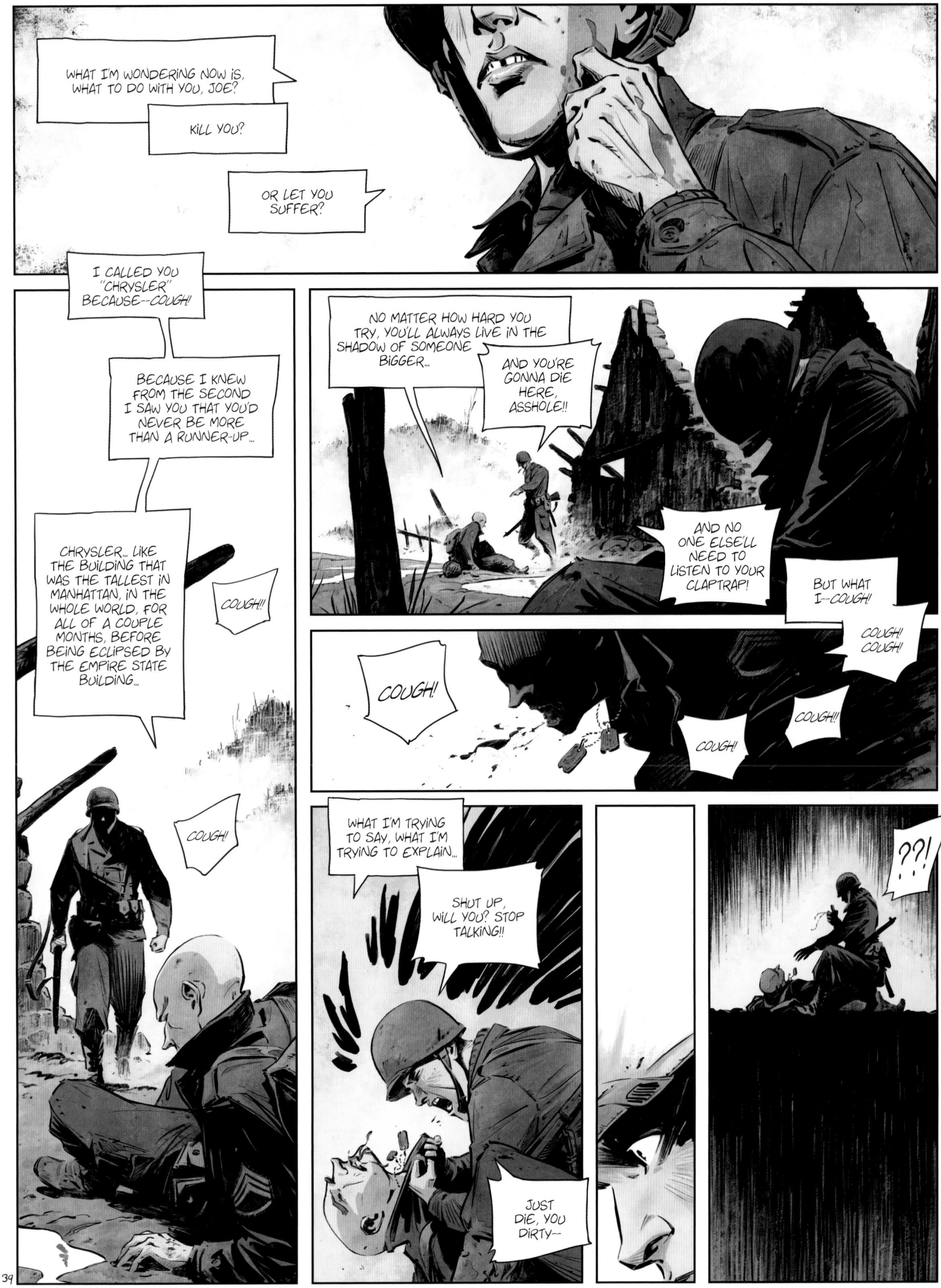
WHAT I'M WONDERING NOW IS, WHAT TO DO WITH YOU, JOE?
KILL YOU?
OR LET YOU SUFFER?
I CALLED YOU "CHRYSLER" BECAUSE--COUGH!
BECAUSE I KNEW FROM THE SECOND I SAW YOU THAT YOU'D NEVER BE MORE THAN A RUNNER-UP...
CHRYSLER... LIKE THE BUILDING THAT WAS THE TALLEST IN MANHATTAN, IN THE WHOLE WORLD, FOR ALL OF A COUPLE MONTHS, BEFORE BEING ECLIPSED BY THE EMPIRE STATE BUILDING...
COUGH!!
COUGH!
NO MATTER HOW HARD YOU TRY, YOU'LL ALWAYS LIVE IN THE SHADOW OF SOMEONE BIGGER...
AND YOU'RE GONNA DIE HERE, ASSHOLE!!
AND NO ONE ELSE'LL NEED TO LISTEN TO YOUR CLAPTRAP!
BUT WHAT I--COUGH!
COUGH! COUGH!
COUGH!
COUGH!!
COUGH!
WHAT I'M TRYING TO SAY, WHAT I'M TRYING TO EXPLAIN...
SHUT UP, WILL YOU? STOP TALKING!!
JUST DIE, YOU DIRTY--
??!
39

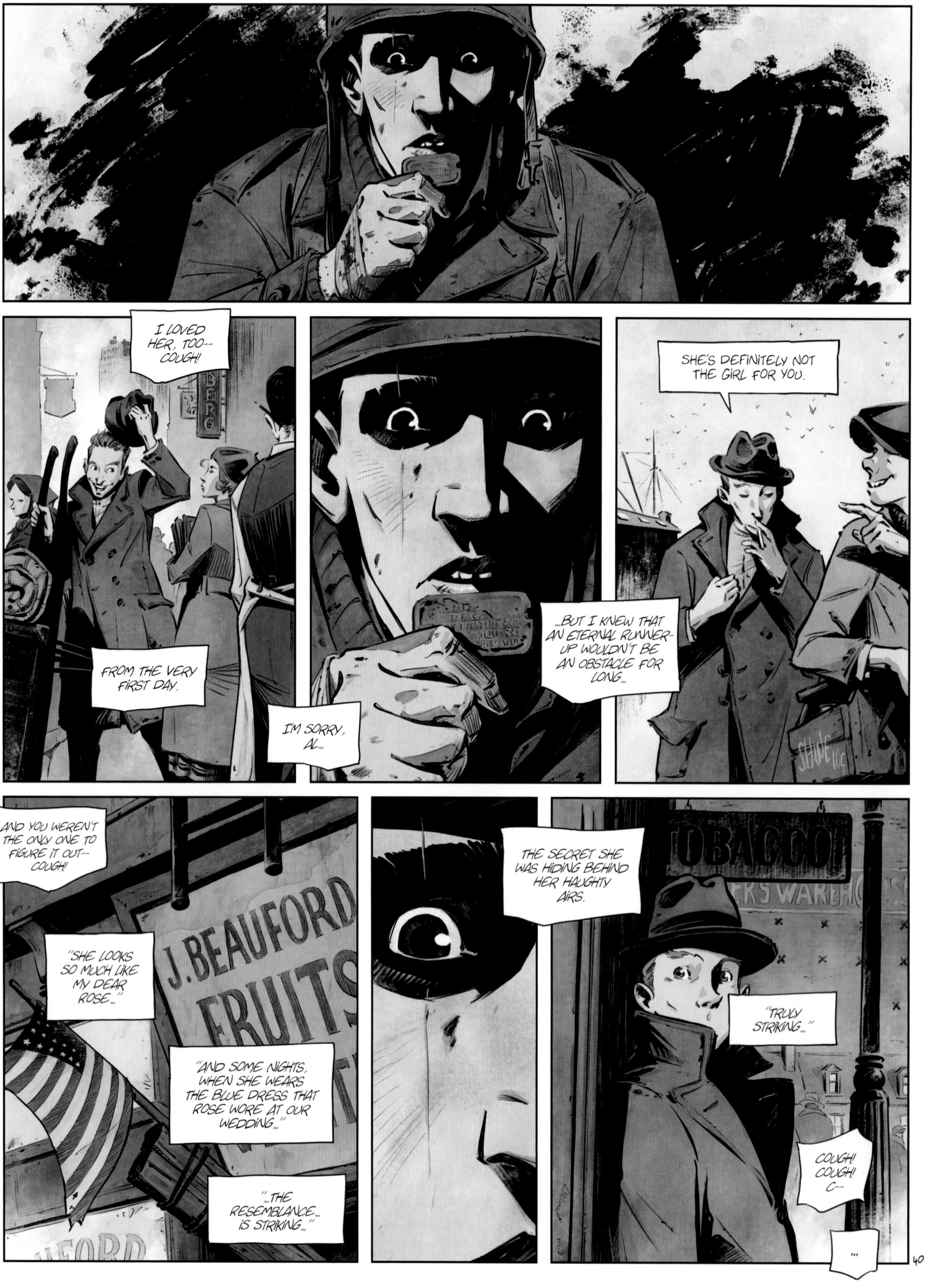
I LOVED HER, TOO-- COUGH!
FROM THE VERY FIRST DAY.
I'M SORRY, AL...
...BUT I KNEW THAT AN ETERNAL RUNNER-UP WOULDN'T BE AN OBSTACLE FOR LONG...
SHE'S DEFINITELY NOT THE GIRL FOR YOU.
AND YOU WEREN'T THE ONLY ONE TO FIGURE IT OUT-- COUGH!
J. BEAUFORD FRUITS
"SHE LOOKS SO MUCH LIKE MY DEAR ROSE..."
"AND SOME NIGHTS, WHEN SHE WEARS THE BLUE DRESS THAT ROSE WORE AT OUR WEDDING..."
"...THE RESEMBLANCE... IS STRIKING..."
THE SECRET SHE WAS HIDING BEHIND HER HAUGHTY AIRS.
TOBACCO
"TRULY STRIKING..."
COUGH! COUGH! C--
...
40

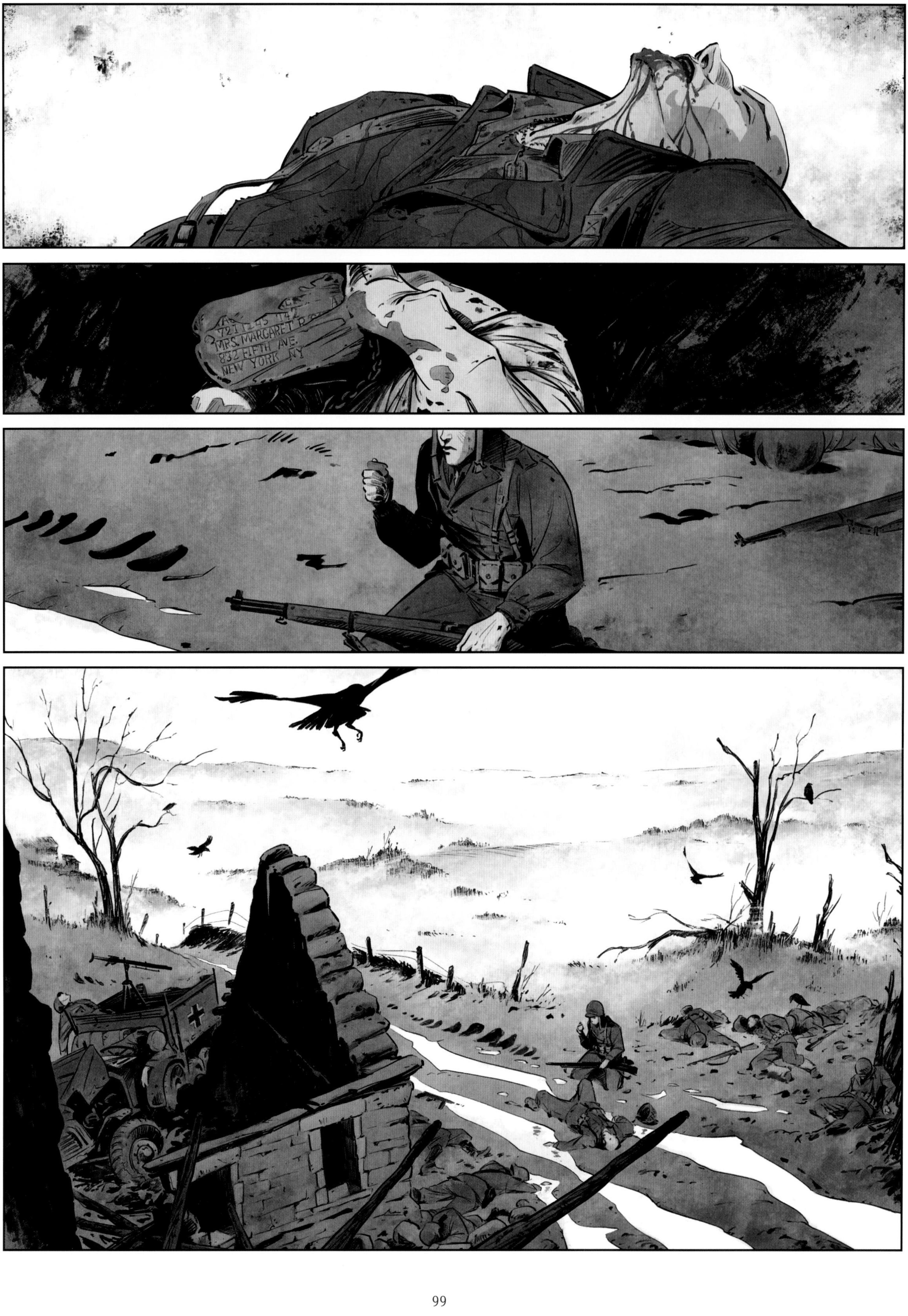
MRS. MARGARET R
832 FIFTH AVE.
NEW YORK NY

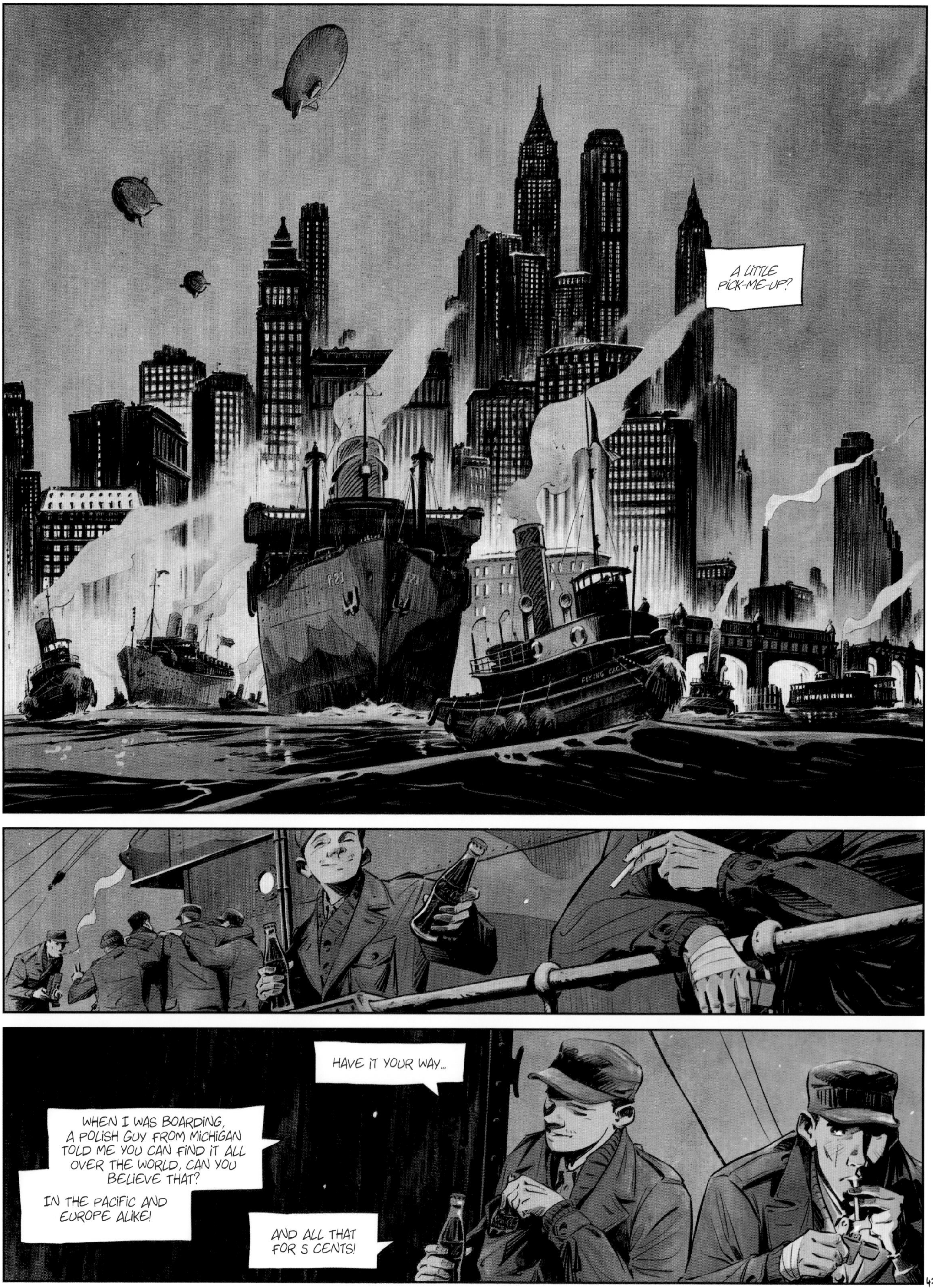
A LITTLE PICK-ME-UP?
HAVE IT YOUR WAY...
WHEN I WAS BOARDING, A POLISH GUY FROM MICHIGAN TOLD ME YOU CAN FIND IT ALL OVER THE WORLD, CAN YOU BELIEVE THAT?
IN THE PACIFIC AND EUROPE ALIKE!
AND ALL THAT FOR 5 CENTS!

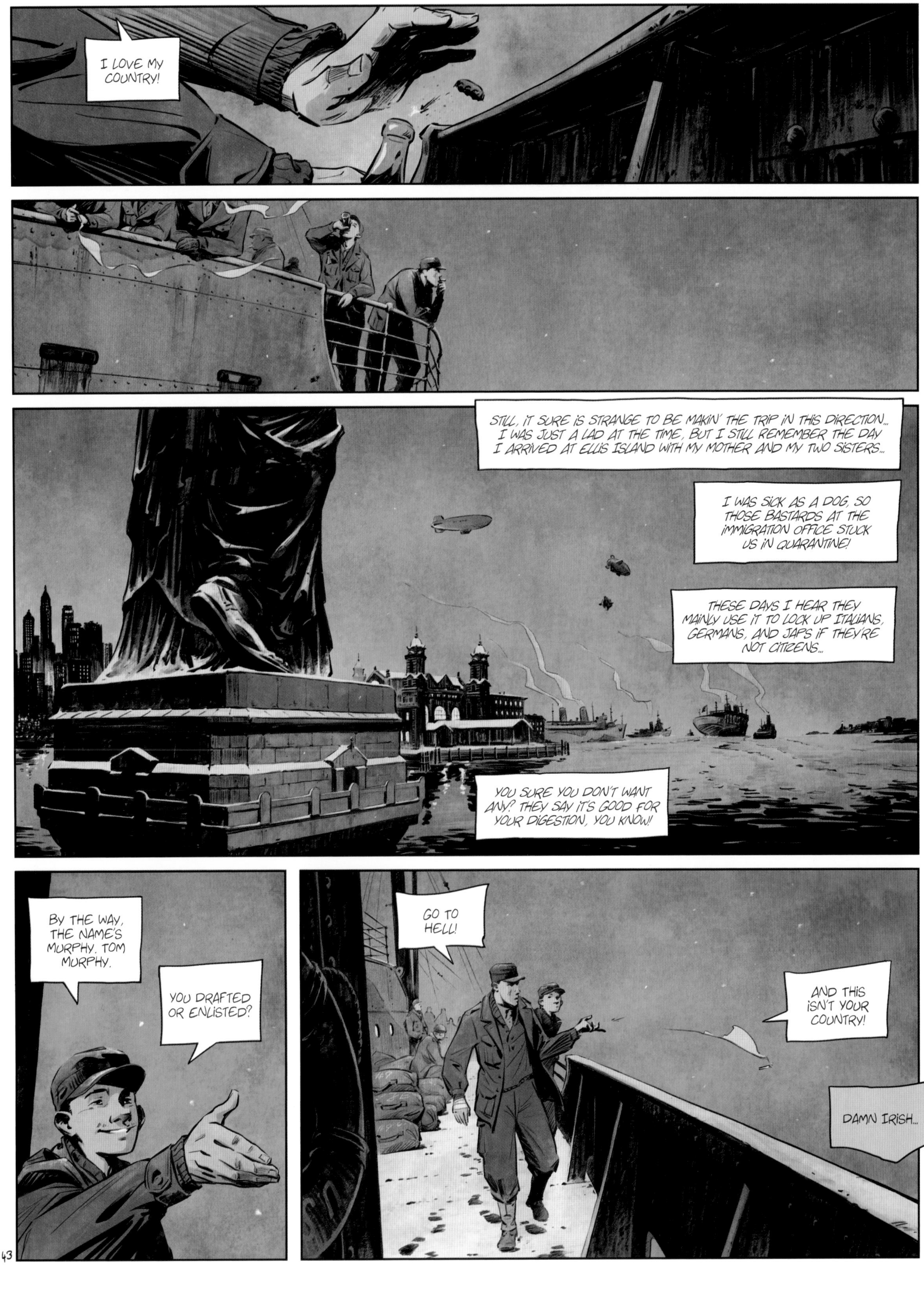
I LOVE MY COUNTRY!
STILL, IT SURE IS STRANGE TO BE MAKIN' THE TRIP IN THIS DIRECTION... I WAS JUST A LAD AT THE TIME, BUT I STILL REMEMBER THE DAY I ARRIVED AT ELLIS ISLAND WITH MY MOTHER AND MY TWO SISTERS...
I WAS SICK AS A DOG, SO THOSE BASTARDS AT THE IMMIGRATION OFFICE STUCK US IN QUARANTINE!
THESE DAYS I HEAR THEY MAINLY USE IT TO LOCK UP ITALIANS, GERMANS, AND JAPS IF THEY'RE NOT CITIZENS...
YOU SURE YOU DON'T WANT ANY? THEY SAY IT'S GOOD FOR YOUR DIGESTION, YOU KNOW!
BY THE WAY, THE NAME'S MURPHY. TOM MURPHY.
YOU DRAFTED OR ENLISTED?
GO TO HELL!
AND THIS ISN'T YOUR COUNTRY!
DAMN IRISH...
43

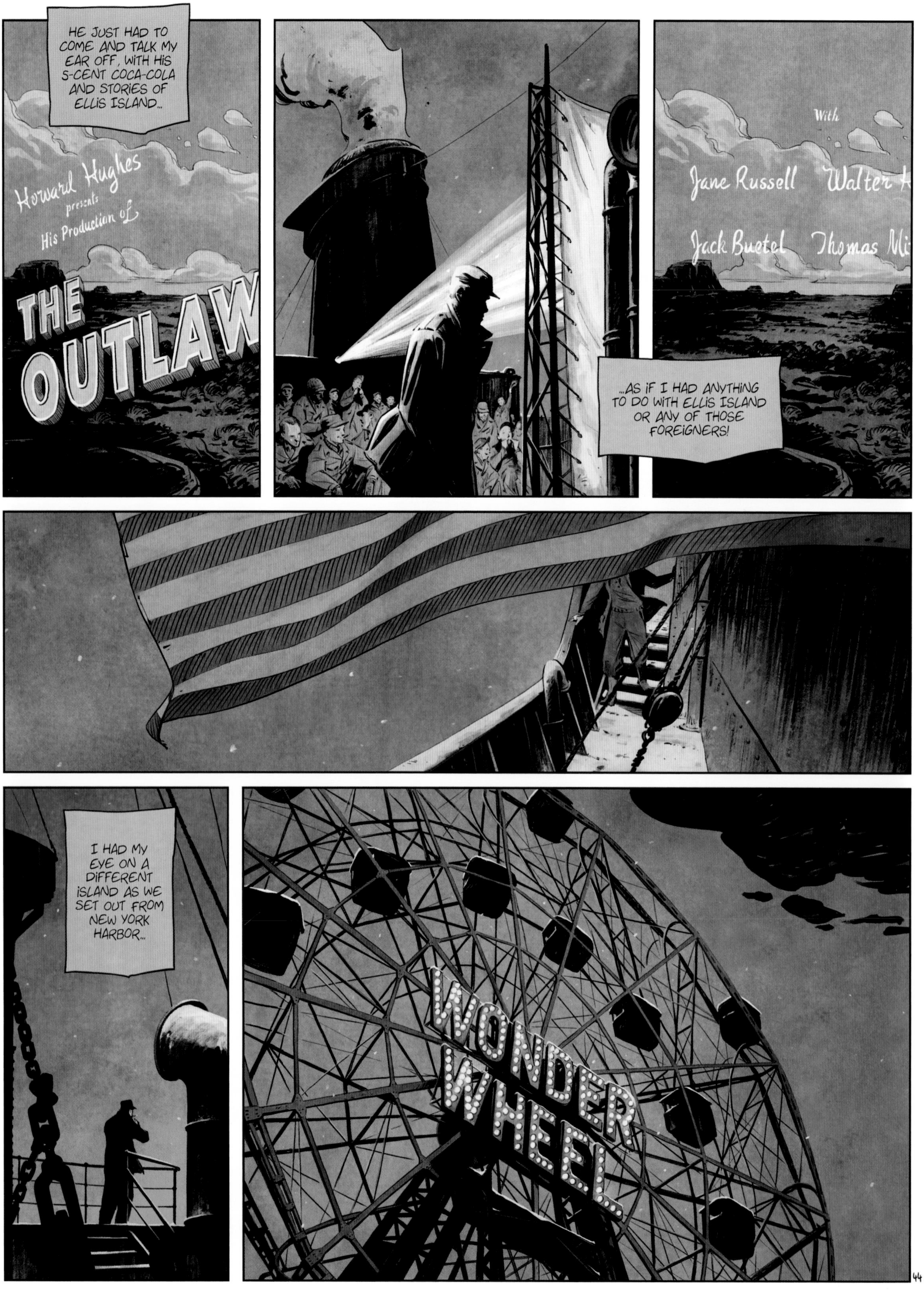
HE JUST HAD TO COME AND TALK MY EAR OFF, WITH HIS 5-CENT COCA-COLA AND STORIES OF ELLIS ISLAND...
Howard Hughes presents His Production of
THE OUTLAW
With
Jane Russell Walter
Jack Buetel Thomas
...AS IF I HAD ANYTHING TO DO WITH ELLIS ISLAND OR ANY OF THOSE FOREIGNERS!
I HAD MY EYE ON A DIFFERENT ISLAND AS WE SET OUT FROM NEW YORK HARBOR...
WONDER WHEEL
44

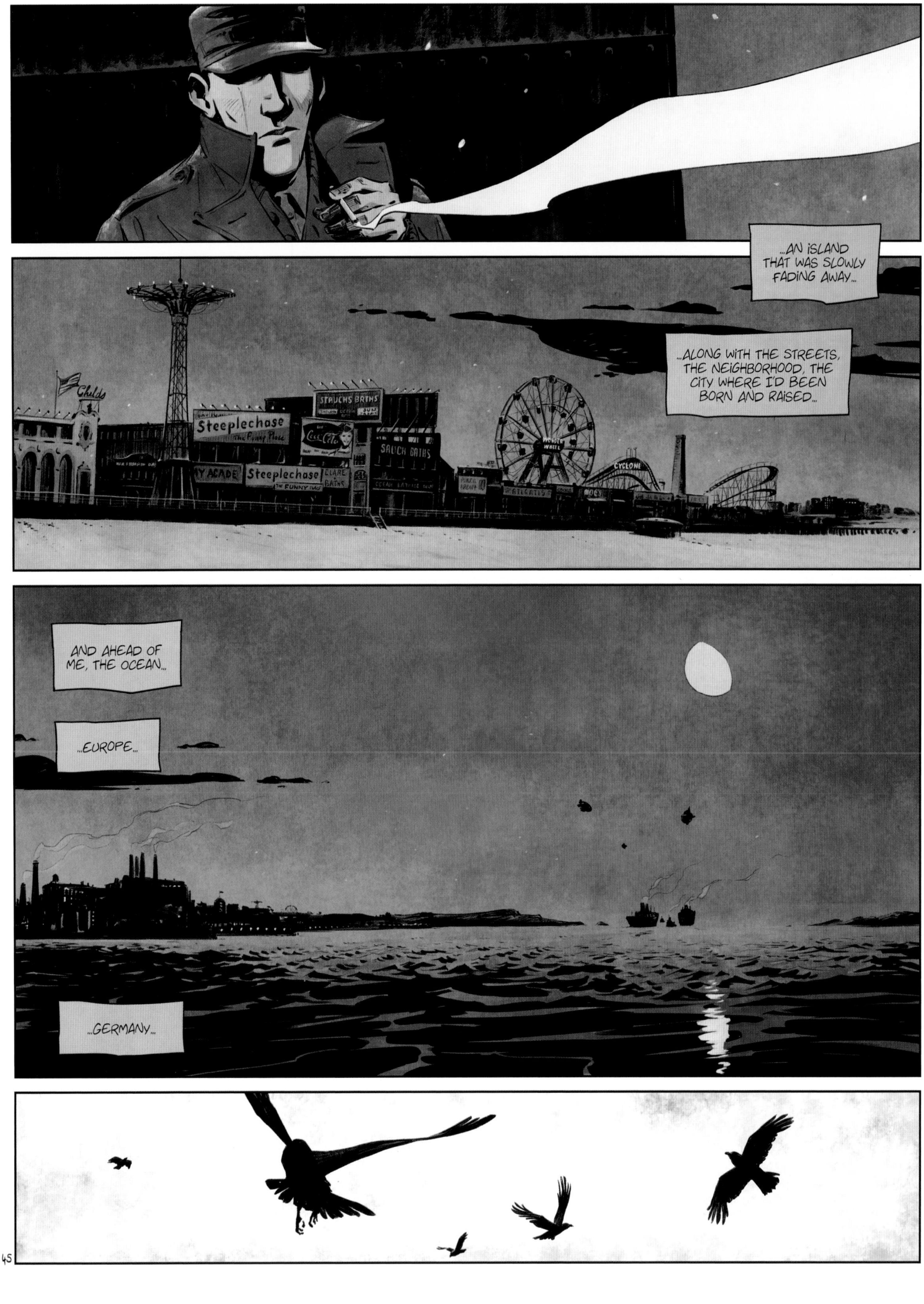
...AN ISLAND THAT WAS SLOWLY FADING AWAY...
...ALONG WITH THE STREETS, THE NEIGHBORHOOD, THE CITY WHERE I'D BEEN BORN AND RAISED...
Childs
Steeplechase
Steeplechase
WONDER WHEEL
CYCLONE
AND AHEAD OF ME, THE OCEAN...
...EUROPE...
...GERMANY...

45

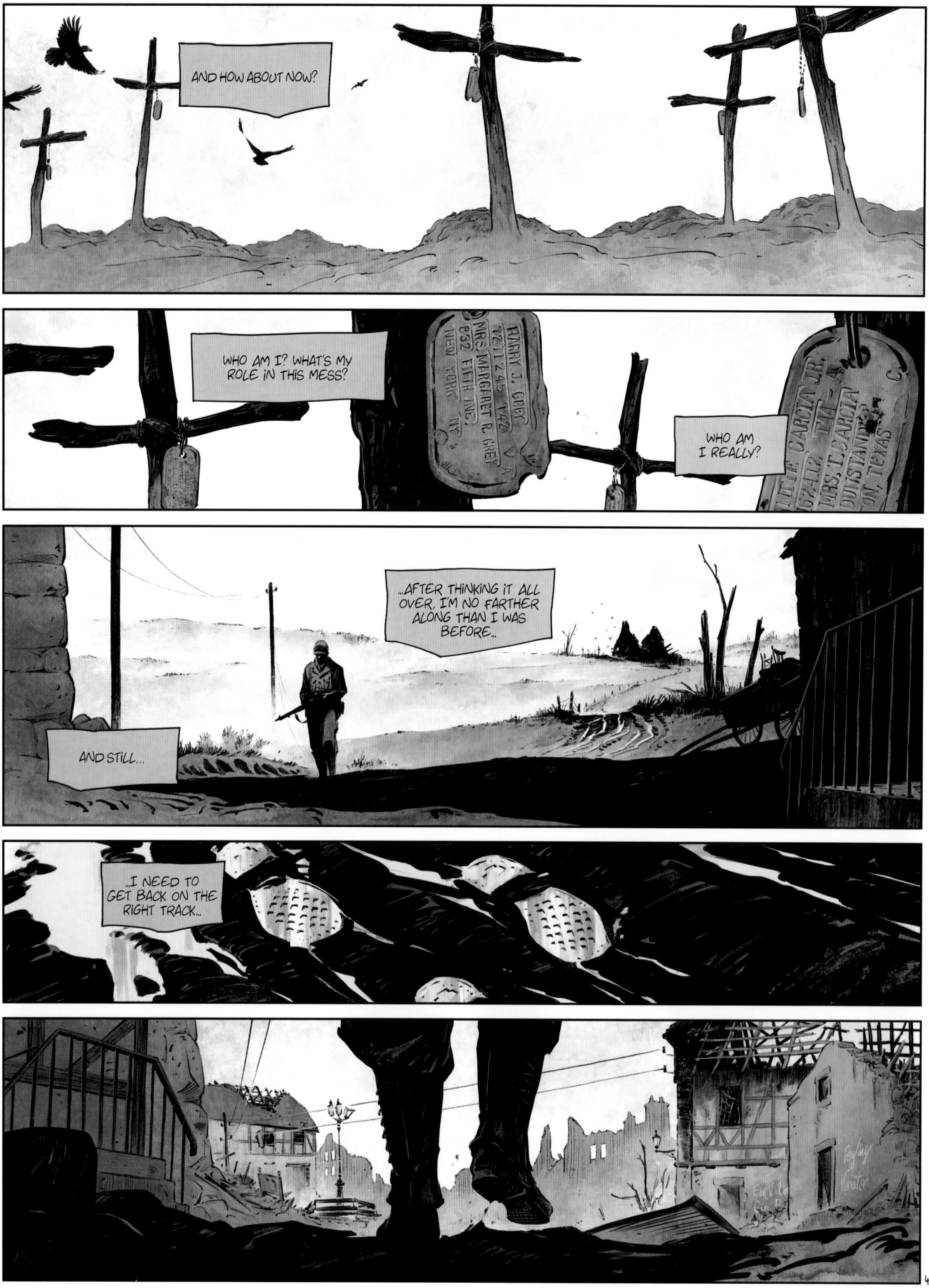
AND HOW ABOUT NOW?
WHO AM I? WHAT'S MY ROLE IN THIS MESS?
HARRY J. GREY
WHO AM I REALLY?
...AFTER THINKING IT ALL OVER, I'M NO FARTHER ALONG THAN I WAS BEFORE...
AND STILL...
...I NEED TO GET BACK ON THE RIGHT TRACK...
46

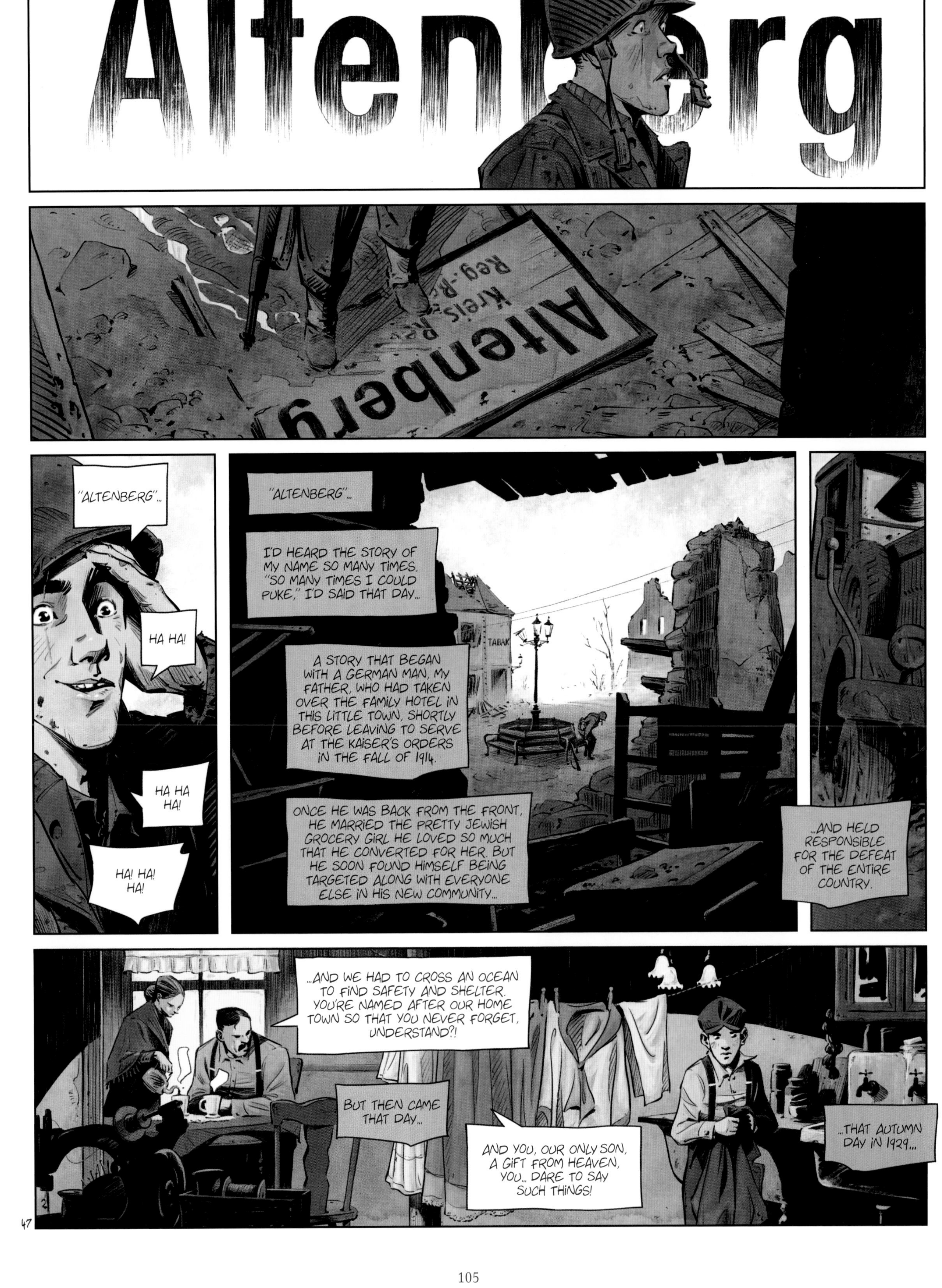
Altenberg
Altenberg
"ALTENBERG"...
HA HA!
HA HA HA!
HA! HA! HA!
"ALTENBERG"...
I'D HEARD THE STORY OF MY NAME SO MANY TIMES. "SO MANY TIMES I COULD PUKE," I'D SAID THAT DAY...
TABAK
A STORY THAT BEGAN WITH A GERMAN MAN, MY FATHER, WHO HAD TAKEN OVER THE FAMILY HOTEL IN THIS LITTLE TOWN, SHORTLY BEFORE LEAVING TO SERVE AT THE KAISER'S ORDERS IN THE FALL OF 1914.
ONCE HE WAS BACK FROM THE FRONT, HE MARRIED THE PRETTY JEWISH GROCERY GIRL HE LOVED SO MUCH THAT HE CONVERTED FOR HER. BUT HE SOON FOUND HIMSELF BEING TARGETED ALONG WITH EVERYONE ELSE IN HIS NEW COMMUNITY...
...AND HELD RESPONSIBLE FOR THE DEFEAT OF THE ENTIRE COUNTRY.
...AND WE HAD TO CROSS AN OCEAN TO FIND SAFETY AND SHELTER. YOU'RE NAMED AFTER OUR HOME TOWN SO THAT YOU NEVER FORGET, UNDERSTAND?!
BUT THEN CAME THAT DAY...
AND YOU, OUR ONLY SON, A GIFT FROM HEAVEN, YOU... DARE TO SAY SUCH THINGS!
...THAT AUTUMN DAY IN 1929...

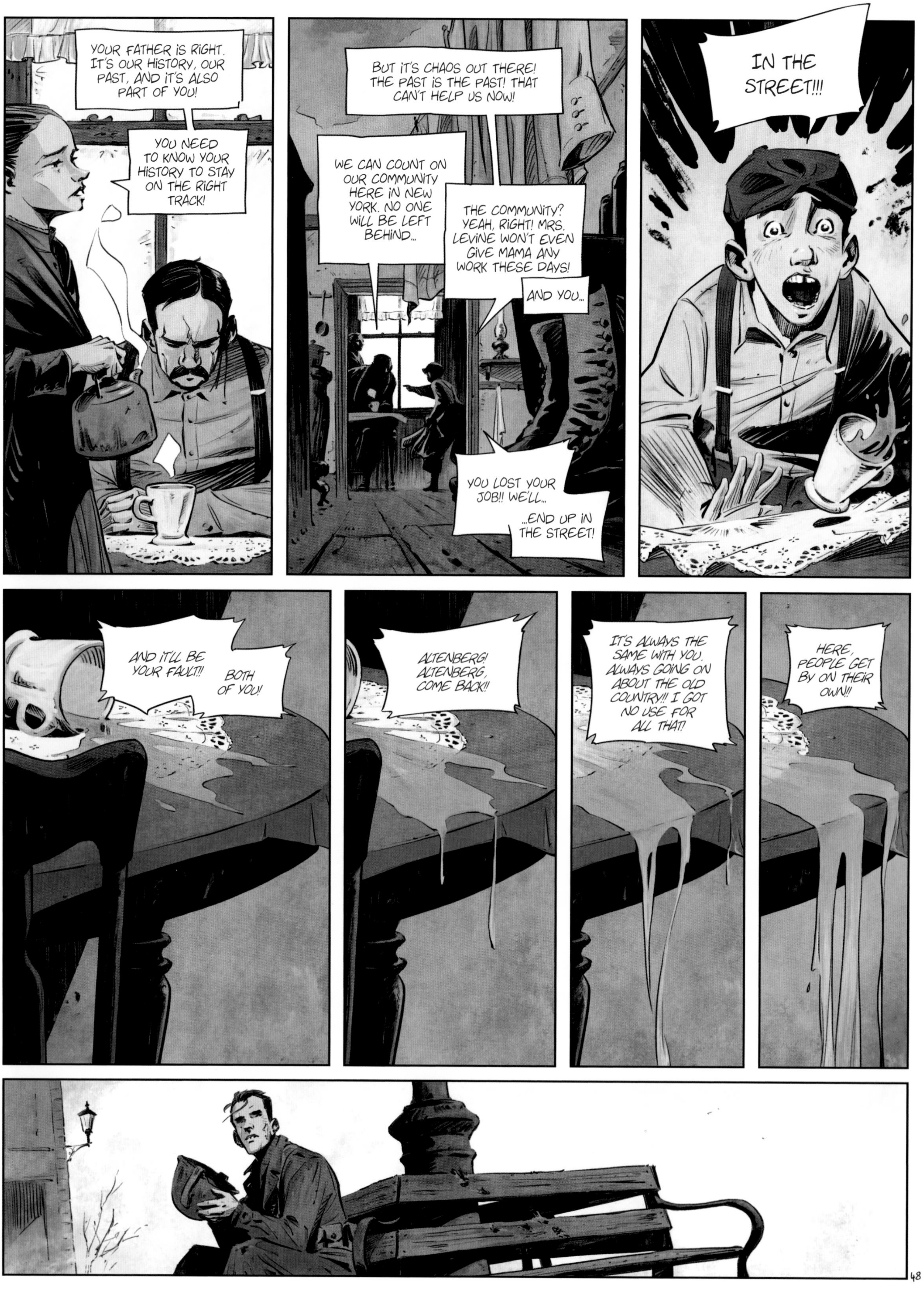
YOUR FATHER IS RIGHT. IT'S OUR HISTORY, OUR PAST, AND IT'S ALSO PART OF YOU!
YOU NEED TO KNOW YOUR HISTORY TO STAY ON THE RIGHT TRACK!
BUT IT'S CHAOS OUT THERE! THE PAST IS THE PAST! THAT CAN'T HELP US NOW!
WE CAN COUNT ON OUR COMMUNITY HERE IN NEW YORK. NO ONE WILL BE LEFT BEHIND...
THE COMMUNITY? YEAH, RIGHT! MRS. LEVINE WON'T EVEN GIVE MAMA ANY WORK THESE DAYS!
AND YOU...
YOU LOST YOUR JOB!! WE'LL...
...END UP IN THE STREET!
IN THE STREET!!!
AND IT'LL BE YOUR FAULT!!
BOTH OF YOU!
ALTENBERG! ALTENBERG, COME BACK!!
IT'S ALWAYS THE SAME WITH YOU. ALWAYS GOING ON ABOUT THE OLD COUNTRY!! I GOT NO USE FOR ALL THAT!
HERE, PEOPLE GET BY ON THEIR OWN!!
48

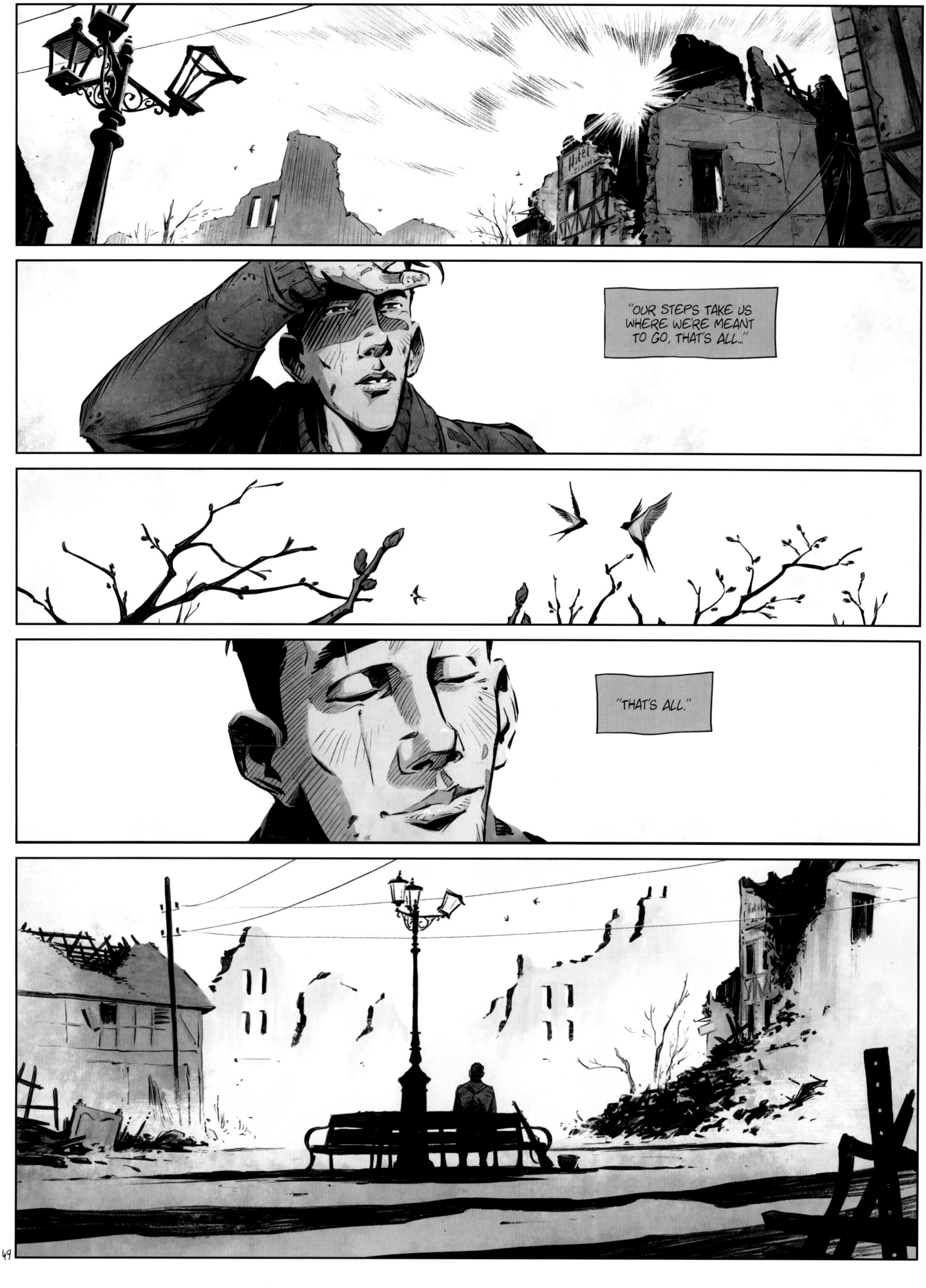
"OUR STEPS TAKE US WHERE WE'RE MEANT TO GO, THAT'S ALL..."
"THAT'S ALL."
49

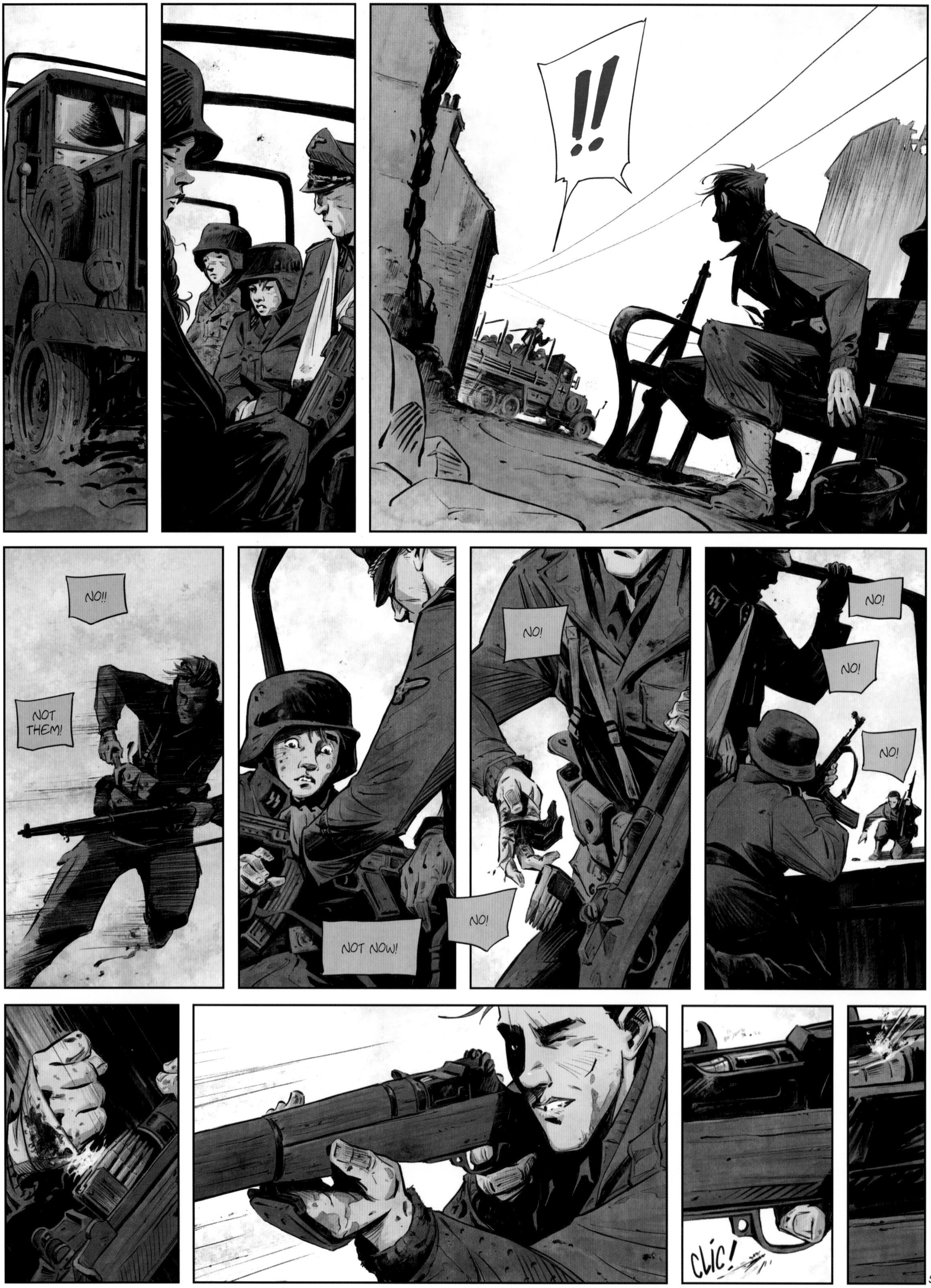
!!
NO!!
NOT THEM!
NOT NOW!
NO!
NO!
NO!
NO!
NO!
CLIC!

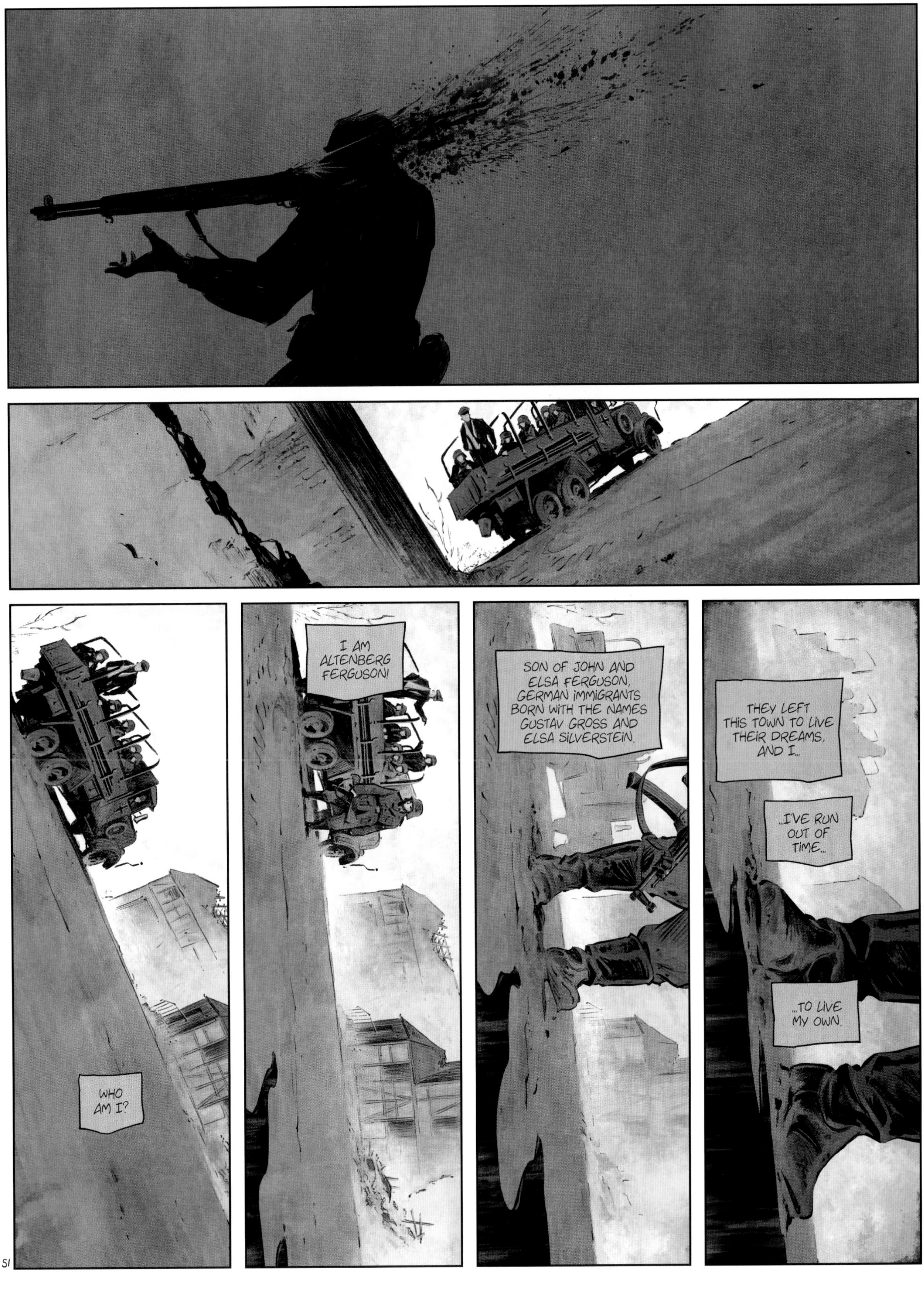
WHO AM I?
I AM ALTENBERG FERGUSON!
SON OF JOHN AND ELSA FERGUSON, GERMAN IMMIGRANTS BORN WITH THE NAMES GUSTAV GROSS AND ELSA SILVERSTEIN.
THEY LEFT THIS TOWN TO LIVE THEIR DREAMS, AND I...
...I'VE RUN OUT OF TIME...
...TO LIVE MY OWN.
SI

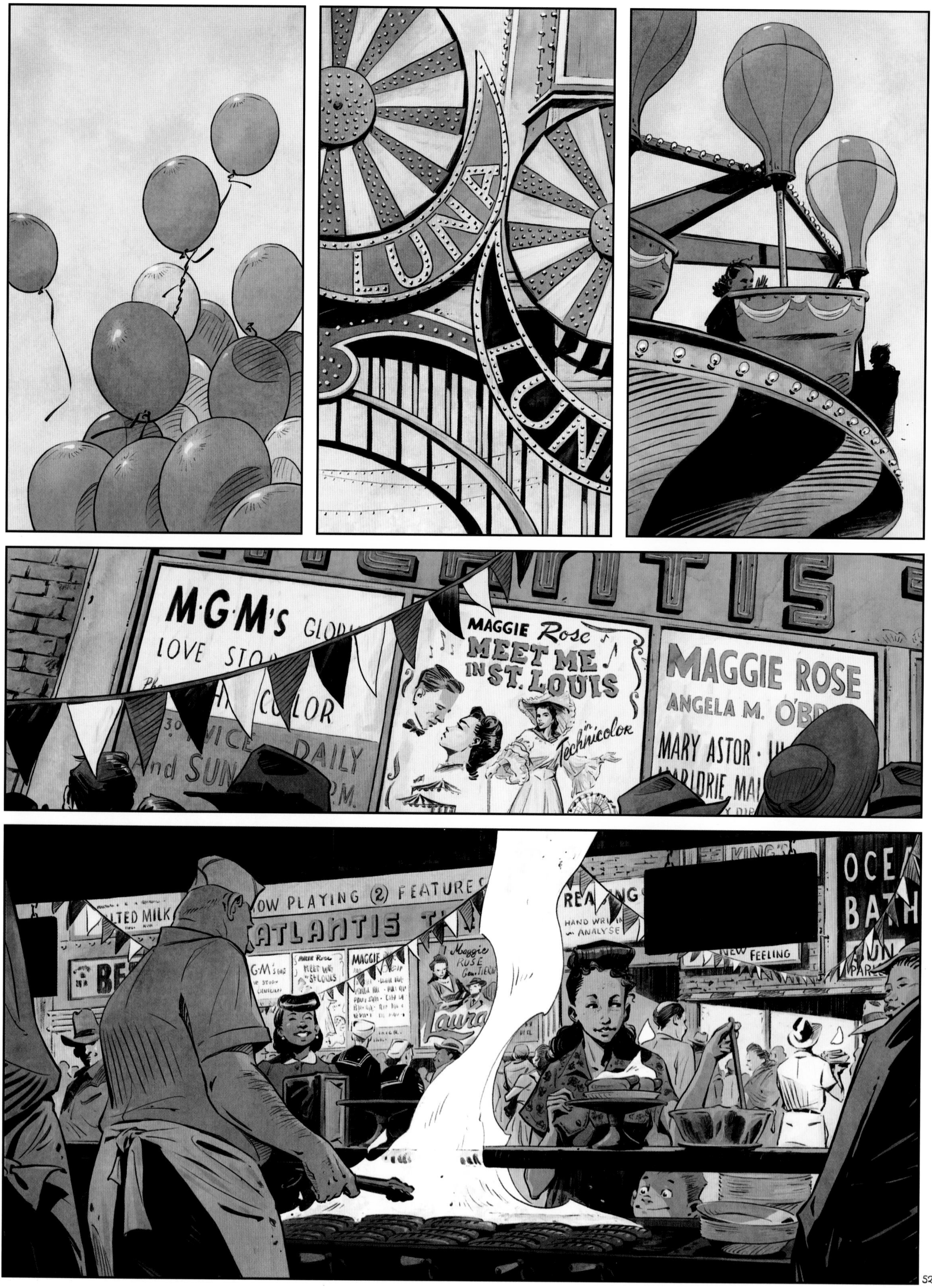
LUNA
LUNA
M·G·M's
LOVE
COLOR
DAILY
MAGGIE Rose
MEET ME IN ST. LOUIS
in Technicolor
MAGGIE ROSE
MARY ASTOR
NOW PLAYING (2) FEATURES
ATLANTIS
HAND WRI
ANALYSE
NEW FEELING
Laura

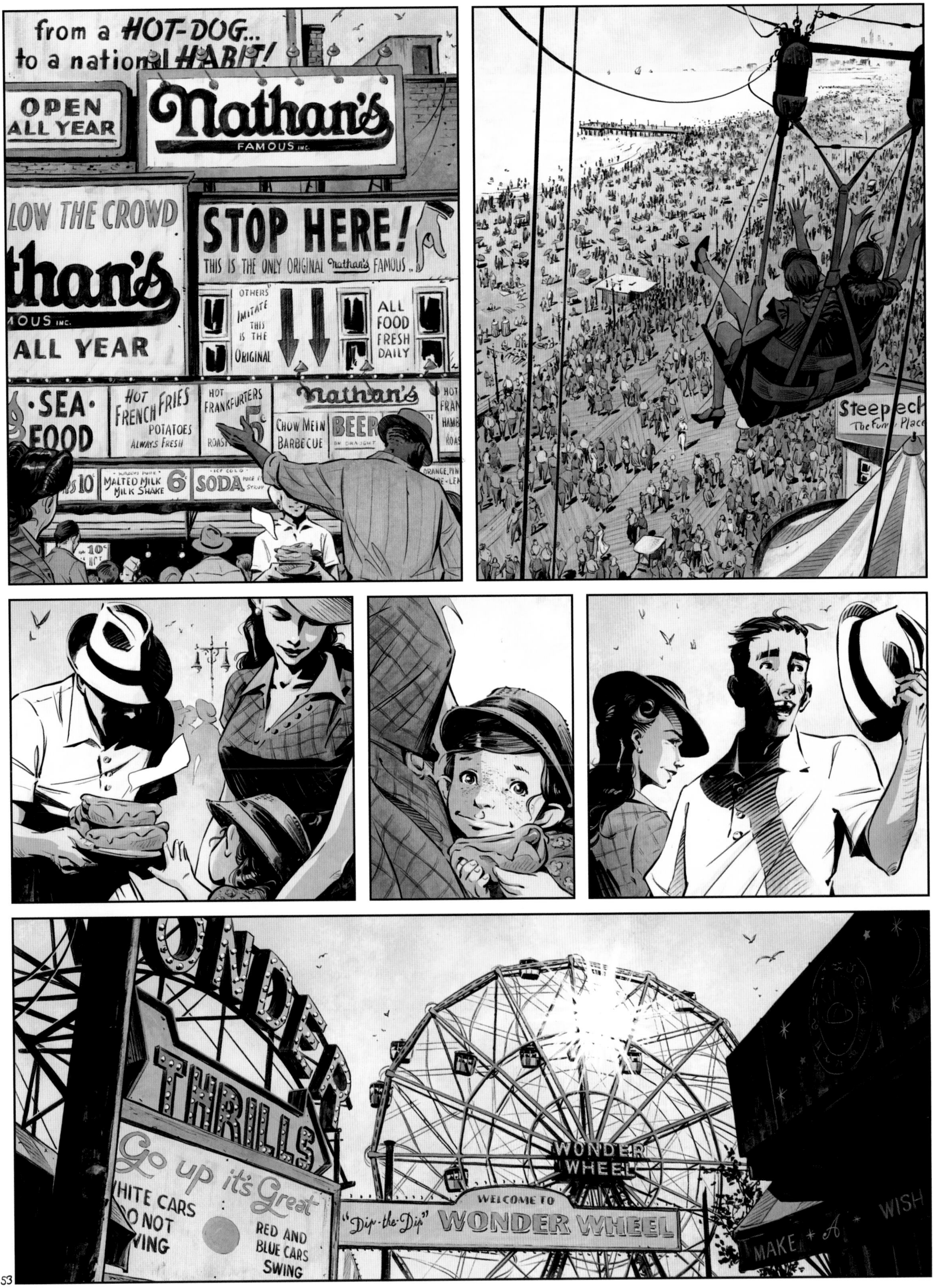
from a HOT-DOG...
to a national HABIT!
OPEN ALL YEAR
Nathan's
FAMOUS INC.
LOW THE CROWD
than's
FAMOUS INC.
ALL YEAR
STOP HERE!
THIS IS THE ONLY ORIGINAL Nathan's FAMOUS..
OTHERS IMITATE THIS IS THE ORIGINAL
ALL FOOD FRESH DAILY
·SEA· FOOD
HOT FRENCH FRIES POTATOES ALWAYS FRESH
HOT FRANKFURTERS 5¢
Nathan's
CHOW MEIN BARBECUE
BEER ON DRAUGHT
MALTED MILK MILK SHAKE 6¢
SODA
Steepech
The Fun Place
THRILLS
Go up it's Great
WHITE CARS DO NOT SWING
RED AND BLUE CARS SWING
WONDER WHEEL
WELCOME TO
"Dip-the-Dip"
WONDER WHEEL
MAKE A WISH

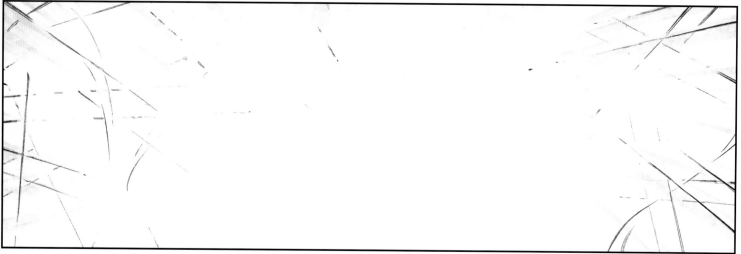

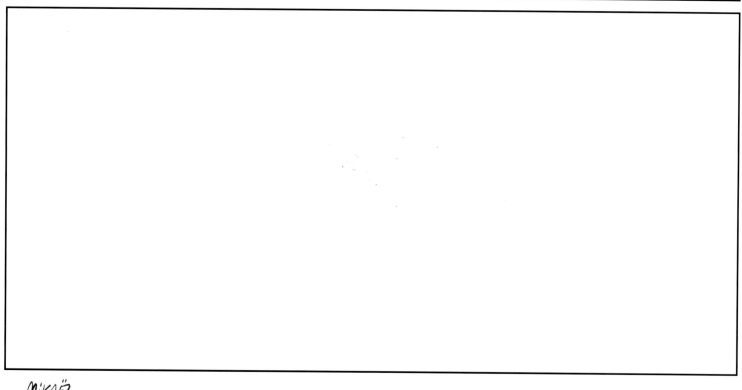

MIKAËL
FÉV. 2020

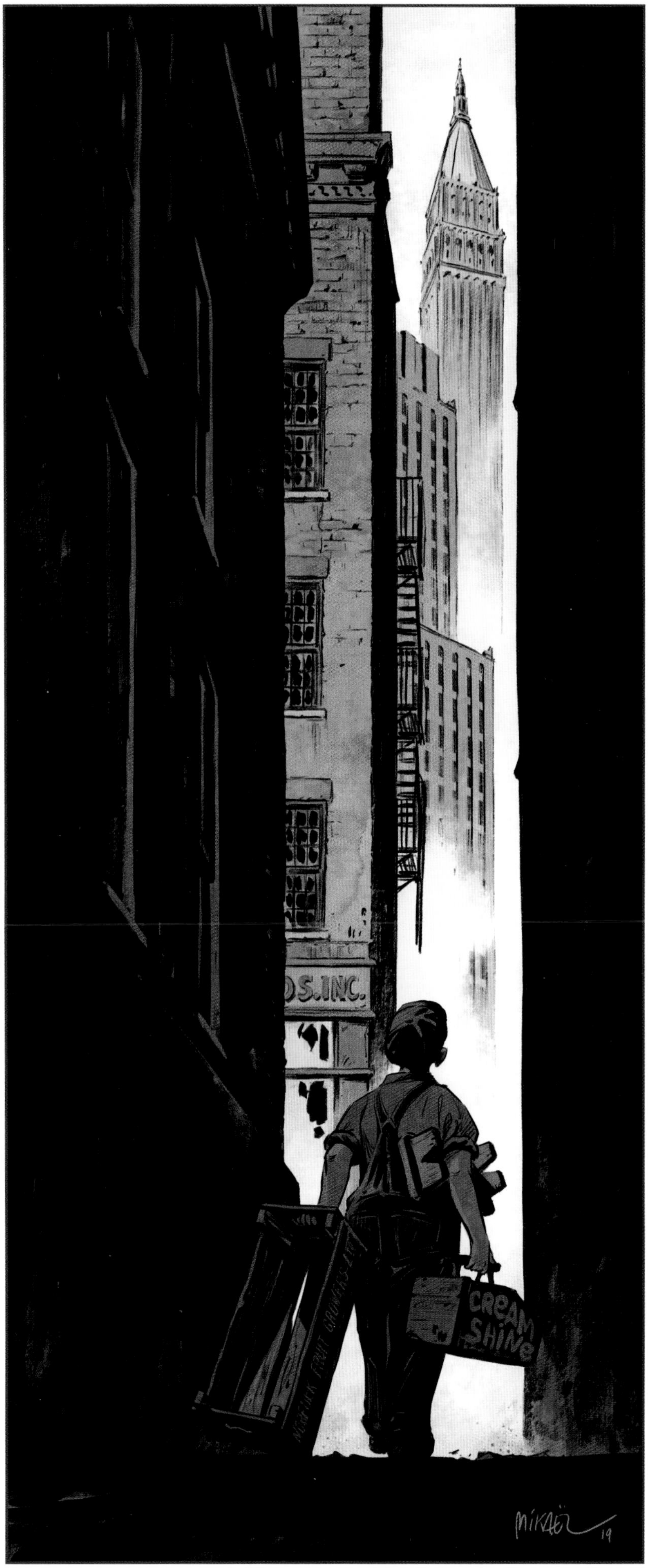
DS.INC.
CREAM SHINE

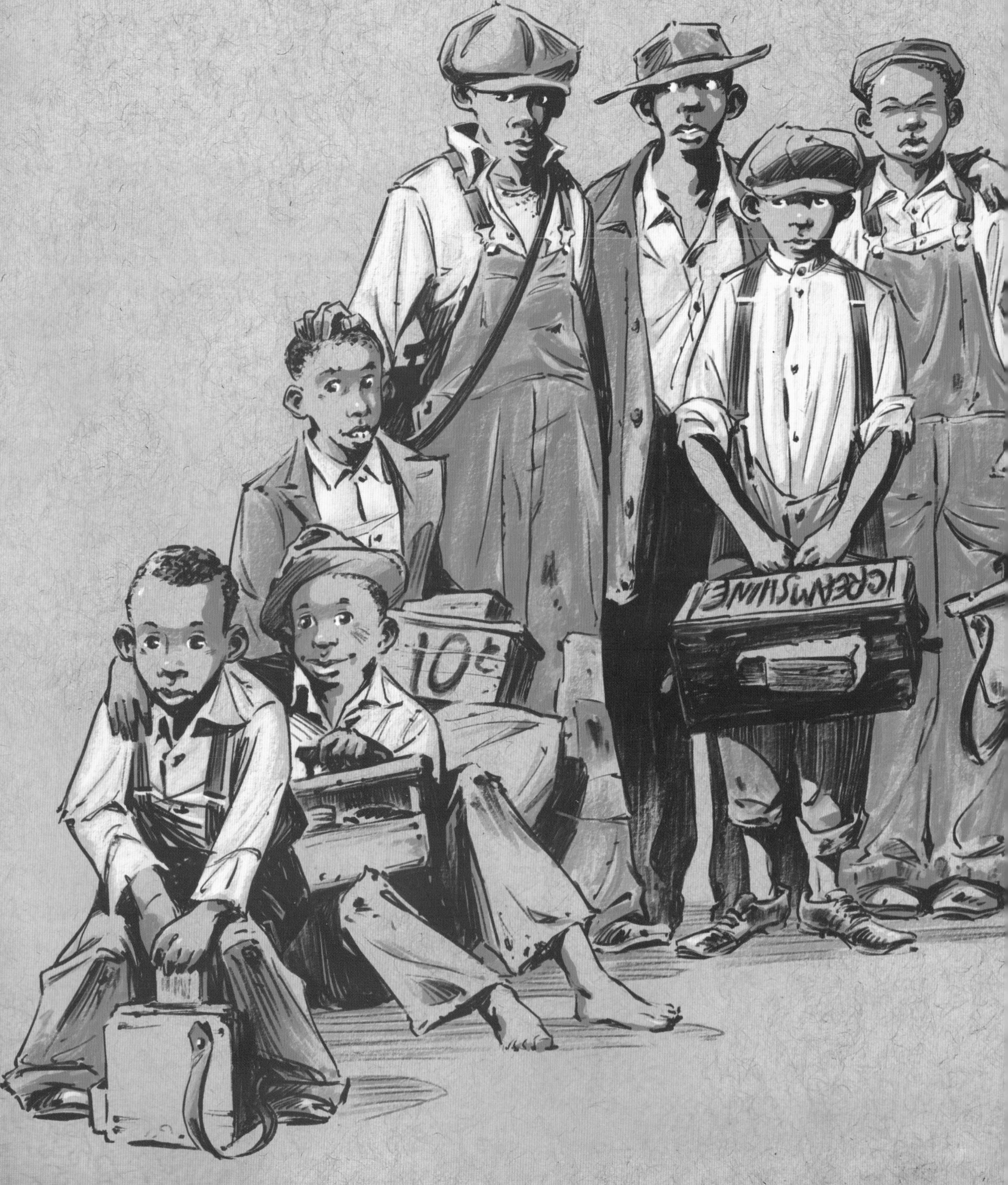
10¢